Clay Walls

CLAY
WALLS

a novel by Kim Ronyoung

UNIVERSITY OF WASHINGTON PRESS
Seattle and London

Copyright © 1987 by Kim Ronyoung
Reprinted by arrangement with The Permanent Press, Sag Harbor,
    New York 11963
University of Washington paperback edition first published in 1990
Second printing, 1992
Printed in the United States of America

Library of Congress Cataloging-in-Publication Data
Kim, Ronyoung.
    Clay walls / Kim Ronyoung.
    p.   cm.
    ISBN 0-295-96927-X (alk. paper)
    1. Korean Americans—History—Fiction.   I. Title.
PS3561.I4153C55   1990   89-39875
813'.54—dc20   CIP

The paper used in this publication meets the minimum requirements of
American National Standard for Information Sciences—Permanence of
Paper for Printed Library Materials, ANSI Z39.48–1984. ∞

*For my mother and father
and their compatriots*

/kɑmˈpetrɪə̯tz/

n. 同胞

PART ONE

HAESU

Mrs. Randolph is taking advantage.

ONE

Just because ~~she~~ Haesu is an Asian, her place is to ~~do~~ that kind of work, no questions.

接 Point 2.

Read

"You've missed a spot," Mrs. Randolph said, pointing. "Dirty." Haesu had been holding her breath. She let it out with a cough. *→MISIZ* *|sten|*

Mrs. Randolph shook her finger at the incriminating stain. "Look," she demanded, then made scrubbing motions in the air. "You clean."

Haesu nodded. She took in another breath and held it as she rubbed away the offensive stain.

"Th-at's better." Mrs. Randolph nodded with approval. "Good. Clean. Very good. Do that every week," she said, scrubbing the air again. She smiled at Haesu and left the room.

Haesu spat into the toilet and threw the rag into the bucket. "*Sangnyun!*" she muttered to herself. "*Sangnyun, sangnyun, sang-nyun!*" she sputtered aloud. She did not know the English equivalent for 'low woman', but she did know how to say, "I quit" and later said it to Mrs. Randolph. The woman looked at her in disbelief.

"I don't understand. We were getting on so well. I . . ." Mrs. Randolph pointed to herself "teach you." She pointed at Haesu. "You do good. Why you say, 'I quit'?"

"Toilet make me sick."

"That's part of the job."

"No job. No toilet. Not me. I go home." Haesu held out her hand, palm up to receive her pay.

Haesu quit this job because of her pride. ↑ 上面.

Mrs. Randolph stiffened as she backed away from Haesu's out-stretched hands. "Oo-oh no. You're supposed to give me adequate notice. I'm not obligated to pay you anything."

They were words not in Haesu's vocabulary. Perhaps she had not made herself clear. Haesu raised her hand higher.

Mrs. Randolph tightened her lips. "So you're going to be diffi-cult. I'm very disappointed in you, Haesu, but I'm going to be fair." She motioned Haesu to stay put and left the room.

Haesu sighed with relief and put down her hand. She knew that Mrs. Randolph's purse was on top of the dresser in the bedroom; the woman had gone to get the money. As she waited, Haesu looked around. It was a beautiful room. She had thought so when she first agreed to take the job. Later, when she ran the vacuum over the carpet, she had admired the peach-like pinks and the varying shades of blues of the flowing Persian pattern. She felt an affinity with the design. Perhaps what some historians say is true, that sometime in the distant past Hittites were in Korea. She ran her fingers over the surface of the table. The mahoghany wood still glowed warmly from her earlier care. She had not minded dusting the furniture. It was cleaning the toilet she could not stand.

Mrs. Randolph returned carrying a coin purse. She gestured for Haesu to hold out her hand, then emptied the contents of the purse into the outstretched palm. The coins barely added up to one dollar. Haesu held up two fingers of her other hand.

Mrs. Randolph gave a laugh. "No. You quit. Two dollars only if you were permanent." She shook her head; it was final.

Carefully, so as not to scratch the surface, Haesu placed the coins on the table. She picked up a dime. "Car fare," she explained.

Mrs. Randolph glared at Haesu. She began to fume. "Why you insolent yellow . . ."

Haesu knew they were words she would not want translated. She turned on her heels and walked out.

The dime clinked lightly as it fell to the bottom of the coin box. Haesu found a seat by the window. She would put her mind to the scenes that passed before her and forget the woman. She enjoyed her rides on streetcars, becoming familiar with the foreign land without suffering the embarrassment of having to speak its lan-guage. In three months, she had learned more about America from the seat of streetcars than from anywhere else.

The ride from Bunker Hill to Temple Street was all too brief for her. Only a few minutes separated the mansions of well-to-do Americans from the plain wood-framed houses of the ghettos. But it might as well be a hundred years, she thought. Her country's history went back thousands of years but no one in America seemed to care. To her dismay, few Americans knew where Korea was. This was 1920. The United States was supposed to be a modern country. Yet to Americans, Koreans were 'oriental', the same as Chinese, Japanese, or Filipino.

As shops began to come into view, Haesu leaned forward to see the merchandise in the windows. In front of the Five and Ten-cent Store, children were selling lemonade. A discarded crate and hand-scrawled signs indicated they were in business. Charmed, Haesu smiled and waved at the children. When she recognized the shops near her stop, she pulled the cord to signal the conductor she wanted off.

Clara's house was several blocks away. Although the rambling Victorian was really the meeting house of the National Association of Koreans, Haesu thought of it as Clara's. It was because of Clara that Haesu and her husband, Chun, were given a room, a room usually reserved for visiting Korean dignitaries. It was because of Clara that Mr. Yim, her husband, had agreed to make an exception to the rule.

The front door was open. Rudy Vallee's tremulous voice filtered through the screendoor. Clara was practicing the foxtrot again. Haesu stepped out of her shoes and carried them into the house.

"I quit my job," she announced, loud enough to be heard over the victrola.

Clara stopped dancing and took the needle off the record. "But you've just started," she said.

Haesu set her shoes on the floor and plopped into the sofa. "It was horrible. That *sangnyun* stood over me while I worked. I had to practically wipe my face on her filthy toilet to satisfy her."

"Oh, *Onni*, how terrible," Clara said, looking as if she had swallowed something distasteful.

The expression on Clara's face made Haesu laugh. '*Onni*', older sister. The honorific title further softened her anger. "The work wasn't hard. I could have done it," Haesu said confidently. "I have to admit the *sangnyun* has good taste. Beautiful furniture. Carpets this thick." She indicated the thickness with her forefinger and thumb. "Such lovely patterns. Like the twining tendrils on old Korean chests. Do you think we have Persian blood in us?"

Clara laughed. "I wouldn't know. You're the one who always says you're one hundred percent Korean."

"I am. But I'm talking about way back. Long, long ago. It would be fun to know." She absent-mindedly picked up one of the round velvet pillows Clara kept on the sofa and ran her hand over it, smoothing down the nap of the fabric. "What difference does it make now?" she said with a sigh. "What difference does it make who our ancestors were? I don't have a job."

"A lot of difference, *Onni.* Your ancestors were *yangbans.* No one can ever deny that. Everyone knows that children of aristocrats are not supposed to clean toilets," Clara declared.

Haesu tossed the pillow aside with such force that it bounced off the sofa onto the floor. "Then what am I doing here?"

Clara picked up the pillow and brushed it off. "How many times are you going to ask me that? You're here . . ."

"Living with you and Mr. Yim because Chun and I can't afford a place of our own," Haesu said.

"Why do you let that bother you? Mr. Yim and I don't mind. We want you here." Clara sat down next to Haesu and slipped her arm into Haesu's. "You're like a sister to me. If you were in my place, you would do the same."

Haesu looked earnestly into Clara's eyes. "I would, that's true. We had such fun in Korea, laughing at everything, worrying about nothing."

"It will be that way again. We haven't been here long enough. I've only been here a year and you've hardly had time to unpack. We'll get used to America." Clara leaped from her seat and pulled at Haesu's arm. "Put on your shoes and let's do the foxtrot. I think I'm getting it."

Laughing as she pulled away, Haesu protested, "No, no. I can't do that kind of dance."

"Yes you can. Just loosen up. You act like an old lady, Haesu. You act like you're eighty not twenty." Clara put Rudy Vallee on again and began dancing around the parlor, gliding effortlessly on the linoleum rug.

Haesu drew her feet onto the sofa out of Clara's way. She reached for the cushion and held it in her lap. Clara's enthusiasm amused her. It also puzzled her. Rudy Vallee stirred nothing in Haesu to make her want to dance.

Haesu stood at the screendoor waiting for Chun. Since Monday she had been thinking about what she would say to her husband. She knew what she would not say to him. At dinner on Monday, when Haesu had explained to Mr. Yim why she had quit her job, Clara had chimed in with, "It's so hard here. Haesu's right. We had such fun in Korea, laughing at everything, worrying about nothing."

Mr. Yim's jaw had dropped, the *kimchee* he held in his chopsticks falling onto his rice, causing a momentary lapse in his usual courtly manners. "Laughing at everything and worrying about nothing?" he had said incredulously. "Then, tell me, what are we doing here?" While Haesu and Clara had searched for an answer, Mr. Yim had sardonically added, "As I recall, no one I knew was laughing at Japanese atrocities. Everyone I knew was worrying about persecution." Haesu had shrunk with embarrassment; Mr. Yim was a Korean patriot who had suffered torture in a Japanese prison, and was now forced to live in exile to escape death. "How thoughtless of me," she had replied. "Please forgive me."

Up until two weeks ago Haesu walked with Chun to Clara's house on Thursdays. Chun had found them work as live-in domestics. But Haesu could not bear being summoned by the persistent ringing of a bell and, after two months, had quit. Chun had insisted upon staying on, choosing the security of room and board and five dollars a month. Haesu now saw him only on his days-off.

As soon as she recognized his slight build and flat-footed gait, she flung open the screendoor and walked out to meet him.

Chun did not stop for her. She had to turn around and walk alongside him, matching her steps to his. "I quit my job," she said.

"Let's talk about it later," he said, speeding up. "I have to go to the bathroom. The damn food makes me sick." He hopped up the front steps and disappeared into the house.

Later that night, when they were alone in their room, Haesu told her husband the details of her quitting.

"You'll get used to the work," he said.

"Never! I'll never get used to cleaning someone else's filth."

"It takes two minutes to clean a toilet. It won't kill you," he said as he climbed into bed.

Haesu felt the heat rise to her cheeks. "I'll never understand how you do it, how you can remain mute while someone orders you to come here, go there, do this, do that . . like you were some trained animal. They call you a houseboy. A twenty-five year old man being called 'boy'."

"They can call me what they want. I don't put the words in their mouths. The work is easy. Work for pay. There's no problem as long as they don't lay a hand on me. Just a job, Haesu. Work for pay."

"Cheap pay and demeaning work," she said.

Chun shrugged his shoulders. "No work, no pay. No money, no house, no food, no nothing. It's as simple as that."

"That's not good enough for me and I won't disgrace my family by resorting to menial labor," she whispered hoarsely, keeping her voice down as her anger rose. She was obliged to maintain the peace of her host's home.

"I haven't met a *yangban* yet who thought any work was good enough for him. Me? I'm just a farmer's son. Any work is good enough for me. Isn't that right?" He pulled the covers over him.

"I don't want to talk about that now. I have an idea. Are you listening? Riding home on the streetcar, I saw these little stands where people were selling things. Nothing big and fancy. Little things. Standing in the sun selling . . . things. It didn't seem like hard work. Why can't we do something like that? Are you listening?" She shook his shoulders.

Chun snorted. "You? Selling things? Out in the sun where all the Koreans can see you?"

Haesu pulled the blanket from his shoulders. "I don't care about that. All I care about is that we be our own boss. Can't you see that? No one will tell us what to do."

Chun pulled the blanket from her. "Let a man get some sleep, will you?" He covered himself then turned his back to her.

Haesu walked over to his side of the bed. She leaned over him and put her lips close to his ears. She spoke softly. "I will never work for anyone. Do you hear me. Chun? I'll never clean someone else's filth. Never! You'll never make enough money as a houseboy to support us. Do you hear me, Chun? As soon as we make enough money, we are going back to Korea. We don't belong here. Just tell me, what are we doing here?" She really had laughed at everything and worried about nothing in Korea; a daughter protected from the world by her parents, groomed in seclusion for marriage.

Chun's answer was a series of rattled breaths followed by deep snores.

In the morning, Chun showed no indication that he had heard her. She raised the subject the following week. She pursued the matter until Chun held up his hand to stop her.

"All right, all right, have it your way," he said. "We'll ask Mr. Yim. See what he thinks."

Mr. Yim was the titular head of the house. In truth, the house was more his than Clara's because he was paid by the National Association of Koreans, the NAK, to maintain the clubhouse. He was fifteen years older than Clara, older than everyone who lived under his roof. He treated them all as he would his own children.

Haesu waited impatiently as Chun explained her idea to Mr. Yim. Ordinarily, Chun's terse speech left her yearning for more. Now she hoped for greater brevity.

Mr. Yim's response was important to her. She's never felt qualified to enter into debate with him about anything. He was a *yangban* higher born than she. And he was a scholar. But his life had become one of contradictions. Ten years ago, when the Japanese confiscated his land, he refused to relinquish his ancestral home to the usurpers and set his house on fire. He left for America with only the money in his pocket and found work in Los Angeles washing dishes. When be began to receive a small stipend from the NAK for his organizational work, he arranged to have a bride sent from Korea. He was beseiged with photographs from potential mothers-in-law who listed their daughters many virtues; they were after his family name. Mr. Yim chose Clara. He claimed that he chose her because of her family background and honest face, but everyone knew it was because she was an exceptional beauty. "You're a classic Korean beauty," Haesu would tell Clara, "with delicate features and skin as smooth and fair as porcelain."

Remembering Clara's unfailing response, "I'd rather have your large eyes," brought a smile to Haesu's lips.

"I see that Chun's idea appeals to you," Mr. Yim said. "What will you sell?"

Chun looked at Haesu. Her mind went blank; lemonade was for children.

"Hmm. How about fresh produce?" Mr. Yim suggested. "Men who work at the produce market often come to the cafe where I work. I could find out how you can get produce wholesale. You can quit your job as houseboy, Chun." He waved his hand in the air. "Don't worry about having food in your stomachs or a roof over your heads. Consider my home yours." He nodded. "I approve of your idea. Selling anything to someone is better than polishing his shoes."

The sky was just turning light as Chun pulled and Haesu pushed the crate of apples up Temple Street. They had invested in a wagon for their new business. Haesu had assured Chun that no risk was involved. If the business failed, she would sell the wagon to some child in the neighborhood.

At Sunset Boulevard Chun said, "This is as far as we go."

By the time they had finished stacking the apples, the sun had risen and shone obliquely on the skins. Haesu had polished each apple the night before. They now glowed a magnificent red. She selected one for its elongated shape, skillfully cut it into a floret then set it atop the pyramid of apples. She stood back to examine her handiwork. *"Ibuji?"* she said, asking Chun to confirm that it was beautiful.

He nodded. "It looks like a lotus."

His poetic reference took her by surprise. Her look made Chun blush.

"Cigarettes," he blurted and dashed across the street to a drug-store.

How strange he is, Haesu thought. They have been married several months and he was as much a stranger to her as when she first learned she was betrothed to him. Her parents had arranged it; she never wanted him. She had begged them to reconsider, reminding them that his family was socially beneath theirs. They would not listen. They would never go back on their word; they could not. Chun had asked his American missionary employer to act as matchmaker and Haesu's parents could not refuse the es-teemed foreign dignitary. When Chun had to leave Korea, Haesu was sent to California to marry him, committed for life to a man she did not love.

Haesu took a lemon from the pocket of her apron and cut it open. She squeezed the juice over the cut apple to keep the white from darkening.

The lotus was a Buddhist symbol of purity, a flower that bloomed even when rooted in stagnant water. Her family were Buddhists before their conversion to Christianity. So were Chun's.

He can't forget, Haesu told herself, he still thinks of home.

She looked up as a streetcar passed. A Chinese woman sitting at a window seat was staring at her.

She'll think I'm part of the American scene, Haesu thought. She couldn't help the smile that came to her face.

—2—

It was meeting night. While Clara and Mr. Yim were in the parlor unfolding wooden chairs and setting them in rows, Haesu and Chun were in their room soothing their weary bodies.

"Oooh, nothing feels as good as this," Haesu murmured, playing her toes in a warm solution of Epsom salt. Chun had been soaking in a tub of hot water and now threw himself on the bed.

"You can't go to sleep," Haesu warned. "The meeting will start soon. You'll have to attend. What will everyone think?"

"They'll think I'm unpatriotic."

"Min Chang Mo is going to be the speaker. He was in Kyonggi Province after the March First Incident."

"I'm tired," Chun said, adjusting the pillow under his head.

"Who isn't?" Haesu said, adding more hot water to the pan.

It had taken them several weeks to learn that if they were to make a profit, they would have to push their wagon from one place to another. In the early morning they were at Temple and Sunset selling apples to workers leaving for work. At mid-morning, they moved on to Grand Avenue to catch the shoppers at lunch. In the afternoon, they made stops in residential districts on their way home. As the day wore on, the apples showed signs of ageing and were sold at reduced prices to children returning home from school.

"If only we didn't have to walk so much," Haesu said. "If only we had a car or truck."

"It takes money. Lots of money," Chun said.

"We could drive around Bunker Hill. Sell all kinds of produce to wealthy customers."

"You wouldn't have to drive anywhere if we had a truck. I could do it all myself."

"What would I do?" Haesu would like to know.

"Stay home like Clara. Like all *yangbans.*"

"How much would it take?"

Chun shrugged his shoulders. "Maybe five hundred dollars."

"Hmph! Might as well be five million. We have all of fifty dollars saved up," she noted.

"Takes money. Everything takes money," Chun mumbled.

Haesu wiped her feet dry with a towel. "You had better get dressed, the people will be arriving soon." But she was too late. Chun's eyes were closed, his breathing turning into loud rasps.

At the first sound of people climbing the porch steps, Haesu quickened her movements. By the time she got downstairs, Koreans had crowded into the living room, hands outstretched, ready to grasp any hand it found in its path, cutting the air with aspirated consonants and mellifluous vowels of their native tongue. Haesu moved through the crowd, taking grip of a dozen hands as she went, exchanging news of family and friends with her fellow countrymen.

Some of the men offered to help Mr. Yim set up more chairs. The ones who couldn't tell one end of the chair from the other chuckled with embarrassment as they tried to figure it out. They let out a startled *"aigoo!"* when the chair snapped open.

Haesu once asked Clara the English equivalent of *aigoo.* Clara thought 'oh my' or 'my goodness' came close but were not exact translations. *Yobo* was another commonly used word for which Clara had searched for an English counterpart. She thought 'you there' was something like it, but laughed when Haesu said, "you there" to Chun and suggested she stick to *yobo.*

As even more Koreans arrived, *"Yobo!"* spanned the room. Additional chairs filled the space intended to separate the speaker from the audience. The remaining chairs were set up on the porch outside of raised windows. Latecomers made their way to the stairs leading to the second floor to sit on the steps. According to Clara, before the March First Independence movement, Mr. Yim had to phone members and beg them to attend the meetings.

On March 1, 1919, Haesu was in Shanghai. She was booked on the S.S. China scheduled to leave for San Francisco when she heard about Korea's Declaration of Independence from Japan. She thought it a substantial reason for canceling her passage and returning home. But political escapees from Korea had dissuaded her. The situation in Korea was worse than ever, they had told her. The Declaration was purely symbolic, a non-violent political gesture that had infuriated the Japanese, causing them to retaliate violently and intensify every atrocity they had ever committed on the Korean people. She was persuaded to give vent to her indignation from America.

Before the meeting was called to order, Haesu took her place on one of the four chairs facing the audience to take a few notes. She was the secretary, appointed by Mr. Yim for her "skillful use of the Korean language and beautiful handwriting". Her accounts of the meetings were published in the Korean newspaper.

The first paragraph extolled the attendance of conscientious Koreans. She then studied the guest speaker as he mingled with the crowd, jotting down notes for later amplification. "Tall. Sturdy physique. Delicate hands. Large expressive eyes. Well-delineated lips of an aristocrat. Honest, earnest expression. Distinguished. According to Korean standards, a fine-looking man."

Not by anyone's standard was Chun a handsome man, she thought. His angular face with eyebrows resembling birds arched in flight gave him a look of perpetual disconcertion. By her standards his teeth were too large and his eyes too small. Only his narrow high-bridged nose deserved admiration. That was all she found to admire by her standards.

Mr. Yim, Min Chang Mo, and K.Y. Yun, the treasurer, filled the seats next to hers, signaling the meeting was about to begin. After the Korean national anthem, Mr. Yim introduced the guest speaker. Haesu listened while taking notes. "Married. No children. Twenty-eight years old. Came from a family of scholars." She underlined 'scholars'. "Destined to be a professor but was forced to flee Korea. Wanted by the Japanese police for sedition."

Min wasted no time getting to his story. "They burned my mother and sister alive," he said bitterly. "I saw it with my own eyes." He told of being there in Kyonggi Province right after the March First demonstration when the Japanese police herded his mother and a score of villagers into a church, his mother carrying his infant sister on her back. He and others were left to witness what was to follow. He was stunned when the police set fire to the church. He was filled with anguish as the searing heat forced him back. His cries of agony matched those of his mother.

A shudder ran through Haesu; she put down her pen. Tongues

clacked and murmurs of indignation rumbled through the audience. Someone yelled, "Those sons-of-bitches!" Mr. Yim called for order, asking for restraint, requesting that Min Chang Mo be allowed to resume his story. Haesu picked up her pen. "Forced to witness the murder of his mother and sister," she wrote.

"Then the Japanese police fired their guns at the pyre of human bodies," Min said. He raised his voice above the obscenities shouted by some of the men in the audience. "I too was enraged. I vowed to destroy every police station in Korea." Half the audience rose to its feet and shouted, "Mansei!" The other half scrambled to join them.

It took both Mr. Yim and K.Y. Yun to calm everyone down. Min went on to say that there were about fourteen thousand military and civilian Japanese police in Korea. He needed more dynamite. He had come to America to collect money for more explosives.

Before the applause had subsided, K.Y. Yun began passing out mimeographed copies of the Treasurer's Report. Before everyone had received his copy, Yun proceeded to read the report aloud. He called off the names of contributors to the Independence movement, waiting for hands to clap after the names of generous donors, then lumped together the names of donors of smaller amounts according to denomination. Haesu was mortified to discover that Chun's name was not on the list. When K.Y. Yun called for new pledges, Haesu promised fifty dollars.

Unable to sleep, Haesu tossed and turned in bed. At three o'clock in the morning, when Chun got up to go to the bathroom, she told him she had pledged the fifty dollars.

"I was going to warn you about that," he said as he left the room.

She felt miserable. The paucity of his response made her uneasy. He gave her the impression that there was more meaning to what he left unsaid, leaving her wondering where she stood in the matter. She didn't know which she wanted most, his approval or his absence.

Chun crawled back into bed without saying a word.

"I couldn't stand not contributing something," she explained. "My family always gave generously. I had to give something."

"You have to have something to give," he said.

She tried to think of some response. She knew he wasn't asleep; his body was taut and she sensed that his eyes were open.

Then she felt his hand on her, crawling over the rise and depressions of her body. When he turned toward her, she protested. "No! They'll hear."

"They're asleep," he said as he groped for the cleft where he would enter. Pressing his chest hard against her nipples and jamming his knees between her thighs, he formed a human vise. She wanted to scream herself free. Instead, she became wooden. Her lack of response only served as a goad, intensifying his determination to arouse her. But the more he tried, the more she wanted to expel him from her. It was over when he could hold back no longer. Grunting like a barnyard animal, he collapsed in a heap on top of her.

She pushed him aside and, almost immediately, he fell asleep. She lay there thinking how much she hated it, more each time than the time before. Finally, she turned on her side and pulled the covers over her shoulders, asking herself, "Who cares about the money?".

—3—

Something was going on with Chun, but Haesu did not ask any questions. One night, he took the money she had pledged to NAK and left. The next morning, when he returned, he handed the money to her. He began to go out several nights a week, often not returning until morning.

"Has he found a second job?" Mr. Yim asked.

"I don't know," Haesu replied. She found herself hoping that it was 'another woman'.

When she mentioned to Chun that Mr. Yim wondered if he had found a second job, Chun said, "He hasn't said anything to me."

"He probably doesn't want to appear as if he's prying," she said. "It isn't easy for anyone to ask you anything."

Chun ran his hands through his hair, scratching his scalp along the way. Then, smoothing his disheveled hair, he said, "It's time for us to move out. Tomorrow you go out and find us a place to live. I'll work by myself."

"We can't afford a place of our own," she said.

"Fifteen dollars a month." He pulled out his wallet and counted off the money. "First month's rent," he said, handing her the bills.

Haesu was about to ask where he got the money, but decided

against it. Whatever fifteen dollars would provide was welcomed; keeping her fights with Chun private and her growing sense of obligation to the Yims were beginning to wear heavily on her.

At breakfast, she explained why she had not gone to work with Chun. "We've imposed upon you long enough. It's time we moved. I'll need you to go househunting with me, Clara."

"I'd love to go with you," Clara exclaimed. Then a pained expression suddenly came over her face. "But what will I do after you move?"

Haesu laughed. "What you always do when I'm not here." She had meant to cheer her friend but Clara turned thoughtful, almost sad.

"Do you know that green crepe dress with the side bow? How do you think that would look with my white shoes?" Clara asked. In the next breath she said, "I don't know if I want to go. I hate it when everyone stares at me. They look at me as if I was some kind of freak."

"Nonsense. It's only because we don't look like other Americans," Haesu said.

"It's these eyes," Clara said, popping hers open as wide as she could.

"Don't be a child, Clara. You're a rare beauty. You're eyes are just right."

"That's easy for you to say. I'll bet no one asks you if you can see with your eyes."

"Who asks that?"

"There. I told you. Children ask me that all the time."

"Children!" Haesu scoffed. "What do they know? Wear the green dress and the white shoes. You'll look beautiful. I'll wear something special too. Come on, Clara, it will be fun."

With a sigh of resignation, Clara said, "All right. Let me know if you want to borrow anything."

Mr. Yim had sat quietly while the women made their plans. He now leaned toward his young wife, placing his hand on hers. "While you are out, if you see something you would like to buy for yourself, please do so." He turned to Haesu. "Clara has not been out of this house for months."

"I know. It's my fault. As soon as we get a truck, Chun says I won't have to work. Then Clara and I will go all over Los Angeles together. As a matter of fact, we can start today. Let's get ready, Clara."

Mr. Yim pulled a gold fob from his pocket. "I'm late for work," he declared. "Don't change your mind, Clara. You're more beautiful than any woman in this country." He put on his hat and walked out the door.

Haesu skipped every other step going up the stairs, unbuttoning her house dress as she went. Going through her limited wardrobe, she made her decisions quickly, taking everything she was going to wear from the dresser and closet and laying them on the bed. The corset was her least favorite garment. Why should she have to reshape her body to fit into a dress? The lacing around her small breasts needed little cinching. It was her hips that required the hardest pull, the part of her body that, in Korea, was hidden under a billowing *chima*.

Her ecru crepe dress glided smoothly over her satin underslip. Ready to step into a pair of black pumps, she discovered her feet were bare. "Forgot again," she muttered impatiently. She sat on the bed to put on the taupe silk stockings. The fine mesh conformed to her legs as she carefully stretched it to her knees. Straightening the seams before securing the stockings to her plain pink garter, Haesu then worked her feet into her shoes.

As careful as she tried to be, she couldn't seem to avoid putting snags in her stockings. Yanking and tugging was how she had put on the padded socks she grew up with, calf-high coverings sturdier than the canoe-shaped shoes they fitted into, socks sewn with up-turned toes to fill the upturned toes of shoes that historians linked with cultures of the Middle-east. She never forgot to put them on.

It wasn't necessary but she put a touch of rouge on her cheeks. She was blushing with excitement. She flattened her lips against her teeth to rub lipstick over them, the way a door-to-door cosmetic saleslady had shown her. She had giggled throughout the demonstration, having had to make such funny faces while the saleslady applied the makeup. She remembered that Clara had scolded her for her lack of seriousness, scolded her *Onni* for being silly. That had struck Haesu as being even more amusing. She was a year older than Clara and entitled to the respect accorded older sisters. The whole event struck her as being a comic drama with everyone playing the wrong role, causing her to laugh harder than ever. She now wore makeup as a matter of course, concerned with wearing the right color and the correct amount.

She put on her wide-brimmed black straw hat, the only hat she owned, setting it carefully over her thick black hair. She decided to borrow white gloves and a white bag from Clara.

She found Clara sitting on the sofa downstairs. "I'm sorry," Haesu said. "I didn't mean to keep you waiting."

"I don't think I'll go with you," Clara said.

"But you're dressed and ready to go."

"I've changed my mind."

Haesu took Clara by the hand and pulled her to her feet. "You're going with me. You can't spend your life in this house dancing alone to Rudy Vallee records. We haven't been anywhere together for ages. Besides, who's going to help me with my English? I'd be lost without you. Now no more of this. Can I borrow your white purse and white gloves?"

"Of course. I'll get them for you," Clara said. She started for her room. "I'll get my hat too," she said as she went.

Haesu heaved a sigh of relief.

Clara's hat was deep cloche. The gray felt brim curved over her brows then ran along her cheeks to below her ears. In profile, only the tip of her nose and a bit of her lips and chin were visible.

"For someone who rarely goes out, you've managed to buy very smart clothes," Haesu said.

"Mrs. Thayer shops for me," Clara said.

"Mrs. Thayer?"

"Our landlady. You haven't met her. She only comes when we need her."

"You look lovely, Clara. If people stare at you it's because you're so pretty."

They had walked a full block when they realized that neither of them had any idea where they were going.

"How did you find your house?" Haesu asked Clara.

"Mr. Yim was living in it when I came to marry him, remember?" Clara stopped in her tracks. "There's no point in going on; we don't know where to go."

Haesu slipped her arm under Clara's. "We're not going back. Do you think your landlady can help us?" She began walking Clara forward. "Where does she live?"

Clara saw that she had no choice but to show Haesu.

Mrs. Thayer lived only two blocks away. She was delighted to be of help, going as far as finding a newspaper and circling all the ads of rentals Haesu could afford. She brought out a map of the City of Los Angeles from her study and marked an X where the rentals were located. "There aren't too many rentals for fifteen dollars," she explained to Clara. "But tell your friend that I will be happy to recommend her to any landlord." She stepped back to look Clara over. "You look darling . . . both of you do. I don't see how anyone could turn you down."

Clara did not bother to translate the last sentence for Haesu.

The first landlord did not have a chance to turn Haesu down. She screwed up her face at the musty odor in the entry and shook her head at the stained carpets. *"Aigoo,"* she gasped and led Clara out the door.

The second landlord turned Haesu down from his living room window. He pulled aside the curtain, glanced at her and the newspaper in her hand, then waved a 'no' before closing the curtain.

"It must be taken," Haesu said.

Clara said nothing as she moved aside to let a woman pass. The woman scanned the newspaper in her hand then rang the doorbell to the landlord's apartment.

"Shouldn't you tell her it's been taken?" Haesu asked Clara.

Before Clara could answer, the man was at the door letting the woman in. Haesu's jaw dropped. Clara took her by the arm. "Let's go. He doesn't want 'orientals' "

Haesu pulled away. "Why not?"

Clara shrugged her shoulders. "Some people do and some people don't. We'll have to find someone who does."

Haesu was dumbfounded. "I don't know whether to laugh or cry. Find someone who will take me? I'm not asking him to like me, I'm finding plenty of people who don't, but if I like a place and I pay what the landlord asks and I take care of his property, he can't turn me away."

"Yes he can. Don't ask me for an explanation. That's just the way it is."

"I would certainly like to know why the Korean Declaration of Independence was modeled after the American Declaration of Independence."

"Let's go home, Haesu. I don't want to look anymore."

"No. I'm not going to do that. We're going to every place your landlady circled." Haesu opened the map. "Show me the places we've already seen." By Clara's indication, only two locations remained. "They're so close to one another," Haesu noted.

"They're in the unrestricted areas," Clara explained. "Some places are for 'whites only'."

Haesu's lips opened with a smack. "All men are created equal."

"You don't have to make any speeches to me," Clara said. "But I do know one thing. Once you've made up your mind, there's no changing it." With a tilt to her head she added, "Maybe we'll find a place you like and the landlord likes you."

"We'll see," Haesu said. "We'll see."

The other apartments didn't particularly strike Haesu's fancy, but the landlord of one of them took down Mrs. Thayer's phone number and said he would let Haesu know.

Haesu omitted no detail as she told Chun what had happened. She ended her bitter account with. "I'm not going to take a place just because it's available to 'orientals'."

Chun sighed. "You'll have to find something soon. A man came up to me today and asked if I would be interested in going into partnership with him. He wants to rent a stall at Grand Central Market."

The length of Chun's statement told her the information was significant. "Korean?" she asked.

"No. I don't know what he is. His name's Bancroft. I'm going with him the day after tomorrow to see the place. You'll have to tend the business."

"Bancroft? He asked you? We're not good enough to live in certain places and Bancroft asks you to be his partner?" Her sarcasm was mild compared to what she felt.

"He likes the way we set up our produce. He says it makes people want to buy them."

"Oh, I see. If we polish our apples nice, that's acceptable. But if we want to live in his neighborhood, that's not acceptable. It doesn't make sense to me. I think . . ."

Chun cut her off with a wave of his hand. "Don't waste your speech on me. I can't do anything about it."

Air escaped from her puffed up cheeks. She had plenty to say about ignorance, prejudice, and discrimination. But Chun was right, it would be wasted on him. To whom then, she wondered. All her thoughts were formed in her native language. In English, she could only utter one or two isolated words, using her hands when words failed her, exasperated that she appeared mentally deficient.

"I'm going to study English," she blurted out.

Her sudden announcement caught Chun off his guard. "English?" It took a few seconds for the information to sink in. "A roof over our heads and food in our stomachs first. English later."

"Come in, Mrs. Thayer," Haesu said. Her 'th' sounded like 'd' but she wanted to address the woman by name; she had not forgotten her kindness.

"I received a phone call from one of the landlords." She held an imaginary telephone receiver to her ear. "He's a robber, my dear. He will let you have his place but he's going to raise the rent. A scoundrel . . ."

"Excuse me, Mrs. Thayer." Haesu left the room to fetch Clara. "Your landlady's here. She seems upset about something."

Clara entered the parlor with her hand extended. Mrs. Thayer clasped it between her hands. "Clara dear, tell your friend that one of the landlords called." She enunciated each word carefully. "He said that Haesu could have the apartment but the rent would be twenty-five, not fifteen dollars." She let go of Clara's hand to indicate the number, folding and unfolding her fingers until she had held up the correct amount.

Clara was puzzled. "Twenty-five?"

"Yes. A thief. He's taking advantage of your friend."

Clara nodded with understanding and turned to Haesu to explain. The color rose to Haesu's face.

Mrs. Thayer quickly added, "It's okay. O-kay. I told him he could take his apartment and stuff it down the sewer." She laughed then realized she wasn't getting through when no one else joined her. She slowed her pace and separated each syllable. "I am going to help you. I will find a place and sublet it to you. No one can refuse to rent to me. You pay me and I pay the owner."

Clara had been following Mrs. Thayer closely. "You be landlady?"

"Sort of."

Clara understood and told Haesu the plan.

"Ask her if it's legal" Haesu said.

Mrs. Thayer's response was emphatic. "To a higher law than the one he's following. By what right does he charge you more than anyone else? Thank God we're not all like him. Yes, legal! I want to do it."

After much explanation, it was settled as Mrs. Thayer wished.

—4—

True to her word, Mrs. Thayer found a place for Haesu and Chun, a rear apartment carved out of a large old wood-framed house. It consisted of a bath, a kitchen that had been converted from a pantry, and two small rooms that were once bedrooms for maids. Haesu would have preferred larger rooms, but being able to look out to the garden made up for any deficiencies. She was pleased that the entrance to the apartment faced the backyard, eliminating the need to use the main entrance and walk a long dark hall to her door. But best of all, there was no necessity to sublet the unit from Mrs. Thayer. The landlord seemed a reasonable man, so Mrs. Thayer confided in him about Haesu and Chun. She later took Haesu to see the place and meet Mr. Simpson. Haesu accepted the apartment and Mr. Simpson accepted her.

Chun borrowed a truck from his new partner, Charlie Bancroft, and with Mr. Yim's and Clara's help, Haesu and Chun moved into their own apartment. They borrowed a bed and some kitchenware from the Yims. "They're really the property of the Korean people," Mr. Yim said, "bought by the money provided by the membership. When you no longer have a need for them, pass them on to another Korean in need."

The only furniture in the living room was an overstuffed chair provided by Mr. Simpson. Chun told Haesu he did not mind, he preferred sitting on the floor in an uncluttered room.

When the Yims were ready to leave, Clara's eyes welled with tears.

Haesu laughed at her. "It's not as if we were moving to another country. We'll be just ten minutes apart."

"I don't know why I'm crying. It's just that the house will seem so empty without you."

"Now that I won't be working, you'll see more of me than ever. I'll come over and you can teach me the foxtrot," Haesu said.

After they had left, Haesu continued unpacking. She looked for a dry corner in the cupboard to store the half-dozen dahlia tubers Mrs. Thayer had wrapped in newspaper. "Mrs. Thayer told Clara that I shouldn't plant them until the soil is warm," she told Chun. "She said I shouldn't pick the flowers right after watering or when the sun is hot. They'll bloom in July. She told Clara that dahlias are a most generous flower. We will have more each year than the year before."

The brilliant orange of the setting sun reflected on the windows. Chun's silhouette was framed in the open doorway.

"It feels good to look out on a piece of land," he said.

Haesu kept her promise and visited Clara regularly. She took spins around the parlor to Rudy Vallee's tremolo but did not find the same pleasure in it that Clara found. She decided that doing the foxtrot was a waste of time and suggested to Clara that they take courses in English.

"It's too difficult," Clara said.

"No, it's not. Look how much you've learned in the time you've been here. I feel like a dunce. I feel like I'm living with blindfolds over my eyes, grabbing at the air and ending up with bits and pieces of whatever happens to fall into my hands," Haesu said.

"Even if we knew English it would be like that," Clara said.

"No, it would not. We would understand what was going on and know what to do about it. We wouldn't have to depend upon people like Mrs. Thayer."

As hard as she tried, Haesu could not convince Clara and began making inquiries on her own. She learned that adult English classes were offered in the evening at the local High School. That may be a problem, she thought. Chun may not approve of her being away when he was home. She wished he would resume his mysterious late night forays, but ever since he opened the stall at Grand Central Market, except for an occasional Saturday night, he was home. Still, learning English would make her feel at home in America. She decided to present her request to Chun as convincingly as she could.

"You won't have to be so dependent on Bancroft, helpless to take his word for everything. I'll only be gone one night a week for two hours. I'd be a fool not to take advantage of the course."

Chun did not answer immediately. He pulled out a cigarette and lit it before saying, "I don't like your being out at night. Who will do the cooking?"

"I'll prepare your dinner beforehand. The school is just a few blocks away. I'll come straight home."

"I guess there's no stopping you then," he said, snuffing out his cigarette.

Haesu was hurriedly preparing Chun's dinner when K.Y. Yun dropped in. What an inconvenience, she thought. It was the first night of her English class and she did not want to be late. But the good manners of Korean gentility prevailed. She greeted him politely, offered him a seat and a cup of coffee. He declined the coffee and sat on the upholstered chair.

"Very nice," he said, admiring the apartment.

"A little small," she said.

He gave a nervous laugh.

"Excuse me," she said and waved her hand toward the kitchen. "I must turn down the heat on the rice."

"I hope I'm not interrupting anything. I thought it would be too early to intrude on your dinner," he said apologetically. He moved to the edge of his seat, causing the cushion to sag to the floor.

Haesu explained that she was preparing Chun's dinner early because she was going to class to learn English.

"How wonderful! An English speaking secretary will be very useful to our organization. Well, then . . ." he stood up, "this is not a good time."

"Is there some news I should know?" Haesu asked as she accompanied him to the door.

"Well . . . I'll just take a moment. It would save me having to make another call." He returned to the chair and sat down. "As you know, money is always a problem. But no political activity can be done without money. And someone must carry out the unpleasant task of collecting the money. Because I believe so strongly in the cause for Korean independence, I have accepted this responsibility."

He had said 'money' enough times for Haesu to guess his mission. "Everyone appreciates your effort. You're a true patriot," she said. She heard water sizzle on the hot grate. "Excuse me, the soup's boiling over." She hurried to turn down the flame.

Yun was on his feet when she returned. "Now that Chun has a successful business, I thought you would consider making a pledge for an annual amount," he said.

"Chun's at work. Grand Central Market. You can speak to him about it there," she suggested. She wasn't going to take it upon herself to make another pledge.

"Oh, no, no," he said, smiling as he waved her suggestion aside. "I don't want to bother him at work. You can speak to him when it's convenient. I know how it is. Men handle the money." He looked around again. "A very nice home. We're lucky to be here. No Japanese police breaking down our doors and dragging us away to prison."

She was relieved when he finally left. He had almost ruined the evening for her. She rushed and managed to get to her class in time. Eagerly, she looked for immigrants like herself but was disappointed to find that the majority of the students were of European descent. The only other Asians were a Japanese couple.

Chun was surprised when Haesu told him about the Japanese couple. "Husband and wife?"

"Yes."

"Why both of them. Takes only one to handle the English."

"He wants to publish a Japanese newspaper and thinks there will be a day when an English section is added. She wants to write about the comparisons between Japanese and American cultures. Their name's Kusumoto."

"Did they tell you all that?"

"I asked them. There wasn't anyone else I could talk to." Haesu was fluent in Japanese. Like most of her countrymen, she had been forced to learn it in school. And, like most of her countrymen, she avoided using the language if possible.

"They must have money," Chun said. "Everyone else has to work for a living."

The mention of money reminded Haesu of her earlier visitor. "Yun was here. He wants a pledge for an annual donation."

"Why doesn't he ask me?"

"I suggested that to him"

"But he wants you to do it." Chun gave a sudden laugh. "What a sore loser."

"What do you mean?"

"He lost to me at poker. He can't take it. Wants to get back." Chun was smiling as he said it; something Haesu rarely saw him do.

"Poker?"

"You know." He made the motions of dealing out playing cards.

"You've been gambling?" She sounded as if she disapproved.

The smile faded from his face. "Do you know of any other way to make enough money to buy into a partnership or pay the rent? You're supposed to be good in school. How many apples would you have to sell before you would have enough to buy a truck?"

"But gambling." She sounded disappointed. It wasn't another woman.

"Never mind. You don't have to think about it. Money is man's affair," he said in a tone befitting the master of the house.

The terms were clear. They did not originate with Chun. Their roles had been handed down through the centuries, made clear by Confucius generations ago, before Haesu was born, before she had a head to think and a voice to speak.

"Only fools gamble," she said quietly, forgetting they were no longer in Clara's house.

"Some fools are luckier than others," he replied.

"I see. Then it depends on what kind of fool you are," she said, her voice growing stronger as she remembered she was in her own house.

"How I make my money is my business," Chun said.

More of those 'terms', she thought. As long as a man provided for his family, he was beyond criticism. A woman, on the other hand, was measured by how well she served the men in her family; first her father, then her husband and, finally, her son.

"Gambling is for those who can afford it, for those of the leisure class or those responsible only to themselves. You belong to neither group."

Chun reached for a cigarette.

"It's my birthright, not yours, to be a member of the leisure class." The words were rolling off her tongue, making room for more. "It was my birthright to marry a *yangban*."

Chun pulled the pack of Camels from his shirtpocket and tossed it on the table.

"My dream was to marry a scholar," she said, unable to stop herself.

Chun lit the cigarette that dangled on his lips. He inhaled deeply then let out the smoke. "Your parents gave their consent," he said, squinting through the haze.

"How could they refuse Reverend McNeil?" she demanded, the soft edge leaving her voice.

Chun rose from his chair. He gathered up his cigarettes and ashtray then walked to the barest corner in the room. He squat on the floor, sitting on his heels, his back to the window, facing the center of the room. Setting the pack of cigarettes and ashtray in front of him, he then folded his arms across his knees and continued smoking.

Haesu had to turn her head to speak to him. "I don't blame my parents," she said. "I blame you. You shattered all our dreams. Mine and my parents'." Thinking of her parents brought tears to her eyes. "It's because of you that I'm in this strange country. It's because of you that I suffer the humiliation of cleaning up other people's excrement."

Chun took the cigarette from his lips. "We've only been here a few months. Everything takes time." He flicked off the ashes.

She sat back and stared at the floor. "We are not even in honorable exile."

He knew what she meant. It was all a mistake. His name had mistakenly appeared on a list of student protestors. The Japanese should have known he was never involved in politics. But guilty or innocent he would have faced imprisonment, perhaps torture, even death. He had no choice but to escape to America.

"What's the point of rehashing that?" he said.

"Here, because of a stupid silly mistake," she said. Then she lost control and began to cry.

Chun stood up, pulled his cap and sweater off the wall hook and walked out.

Haesu cried most of the night and spent the following morning putting cold packs over her swollen eyes. She stayed indoors, not wanting to see anyone or have anyone see her. She dreaded Chun's return, yet was miserable at being alone. She hadn't planned the

confrontation, but why hadn't it led to greater understanding between them? If only he would express his feelings. As long as he
kept his thoughts to himself, he would remain a stranger to her.

Chun did not come home that night or the next. On the third
night of his absence, Haesu decided to attend her English class. She
returned to an empty apartment. Exhausted, she went to bed and
fell into a deep sleep. She was awakened by the grip of Chun's
hands around her waist. He turned her on her back and held her
firmly as he entered her. Mechanically, he thrust himself in and out
until semen seeped from him. He then fell away from her. Without
a word, he turned his back to her to go to sleep.

Haesu lay in the dark, humiliation crawled over her like damp
moss. Bitterly, she vowed she would never respond to his advances.
She did not know the word for what he had done to her. "That
thing" is how she referred to coitus. She didn't know the word for
rape.

In the morning when Haesu awoke, Chun was gone. There was
no evidence of his having made breakfast for himself. All that lay
on the kitchen counter was a crisp one hundred dollar bill.

Haesu had difficulty concentrating on her homework. Absent-
mindedly, she recited the phrases assigned to her. "Good morning,
Mr. Smith. How are you? I am fine, thank you. Will you and Mrs.
Smith join me for tea?" But her mind was on the events of the night
before. She swore to herself that she would make Chun pay for
debasing her. He would never have her respect, not after what he
had done to her.

That evening, Chun came home from work at the usual time,
giving no indication anything was amiss. They sat silently through
dinner. She then buried herself in her books until Chun went to
sleep. In the morning, she prepared breakfast but waited while
Chun ate alone, waiting until he left for work before sitting down
to eat. No word had passed between them. She would never raise a
subject that had been so demeaning to her.

As the days passed, the pattern of their daily routine remained
unchanged. A word uttered now and then slowly broke the silence
until, seemingly, things were as they were before. Haesu re-
lentlessly searched her mind for some recourse and found only two
open to her: never to forgive or forget. Grievances from then on
were dated after "what he did to me."

"Haesu?" Mrs. Shelton's voice called to her. "It's your turn to reply to Mr. Kusumoto. Lesson Nine, beginning with 'today is a lovely day to go to the park'."

Haesu ran her finger over the page to find the place. She cleared her throat. "Today is a lovely day to go to the park," she read, repeating easily what she had heard.

"Go on," Mrs. Shelton instructed.

Haesu felt the heat rise to her face. Paralysis seemed to creep over her tongue. "Many . . . trees . . . gu-ro . . . d . . . th . . . there. My pavorite . . ."

"Favorite. Ef. Fa, fa, not pa, pa. And, you're right, 'th' is not 'd'. Flip your tongue behind your upper teeth." Mrs. Shelton opened her mouth to demonstrate.

Haesu had practiced her 'f's all week to no avail. There are no 'f' sounds in the Korean language.

"Hard for me," Haesu said with a smile.

"Practice," Mrs. Shelton said. "Practice, practice. One cannot master speaking a language unless one train's the muscles of one's mouth." She looked around the room. "Mr. Jankowsky. You're next."

Haesu felt a failure. She had not missed a single class, completed every assignment, yet she was still third lowest in the class. She didn't tell anyone that, not even Clara. The Japanese couple were at the bottom. There native language seemed to develop a tongue that made forming English words impossible. During the break, Haesu sought them out, speaking to them in Japanese.

"Reading is so much easier," Haesu said. She had mastered the alphabet quickly.

Mrs. Kusumoto nodded. "I can understand what I read. I just can't say it."

"Useless phrases," Mr. Kusumoto complained. "Last week's took the prize. 'I would like roast beef, peas, and mashed potatoes.'"

Mrs. Kusumoto smiled. "Imagine what he would get with that pronounciation."

They laughed.

"At least you remember last week's phrases. I repeat and repeat what we learn only to forget them when I repeat and repeat the next week's lesson." Haesu said.

"It's because you don't have a chance to use it," Mrs. Kusumoto said sympathetically. "At least Mr. Kusumoto and I can practice with each other."

Haesu nodded.

At the end of the break, Mrs. Shelton called everyone back into the room. "It's time for everyone to read his own composition aloud."

Haesu sighed. She wasn't confident of what she had written. Taking lessons had not helped; she was still a dunce in English. In Korea, she had been among the top students of her class.

Several weeks later, the discovery she was pregnant almost came as a relief. She completed the first and second sessions, then quit her English class to await the birth of her baby.

"I know enough English to get by," she told Chun, explaining her reason for dropping the class. "Good enough until we go back to Korea."

"Everyone's trying to get out of Korea and you talk about going back."

"When the situation changes, people will change," she said.

Freed from the long hours she had been spending on grammar texts and workbooks, Haesu had more time for Clara again. While Haesu had been struggling over her assignments, Clara had discovered the movies.

Haesu stood by as Clara threw aside the bedspread to pull a cardboard carton from under her bed. "Mr. Yim doesn't want anyone to see it." Clara explained. "He says it's not in good taste." She drew Haesu down beside her to share her cache of newspaper clippings. She reached into the box and took out a large album. "Scrapbook" was scrawled in gold over the cover, inside were pictures of movie stars. Clara repeated gossip she had read about the stars as she pointed to their photographs, giving an account of each as if she were going through her family album.

"They're very good looking," Haesu commented.

Clara gave her a look of incredulity. "Good-looking? They're perfect! Wait until you see them on the screen."

Later at the matinee, while Clara went into ecstasy over the mere appearance of Douglas Fairbanks, Haesu made a delightful discovery. She was able to follow the story by reading the captions, able to make connections between what a person said and what he did. Settling back into her seat, she found movies were an entertaining way to learn about life in America, much more satisfying than from rides on streetcars, and much less embarrassing than reciting in front of a class.

—5—

An emergency meeting had been called. Haesu offered to help set up chairs, but everytime she would bend over, a wave of nausea came over her.

"You sit down," Clara insisted. "Mr. Yim and I can take care of it."

"I don't think we'll need many more," Mr. Yim said. "No guest speaker tonight. I doubt it will be as crowded as the night Min Chang Mo was here."

"How is he doing? Has he collected enough money to return to Korea?" Haesu inquired. In her purse was an envelope containing the hundred dollar bill Chun had left on the kitchen counter the morning after 'what he had done to her'. She planned to donate it toward explosives.

Mr. Yim shook his head. "I'm afraid not. He got as far as Fresno when someone told him about a scholarship set up by missionaries. He was having such poor luck collecting money that he decided to abandon his project and attend school. It must have been his destiny. He was meant to be a scholar."

"Then tonight's meeting doesn't have anything to do with him," Haesu said, disappointed.

"Not him. But, as usual, money and politics. It seems that everyone is trying to start a party of his own. At the slightest disagreement a new party is formed and appeals go out for money. They don't understand that unity is our only chance for survival. Well, I'll save it for my speech." He sucked in his breath, his lips moving as he counted the chairs to himself. "I think we have enough."

Thirty wooden chairs had been distributed around the parlor. The meeting was scheduled to begin at eight-thirty. At nine o'clock, two-thirds of the chairs were filled. Mr. Yim decided to start the meeting. Even as some still held onto the last note of the Korean national anthem, Mr. Yim began his speech.

"We have serious business before us," he said. Shaking his head disconsolately, he went on. "We Koreans are among the ill-fated people who have been driven from their country." His cadence

became that of a Korean orator. His voice grew loud and vindictive
when he spoke of the Japanese, rolling the vowels at the back of his
throat and spitting out the consonants. Words that recalled his
'beloved' Korea were soft and lilting. His tone became that of a
reasonable man when he said, "Koreans differ on some issues, but
on our country's freedom we have no argument. We are an inde-
pendent people. We cannot bear oppression from anyone. Unity is
our strength. Please keep this in mind as K.Y. Yun gives his report."

Haesu caught her breath. She had forgotten Yun's request for an
annual pledge, dismissed it from her mind after passing the information on to Chun.

Yun began by enumerating the projects that were in need of
funds. The list was not long, but the initial commitment had been
large, made in the flush of patriotism after the Korean Declaration
of Independence. "In need of financial help are: 1. The School of
Aviation in Willows, California, established to train Korean pilots.
2. Korean farmers who, combined, had planted almost eight thousand acres of rice that were totally ruined by early rains and
freezing temperatures."

As Yun continued his list, Haesu clacked her tongue sympathetically. She wished she had the money to bail everyone out. She
jotted down notes for her report to the newspaper, underlining
words such as patriotism, freedom, unity, and sharing.

After he had reported on the crises, Yun read the list of donors
who had already given money. Chun's name was not on the list.
When Yun asked for donations, Haesu took the envelope from her
purse and handed it to him. He opened it carefully and peeked at
the contents.

"A hundred dollars from Chun Haesu," he announced loudly.
"It's sacrifices like this that will bring our country freedom," he
added, smiling at her.

She did not smile back.

In September when the baby was born, the dahlias Haesu had
planted in April were blooming in profusions of reds and yellows.
A blue layette turned out to be the right choice. Haesu gave birth to
a boy. Chun named him Chulyong, but the nurse suggested he be
given an English name as well. The only name Chun could think of
was Charlie, after his partner. Haesu turned down the suggestion.
"In movies, it's the name they give Chinese houseboys," she said.

She remembered that Mrs. Thayer's full name was Mrs. Harold Thayer, so the Chuns named their first American-born child Harold.

Soon after the baby's arrival, Chun and Charlie Bancroft sold their stall at Grand Central Market at a profit, formed the B & C Wholesale Produce Company and moved to Ninth and San Pedro. This meant that Chun would be working nights at the market and sleeping at home during the day.

A baby's cry could make sleep difficult, but nothing Harold did angered Chun. He held his son whenever he could, sometimes falling asleep while holding him. A near accident, when he almost dropped the baby, led to his habit of lying in bed with the baby on top of him. Haesu made periodic checks to see that the baby was safe. Despite Chun's attentiveness to Harold, he never bathed, changed, or fed the baby. Those matters were left to Haesu.

When Harold was old enough to toddle about, Chun told Haesu, "You'd better find a bigger place for us."

It was a thought that had been growing in her mind. She could not remember ever having shared the same thought with Chun. The baby's arrival had not brought Haesu any love for her husband, but their mutual concern over their child had formed a tolerable alliance.

"A house?" she asked.

"A house and yard. Buy not rent," he replied.

His wholesale produce business was prospering. Haesu was convinced that Harold was born under a lucky star.

There had been only a slight improvement in Haesu's English since she last went looking for a place to live, but she was confident she could speak for herself. She anticipated no problem as long as she confined her search to 'unrestricted' districts.

In her opinion, Temple Street was becoming too congested. When she heard that several Korean families had moved to a quiet area near Exposition Boulevard, she learned the bus and streetcar routes and made her way there.

A 'For Sale' sign pierced the front lawn of 1337 W. 37th Place. Haesu was drawn to the pale green wood-frame house trimmed in white. The door was open and as she inspected the property, she visualized her life there. The three bedrooms allowed for a growing family. The large backyard would be a haven for children; safe at play while she watched from the kitchen window. She would border the stretch of lawn in front of the house with flowers, transplanting her dahlias to her new home. The narrow walk that led from the porch steps to the curb presupposed the ownership of an automobile, for now, Chun's truck. The living room window faced the street, as did all the houses in the neighborhood. From inside her own home, she would look out to the world. A public sidewalk connected the front walks of all the houses, linking 'hers' with the others.

The numbers were lucky, she thought. The repeat of 3's and 7's in the address were propitious signs.

"Can I help you?" A man approached her from the sidewalk. Except for his sloppy dress, he reminded her of Adolphe Menjou.

"You know how much this house?" she asked.

"You don't want this house. It's too expensive."

"How much?"

He folded his arms and looked at her askance. "Five thousand."

Haesu contained her whistle. "You owner?"

"Yep, I saw you snooping around from my house. I live over there." He pointed to a house on Dalton Avenue, a street that ran perpendicular to 37th Place. "The one with a palm tree in front of it." The fronds of the thick tree kept the sun from shining on his house.

Although she thought it dark and gloomy, Haesu said, "It's nice house." She scanned 'her' house again. "I see everything already. I let you know."

Later, she described the place to Chun. "You can look out to a piece of land from the front door and the back. The lot is deep with lots of room to plant whatever we like. I'm going to plant _mugung-wha_ on either side of the front steps. I wonder if they grow here?" She couldn't remember ever seeing any in Los Angeles. On the hills surrounding her hometown, Sunchoun, Korea's national flower bloomed wild in shades of lavender, pink, and white. She could still see the azalea-like blossoms in her mind.

"Five thousand dollars is a lot of money," Chun said. "Maybe he's overcharging you. I'd better ask Charlie about it."

Haesu had never met Bancroft to form an opinion about him. Chun trusted him. She had no choice but to do the same.

Haesu began preparations for the move. They would be getting out of the apartment none too soon. Whenever she bent over a packing box, a wave of nausea would come over her. She recognized the sensation; she was pregnant.

"Might as well unpack." Chun said. He had returned from taking Charlie Bancroft to see the house.

"What do you mean?" She swept her hand over the row of boxes lined up near the door. "I'm almost finished."

"First of all, the house was overpriced. Charlie figured three thousand was more like it. I stayed out of sight while he talked to the owner. He told Charlie the price was three thousand five hundred. Charlie didn't know what to say so he told him he'd be back in a few days."

Haesu gave a sigh of relief. "I didn't expect to move right in. I just wanted to give myself plenty of time." She squatted and resumed her packing.

Chun hung up his cap, changed into his slippers, and sat down. He began tapping his fist against the palm of his other hand.

"Something else?" Haesu asked.

"They won't sell the house to us."

Haesu grabbed the arm of the upholstered chair and pulled herself to a standing position. "They won't sell the house to us?"

"They can't sell the house to us. We're not citizens."

"Who says that?" she demanded to know.

"The bank. It's the law."

"Even if we pay five thousand dollars?"

"It's not the money. It's the law."

"What are we going to do? We can't stay here. I'm going to have a baby."

Chun looked at her, slowly comprehending what she had said. His lips curled with irony. "It's getting so I can't separate good and bad news."

Haesu dropped into the chair. "I hate it. Everytime I think things are working out, we run into a wall. What's wrong with *our* money? Why can't it buy for us what it buys for others?"

Chun lit a cigarette. "Charlie can buy the house . . ."

Haesu scoffed. "That's what I mean."

Chun went on. "He can buy it. We'll live in it and pay him"

Haesu sighed. "Money down the drain every month."

"No. We'll buy the house through him. When Harold comes of age, Charlie will transfer ownership to him."

Haesu sat up in her chair. "Is that legal."

"Harold's a citizen." Chun said matter-of-factly.

"Can we trust Bancroft?"

The phone rang, jolting Haesu. She still wasn't used to having a telephone in the house. She ran to answer it.

Mr. Yim was on the other end of the line, sputtering out news so quickly that Haesu had to ask him to slow down.

"The scandal will destroy the NAK! The monies Yun has been sending to Shanghai never got to our leaders!" he exclaimed.

"Yun is guilty of stealing?" Haesu asked, trying to grasp the situation.

"Not Yun but the man he's been sending the money to in China. Confiscated everything and disappeared." Mr. Yim fell into a coughing spasm. "We're having an emergency meeting tonight. We'll need you to record everything," he gasped.

"Of course. I'll be there," Haesu promised and hung up. She ran to the bedroom and shook Chun. "*Yobo, yobo,* the NAK is in trouble."

Chun mumbled, "Is it already time for me to get up?"

Pretty soon," Haesu said. "That was Mr. Yim on the phone. All the money Yun's been sending to China has been stolen."

Chun turned over to lie on his back. "How did they find out?"

"I don't know. What does that matter? The money's gone."

"Yun? Did he have anything to do with it?" Chun was now wide awake.

"Mr. Yim says not," Haesu replied.

Chun threw the blankets aside and got out of bed. "China! Should have kept the money where everyone could see it," he said.

After dinner, Chun dropped Haesu and Harold off at the Yim's on his way to work. "You'll have to find someone to take you home," he said.

"Don't worry, I can always find a ride," Haesu assured him.

As usual, the meeting began with the singing of the national anthem, but everyone was singing as if they wanted to hurry and get it over with. The crisis had brought Min Chang Mo from Fresno and NAK representatives from Delano and Reedley. Mr. Yim dispensed with the Treasurer's Report. K.Y. Yun did not take his customary place facing the audience; he sat near the stairwell, facing the steps.

The women took turns amusing Harold to allow Haesu to take the minutes. Haesu had little difficulty recording the discussion at first. Then the accusations began. Blame was being passed too quickly for her pen to keep up. She appealed to everyone to slow down, but no one paid any attention to her. Mr. Yim repeatedly called for order but lost control of the meeting when he shouted for everyone to remember the cause for Korean independence.

Suddenly, Harold began to cry. Haesu beckoned to him and held him close to calm him down. She shamed the men by saying, "Even a child cries for peace."

His voice now hoarse, Mr. Yim once again pleaded for reason. Min Chang Mo asked permission to speak. "This organization has been run by reactionaries for too long," he began. "Their ideas creak with age and their methods are childish. I myself have been guilty of naivete, thinking that I could rid Korea of the enemy by bombing police stations. We have to develop plans for a new Korea based on modern concepts. This business of someone confiscating money is of minor importance. Sending money to our government in Shanghai was only payment to keep our conscience clear."

There were boo's and shouts of "traitor" but Min continued. "Korea's traditions are based on a feudal society. We need a revolution of ideas to rid ourselves of outmoded thinking. If we do not, we will end up with the same problems of class distinctions. Every Korean should be guaranteed equal rights and equal property. Share the work and share the profit . . ."

"Communist!" several voices shouted. It was the signal for a half-dozen men to rise to their feet and shake their fists at Min.

Harold began to cry again. Haesu walked the floor with him but the angry shouts grew louder and Harold tried to bawl above them.

Min, the man Haesu had once portrayed as a soft-spoken but spell-binding orator, raised his voice above everyone. "This organization is dead! All of you who agree with me will walk out as I do now." Three men stood up to follow him. As he came by Haesu, Min paused to chuck Harold under the chin. "Poor little boy, He should be home in bed. Do you need a ride?" he asked Haesu.

The pitch of voices had risen again as epitets were being hurled at the dissidents. Order was out of the question. Haesu nodded and followed Min out the door.

Gossip about the meeting ran rampant among the Koreans. Everyone took sides whether or not they were at the meeting. The talk even reached Chun at the market.

"I hear you're a communist," Chun said at breakfast.

"I don't even know what that is," Haesu said, pouring his coffee. "I left the meeting because Harold was miserable and I needed a ride home. Mr. Yim is already trying to get another meeting together, but he doubts he can even get a quorum. It's too hard for me to take care of Harold and the minutes too. As soon as the new baby is born, I'm going to resign."

Chun raised his eyebrows. "You're giving up on Korean independence?"

"Never. Min Chang Mo is moving to Los Angeles to form a new group. They'll be meeting here. It will be easier on Harold and me." She poured herself a cup of coffee. "His ideas make sense to me. I believe in equal rights and the equal sharing of property."

"Meeting here?"

"They won't interfere with your sleep. We'll be holding them in the evenings."

"How many members are in this organization?"

"Five at the moment."

"Five?"

Haesu caught the smile that fleeted across Chun's face. "That's enough for a start," she said defensively. "It took only Adam and Eve to start all humanity." When she realized the implication of what she had said, she became flustered. "I mean, every organization starts small."

"I didn't say they didn't."

John was born on February 23rd, 1923. Haesu named him after John Barrymore and Chun named him Keeyong. Unlike Harold, everything John did seemed to get on Chun's nerves. He rarely held the baby and when John became old enough to toddle about, Chun held him responsible for infractions that were clearly Harold's doing. Haesu blamed it on Chun's abnormal working hours.

"You don't get enough sleep. You're in bad humor and take it out on John. Change your business. You're ruining the child," she said.

But Chun would not listen. Charlie Bancroft had announced that after three years of the unnatural schedule, he could no longer take it and sold his partnership to Chun. B & C Wholesale Produce became Chun's Wholesale Produce.

"I can't quit now," Chun told Haesu. "The business is all I'll have to leave my sons."

Haesu decided to drop the matter until she could think of something better to suggest.

One Sunday afternoon, after the dishes had been stacked in the sink and the boys had been put to bed for a nap, Haesu and Chun sat on the porch to enjoy rare moments of quiet. Except for an occasional passerby, the scene was as still as an image seen through a stereoscope.

The hum of an automobile engine drew their attention. A four-door Pierce Arrow convertible came into view. Their eyes were fixed on the luxurious car until their gaze became obstructed by Chun's truck parked at the curb.

"Who was that?" Haesu wondered aloud.

"No one we know," Chun said. "He must have taken the wrong turn."

"A car like that must cost a great deal," she guessed.

"Money's written all over it."

"Could we ever own one?"

"Not unless your name's Rockefeller or you become a movie star."

Haesu was quiet while she let her imagination run free then declared, "It wouldn't be right."

"What wouldn't?"

"To buy a car like that when Korea isn't free."

The distant rumble of the Pierce Arrow was drowned out by the chug of an approaching Model T. A smaller version of Chun's truck pulled into the driveway. The driver waved from his seat and, as he turned off the ignition, shouted, "I've brought you a special visitor".

Haesu doubted it would be of concern to her. She did not know Karl Kang well. Like Chun, he worked at the market and seldom attended community events. Unlike the men who work at the market, the young man in the passenger seat was dressed in a suit and tie, a suit cut by a tailor unfamiliar with western styles, a wool suit too heavy for this warm summer afternoon.

His hat in hand, the stranger jumped out of the truck and quickly ran his fingers through his hair, undoing the tangles formed during the open-air ride. "*Nu nim*, how are you? It's been such a long time," he said.

Haesu looked hard at the stranger who called her 'elder sister'.

He pointed to himself. "Kim Samsung. Remember me?"

Haesu gasped. She ran down the steps. "*Aigoo, aigoo*. Samsung-ah!" She threw her arms around the young man, held him close, pushed him out at arm's length to look him over, then hugged him again. He laughed as he was tossed to and fro. She laughed with him. When she finally released him, they both had tears in their eyes.

"When did you arrive? Why didn't you tell us you were coming?" Haesu took him by the arm and led him up the steps. "Chun, you remember Samsung.—lives in Sunchoun, next to my house, practically my baby brother."

Samsung bowed low to Chun, greeting him respectfully.

"I wasn't sure I would make it to America. As soon as I found passage, I had to leave. There wasn't time for letters. I arrived in San Francisco in December," Samsung explained.

"But that's six months ago," Haesu exclaimed. "Surely you could have let us know."

Chun pushed air between his teeth. "A man who's traveled over half the world isn't going to sit down to write letters," he chided her.

Karl laughed. "I knew you would never expect to see someone from your hometown. I ran into him at Hank's Cafe. As soon as I heard he was from Sunchoun and was asking about you, I brought him right over. You'll have a lot to talk about." He backed toward his truck.

Chun waved everyone into the house. "Come on in, Karl. You can hear the news from home with us."

Haesu's inquiries tumbled out one after another. Questions about the appearance and health of her family and friends fired a desire to see them again, to include them in her daily life and conversations, to be able to look out to Dalton Avenue and see Samsung's family instead of the landlord whom they tricked into selling his house to Bancroft. She used to write home every month, long letters with descriptions of America and her people. She had marveled at modern technology, even extolled the virtues of flush toilets until she had to clean them. The letters became more brief when she had only the events of her and Chun's life to write about. A flurry of short notes had followed Harold's arrival, hurriedly written descriptions of his appearance and progress. Then a lull until she sent home news of John's birth.

Letters from Korea were even less frequent, usually bearing news of a birth or death of a relative.

"I've had almost no news from home. What are the conditions there? Is it time to return?" she asked.

"Return? Who's thinking of returning?" Samsung asked.

"All of us. All of us think of returning home," she replied.

Samsung sadly shook his head. "Korea is no longer for Koreans. If conditions have improved, only the Japanese have benefitted. Any profit made is reaped by the Japanese. If there is a bumper crop of rice, we still eat millet or starve."

Karl threw his hands into the air. "No point in going to Korea, then. Why go all that distance when we can have here what we would have there?" He meant it to be amusing but no one laughed.

"At least there, we would be home," Haesu said.

"Be it ever so humble, there's no place like home. Is that it?" Karl asked wryly.

"Once Haesu gets an idea into her head, she can't let it go. How about some coffee, Haesu?" Chun's request was clearly meant to be an order.

As she made her way to the kitchen, Haesu said, "Samsung, remind me to tell you about our new organization."

"I have no interest in joining a political organization," he answered.

When she served the coffee, Haesu picked up the conversation where Samsung had left off. "Why don't you want to join? Don't you want Korea to be free?"

Samsung poured two heaping teaspoons of sugar into his coffee and began stirring his spoon slowly, watching the brew as it formed an eddy. "The truth is, we are powerless. No matter how many of us are jailed, or have bamboo sticks driven under our nails, or have water hosed into our bodies, we are still powerless."

"More reason to organize," Haesu insisted. "Our strength is in unity . . . We . . ." Chun interrupted her. "Pour Karl some hot coffee."

Karl waved his hand to indicate he wanted no more.

"We'll talk about it after you get settled, Samsung," she said.

Haesu brought up Samsung's name at the next meeting. "We may have a new member," she announced. The group had not grown from the original five, but the membership was an illustrious one and she was proud to be part of it. They never held an election; everyone agreed on who should be what. Min was the chairman, Haesu the secretary, Lee the editor of their bi-monthly newsletter, Yang the treasurer, and Kim the librarian and chairman of culture. They created the position for Kim. It did not seem right that everyone should have a title except him. In Haesu's opinion, he was the least illustrious of the group. A mere spectator at a student protest march, he had turned his head to spit. His sputum landed on the shoes of a Japanese officer and Kim was carted off to jail. He managed to escape and make his way to America, becoming a self-proclaimed patriot. He now worked as a waiter in a Chinese restaurant; an impatient one. If one did not order quickly, Kim would do it for him.

Wiry, hot-tempered Lee was a brilliant writer. He fled Korea with the Japanese hot on his trail, 'wanted' for writing seditious literature. He was currently a janitor-journalist or journalist-janitor. If anyone asked him, it was plain journalist or "none of your business".

Level-headed Yang ran a liquor store. He made more money than the others but shared what he had. He had gone into hiding after the March First demonstration, 'wanted' for distributing copies of the Declaration of Independence at Pagoda Park in Seoul. With the help of friends, he escaped to China then came to America.

They called themselves Koreans for Progressive Reforms. Clara told Haesu that others called them the "Five Cave-dwellers", a reference to the homeless Koreans who had carved shelters out of earth-mounds outside of Seoul. Some said it would be the kind of situation everyone would be in if property were shared equally as advocated by the KPR.

Haesu ignored the gibes. She would miss the intellectual stimulation of the meetings if she resigned. On some nights, when politics took up little of the agenda, they would compose poetry. Samsung was a gifted poet. She mentioned that when she brought up his name.

"Excellent! He will be a great addition to our group," Min said.

But their group of five never became six. Chun found Samsung a job at the market. With his working at night, Samsung could not attend meetings and, therefore, could not join the KPR. He sent his regrets.

—7—

Faye was a Spring baby, born on April 5, 1926. Haesu gave her the name of a movie actress and Chun named her Inyong.

"A girl, at last," Chun said, holding his daughter close. He had come to the hospital directly from the market where he had closed the biggest deal of his life. His company had won the contract to provide the produce to all the Navy bases in southern California. "It means big money," he told Haesu.

"Faye must be born under a lucky star," was her reply.

John was moved into Harold's room to give Faye a room of her own. When the boys protested, Haesu informed them that in Korea, boys and girls have separate quarters. The matter was settled when Chun told his sons that that was the way it was going to be. The boys never argued with him.

Haesu knew from her own experience how girls should be raised, but she had little inkling on how boys should be reared. Faye was her responsibility, Harold and John were Chun's. There would be some common goals. The children would learn to obey their elders and to protect those younger than they. This meant that it would be everyone's duty to protect Faye from harm.

As the children grew older, their needs became more demanding. Haesu was overwhelmed with guilt when Clara called her one day. She quickly blurted out, "I've meant to call you many times. I don't know where the time goes. The children keep me so busy. How have you been?"

Her question was met with silence.

"Clara? Are you still there?" Haesu asked.

Through a sudden burst of sobs, Clara managed to say, "Mr. Yim had a heart attack."

Haesu pulled a wooden chair to her and sat down. "Is he all right?" Suddenly she remembered her dream of the night before: her dahlias had been plucked clean of their blossoms.

Clara's voice came quavering over the phone. "He died in the ambulance on the way to the hospital."

"Oh, Clara, how terrible. I'll have Chun pick you up and bring you here. Pack a bag," she instructed her, "you're going to be staying with us."

Clara moved into Faye's room and K.Y. Yun took care of all the funeral arrangements. Friends dropped in all hours of the day, interrupting Chun's sleep. He decided to stay at the market and sleep in his office until after the funeral.

Mr. Yim's funeral was the first to be held among Koreans in California. Every Korean in Los Angeles, and dignitaries from Reedley, Delano, and San Francisco attended. The services were held at Clara's house. Some of the women appointed themselves wailers and threw themselves upon the coffin. As the wife of the deceased, Clara should have joined in the mournful cries. But she sat in her chair and sobbed quietly. Haesu had managed to find her a white mourning dress, but she could not dissuade Clara from wearing a black veil over her face.

After the eulogies, Samsung found one of Mr. Yim's coats and went outside to climb to the roof. He could not find a ladder so he stood on the porch railing and shouted three times that Mr. Yim was dead. With each shout, he waved the coat, inviting Mr. Yim's soul to depart.

Haesu saw to the banquet after the funeral.

On the days that followed, Haesu encouraged her children to talk to 'aunt' Clara, to try and cheer her up. She encouraged Clara to read to the children. A week later, Clara announced that she was going back to her house. "You've been wonderful, Haesu, but I can't impose upon you any longer."

"Don't talk nonsense. How many months did Chun and I live with you?"

"There were only us then. You have the children now. I'll have to make arrangements to move out of the house. The NAK will be wanting it."

"Live here with us," Haesu pleaded.

"No, *Onni*, I'll have to learn to take care of myself. I'll ask Mrs. Thayer to help me find a place."

Chun took Clara and her belongings to her house. When he returned, Haesu said, "I'm worried about Clara. She's so fragile."

"She'll call if she needs you," Chun said.

It turned out that Clara did not need Haesu. Not only did Mrs. Thayer find a small flat for Clara, she found her a job as a packer in a firm that manufactured bobby pins. According to custom, two years would have to pass before Clara could even consider remarrying. Haesu would not have to concern herself with the major decision until then. She would, however, keep her eyes and ears open for a suitable mate for Clara. Haesu believed that, unlike herself, Clara was one of those women who needed a man.

Barely two years had passed when Clara found a man for herself.

"Robert Scully?" Haesu said incredulously. "What kind a name is that?"

"I love him," Clara said.

"How could you love him?" Haesu wanted to know. "He's not Korean."

"He's nice to me, Haesu. He's my age and very good-looking."

"Don't do anything rash, Clara, It may be just an infatuation."

"We're not planning to get married. Not yet, anyway."

"Promise I'll have a chance to meet him before you make any decision," Haesu said. "What does he do?"

"He's a salesman for the company I work for."

"Clara, be careful."

Haesu tried to like Scully when she met him, but she couldn't. She told Chun, "There's something about him I don't trust. He doesn't laugh right. It's not sincere. He does this." Snorting air in and out of her nostrils, she gave a faithful imitation of Scully's noncommittal snicker.

"Can't hang a man for that," Chun said.

"I can't understand how Clara can give herself to a . . . a foreigner, a white man. It's like giving up everything she is. It's capitulation," she said.

"It's Clara's business," said Chun.

Haesu said nothing but she didn't really agree. She could not explain the sense of loss that had come over her, not the loss of Clara but of something indefinable, something that had been gained through years of history and passed on through generations, something that formed the senses and temperament that made her Korean and not Japanese, Chinese, or anything else.

"It's just not right," she said aloud, but somehow she had an uneasy feeling that it made no difference what she thought.

—8—

Harold brought his first note home from school, when he was eleven. He had been in a fight and the principal wanted Haesu and Chun to come to his office for a conference. " . . . before your son becomes a disciplinary problem," he wrote.

"What kind of problem?" Haesu asked.

"Disciplinary. He means before I become a bad boy," Harold explained.

"Bad boy? You?" Just yesterday she had mentioned to Chun that they were fortunate to have a son as dependable as Harold.

"What was the fight about?" Chun asked.

Harold lifted his shoulders as if he were trying to bury his head between them. He looked at the ceiling then dropped his shoulders and cast his eyes downward. "A kid called John a 'chink' and wouldn't take it back."

"A chink?" Haesu asked.

"It means Chinese but not in a good way," Harold said.

"Why didn't you tell him John's Korean?" she wanted to know.

"Aw, Mom, it wouldn't have made any difference."

"What did John do?" was Chun's next question.

"He called the kid a name. The kid was a lot bigger than John, even bigger than me."

"Go get John," Chun ordered.

"Okay, Papa." Harold ran out of the house to find John.

"Why John?" Haesu asked. "The note was about Harold."

"Harold didn't start the fight. He was protecting his brother."

She began to comprehend the situation. "What shall we do about this?" She held the note from the principal in the air.

"Throw it away. The principal won't understand. Besides, it's none of his business."

When he confronted John, Chun made it clear that no one should start a fight he could not finish. But he was speechless when John asked him what he should do when a kid bigger than he calls him a 'chink'.

It was the first time Haesu had ever seen Chun squirm in his seat. Finally, he said, "Go out and play." As John went out the door, Chun added, "And stay out of fights."

"You didn't give him an answer," Haesu said.

"Do you have one for him?" Chun snapped back.

She searched for an answer and found none. The more she searched, the clearer the dilemma became. It was then that she remembered the billboard. Whenever she went downtown, she passed an enormous picture of a handsome cadet standing in front of the gate to a school. He solemnly invited parents to enroll their sons.

Boys attending private schools would surely come from good homes, she thought. They would come from families that did not

use words like 'chink'. She made up her mind to visit the school, see
how she liked it, and find out the cost of tuition.

As soon as she had the chance, Haesu took the streetcar and rode
toward town, getting off at the corner where the billboard rose
above a brick building. She stood back from the giant sign to read
the name and address of the school and wrote them down. She
stepped back further and studied the painting of the gate and
building behind the cadet. She wanted to be able to recognize the
place when she went looking for the school. On the ride home, she
repeated, "Edwards Military Academy" to herself until she had it
memorized.

A week passed before Haesu felt ready for her visit to the
Edwards Military Academy. She dressed carefully for the occasion,
spreading out several dresses on the bed before deciding on the
navy blue crepe. A white satin collar was its only decoration. No
one, she felt, would question her good taste.

The school was in Hollywood. She wasn't as familiar with the
streets there as she was with those that radiated from Seventh and
Broadway in downtown Los Angeles. She showed the bus driver
the address of the school, relying on him to alert her when she was
at the right stop. She took her seat and with heightened interest
observed the scenes on Wilshire Boulevard, looking at what her
sons would see should they attend the Academy. At Highland
Avenue, she caught the driver's eyes looking at her through his rear
vision mirrow. "Edwards Military Academy," he announced.

The bus came to a stop and the door swung open. They were in
front of a shop. The sign said. "Sarah Mills School Uniforms". Still
holding onto the metal safety rail, Haesu looked at the driver.
"School?" she asked. He made a sweeping semi-circle with his arm,
indicating it was around the corner. She thanked him and stepped
off the bus.

Displayed in the window of the shop was a khaki uniform with
the same brown leather shoulder straps worn by the cadet pictured
in the billboard. She lingered to admire at close range the uniforms
her sons would be wearing should they attend the Academy. Chun
may object to the brass buttons but she thought they gave distinction to the uniform, and the uniforms would give distinction to her
boys.

She turned the corner and was relieved to see the gate that

confirmed she was at the right place.

The grounds had not been pictured on the billboard. The stately tropical trees and profusion of brilliant flowers, all carefully placed to form a perfect landscape, made her feel she was in paradise. She walked under one of the series of arches of the Spanish style building and imagined Harold and John walking the same path. They'll like it here, she thought.

The carved wooden doors were open and locked in place. She tried to be inconspicuous but the heels of her shoes snapped sharply against the tile floor and echoed through the hall. At the reception desk she was directed to a seat opposite a meaty man whose gray hair gave distinction to his ordinary face. He sat behind a mahoghany desk that had his nameplate on it: Colonel Leland-Admissions Officer. With her back straight and sitting forward in her seat, she told him her name, spelling it for him slowly, C-H-U-N, then told him why she had come.

He listened attentively, smiling with understanding as she struggled with her English. He sighed deeply when she finished what she had to say. "The school was established for Anglo-Saxon Protestant boys," he said.

"Yes," she said. "Presbyterian."

He gave her a puzzled look, "Anglo-Saxon," he repeated.

She cleared her throat, "I don't understand."

"It means . . . it means we, that is, the Academy does not accept orientals."

She smiled. "No, not my sons. American-born. Right here in Los Angeles."

"Mrs. . . . uh . . . Please try to understand," he said, impatience in his tone. "Anglo-Saxon, uh . . . Caucasian." He seemed to be searching for the right word. "White," he said, finally.

As she began to understand, her face turned hot. She felt her pulse throbbing in her throat, choking her.

"I'm sorry Mrs . . , uh . . . Mrs. It is the policy of the school. It is out of my hands." The Colonel seemed to squeeze the patronizing words from the upper chambers of his tightened nostrils as he shrugged off any responsibility.

Everything she wanted to say came to her in Korean. She glared speechlessly at the pale, freckle-ladened, flabby-skinned Colonel Leland.

He leaned back in his chair and folded his hands piously in front of him. "Mrs . . . uh," he began.

"Chun!" she snapped.

"Mrs. Chun," he said condescendingly, "your boys would not be happy here. They'll want to be with boys like themselves. You ask them. I'm sure they'll agree with me."

Haesu's eyes grew enormous. Who was he to say what her boys would want, she silently demanded to know. She couldn't find the words to say it aloud. He hadn't even given her a chance to find out how much the tuition was. She wanted to be able to tell him that whatever it was, it was more than the school was worth.

Leland shifted in his seat then began to rummage through some papers, signaling he was through with her. His coat fell open as he reached for a paper he had dropped, exposing the wet stain under his arm. The air became suffocating; she rushed out.

Disgraceful. She thought that was the only word for it. As disgraceful as having to rely on Mrs. Thayer to find her and Chun a place to live. As disgraceful as having to buy their house in Charlie Bancroft's name. She had thought it all necessary because she and Chun were not American-born. But that wasn't it, not all of it. Her boys were American citizens and they were no better off.

She was blind with rage, missing her stops, stalking back to where she should have made a transfer, taking any seat that was empty whether or not it was next to a window. In her preoccupation, she missed her stop and rode into the 'whites only' residential area. She didn't care; it was all L.A. to her. She got off the bus and crossed the street to stand with a group of 'Anglo-Saxons' to wait for the bus that would take her back to the 'unrestricted' section.

Chun was still asleep when she reached home. Harold was looking after Faye. "Where have you been, Mom?" he asked.

"Hollywood," she said and walked directly to the bedroom. *Yobo! Yobo!* She shook Chun hard, shattering his sleep. His eyes snapped open and she quickly assured him that the house was not on fire and that no one was hurt.

Dazed, he raised himself on his elbows. "You could kill a man waking him up like that," he grumbled.

She knew that sleep was what he desired most. He always said that it was 'sweet' sleep for those who had it at night when the world was silent. He complained that it was never a deep sleep for those who had to shut out the daytime world. But she said, "I can't wait. I have to talk to you."

Chun sat up, lit a cigarette, then prepared himself to listen.

She began by describing the billboard that had set her on her quest. Then she went over everything that had happened at the Edwards Military Academy. She did not bother to describe the grounds or buildings of the Academy, but she gave every detail of Leland's mannerisms. She pinched her nostrils and raised her voice to a pitch that matched Leland's. "We don't take orientals. Oh, so sorry, Mrs . . . uh . . . Mrs . . . uh, but your boys are not allowed here." She removed her fingers and in her natural voice said, "He was sweating so bad I had to leave."

Chun ran his fingers through his thinning hair. "You woke me up to tell me this? What did you expect?"

"I didn't expect that. Not for our sons. Not for our American-born sons. It's not right. I'm sure they can't do that and get away with it. I should have told him . . . I should have said . . ."

Chun ground out his cigarette, forcing threads of tobacco to burst through the white paper. The words seeped slowly through his clenched teeth. "Told him what? That's the way those sons of bitches are. You can't tell them anything." He slid under the covers and turned his back to her.

Haesu felt her anger rise again, this time at Chun. She shook him. "*Yobo!* Don't you care about the children? How can you allow anyone to treat them like that? How can you sleep when you've been told your children are not good enough?"

He waved her away. "We can't do anything about it. You should have known that. Why go out of your way to ask for it? Now let a man get some sleep." His tone was sharp. There was to be no mistaking his authority.

She wished she could yank him out of bed, make him take hold of the situation and change it. "You and that Colonel Leland are two of a kind," she said and walked out of the room.

That night, the sound of Chun's truck fading into the distance brought a sigh of relief to Haesu. She plumped the pillows on the sofa then went to the kitchen to prepare something to eat. She had called a special meeting of the KPR.

All four men appeared together. She waited while they distributed themselves around her parlor, waited while two of them settled into the blue mohair sofa. One took the matching chair and the other sat in the tapestry wing chair. She waited while they filled the room, reminding her how empty her house was without them.

As she pulled up a chair for herself, she started right in.

"I went to the Edwards Military Academy today to see about enrolling my sons. I . . ."

Lee interrupted her. "A private school?" he asked, raising his eyebrows. "What a bourgeois idea."

"Yes, I know. But my boys were being called names at school and . . ."

With a knowing smile on his face, Kim said, "Ching-chong Chinaman." He pushed up the ends of his eyes with his fingers.

"Something like that," she said. "I talked to this awful man in charge of admissions. He told me that the school did not take orientals. Sons of bitches aren't they?" She looked at them expectantly. Their expressions remained blank. "Don't you understand? They do not take 'orientals'. My sons are American citizens."

"We understand," Lee assured her. "They only want whites."

"Saved you a lot of money, Haesu. Private schools are expensive," Kim said.

"But that's for me to decide. They can't tell me what to do with my money. And they should not be allowed to tell me that I can't send my boys to their school." She could not understand why the men could not see it. They were men of history who had been disenfranchised and persecuted by an enemy of freedom. "Don't you understand?"

"Of course we understand," Min said. "I'm wondering what we can do about it."

"I could write an editorial for our newsletter," Lee said. He had a grin on his face.

"That won't do any good. Only Koreans read that," Kim said.

"You don't think the L.A. Times would print it, do you?" Lee asked sarcastically. "Haesu, where have you been? Are you only now beginning to wonder what happened to 'America, the land of the free'?"

"I'm not talking about me, I'm talking about my children," she retorted.

Yang's eyes blinked involuntarily as he said. "Before we came, the only thing we knew about America was what the missionaries told us. "Freedom" and "opportunity" they said. They forgot a few things, but we've been here a few years now, long enough to know what to expect."

"That doesn't make it right. That doesn't make it right," she insisted.

"Maybe they didn't know," Kim said.

"What are you talking about?" Lee asked impatiently.

"The missionaries. What did you think I was talking about?"

"Is that supposed to be funny?" Min looked at Kim the way a teacher looks at an unthinking student.

"No, I'm serious," Kim insisted. "They were never discriminated against. They were never told they can't have this job or live in that place, that they must be this and can't be that."

"Can we talk about the school?" Haesu pleaded.

Lee ignored her to respond to Kim. "Don't be a jackass. Where have *you* been?"

"The school. Let's talk about the school," Haesu said.

"Of course, Haesu. You do have a point," Min said thoughtfully.

Haesu was heartened. She knew she could count on him.

Min went on. "The school is guilty of abusing individual rights. Discrimination based on color. They really should not be allowed to get away with it."

Yang nodded his head in agreement. "No question about that."

"Well, what shall we do?" Haesu eagerly asked.

Min inhaled deeply and slowly blew out the air to a steady whistle. Lee tapped his fingers on the arm of the sofa, sucking air between his teeth. Yang, with his arms folded tightly across his chest, blinked harder than ever. Kim took off his glasses and blew his hot breath on them.

They need time to think, Haesu thought. She went to the kitchen to brew some coffee, leaving the swinging door open so she would not miss any conversation. She heard Min as he began to speak slowly and deliberately. "Intentional separation of the non-privileged from the privileged. Power to be perpetuated in the hands of those who can afford it."

"I can afford it," Haesu shouted from the kitchen. She lit the gas under the coffee pot and returned to the parlor.

Min's lips smacked as he opened his mouth to explain. "I'm talking about the kind of money and power you and I will never have. We are not part of *their* system, *their* institutions. If money doesn't keep us out, other reasons have to be invented."

"They don't have to worry about 'other reasons'. It's hard enough for us to just eke out a living," Lee said.

Kim heaved a sigh as he put on his glasses. He folded his hands behind his head and leaned against the blue upholstery. The thick lenses of his glasses magnified his eyes, turning his questioning look into a frightful expression. He reminded Haesu of the clay chimeras of ancient China, guardian figures that were meant to frighten away evil spirits, but in their exaggerated ferocity, managed to look comically unconvincing. The green of his sweater matched one of the hues of the three-colored ware, heightening the resemblance. "What can we do?" Kim asked. "What can we do to affect anything in this country? We're not even citizens."

Haesu was about to remind them again that her children were citizens when she heard the water boil over and sizzle on the burner. She ran to the kitchen. She heard a thud as Lee brought his fist down on the arm of the sofa. "Exactly! That's the real issue. The school is a small matter. Discrimination as it affects the rights of citizenship for 'orientals'. That's the issue. And, most important to us, the recognition of Koreans as separate from the Japanese. We can't waste our time with these puny isolated incidents."

Haesu quickly lowered the flame and glanced at her watch—she always let the coffee percolate for seven minutes. She hurried to the parlor.

"Forget the school, Haesu," Lee said, setting the matter aside with a wave of his hand.

Haesu's mouth dropped open. "Forget the school? Is that all you have to say? You can't just leave it at that." She felt her pulse quicken. "Be realistic?" she said incredulously. "I'm beginning to think you're willing to accept a status of inferiority. You seem to think that unequal treatment is normal . . . realistic. You sound as if you agree with people who discriminate against you. That's what I'm beginning to see as 'realistic'. All your cries for freedom has to do with the Japanese. They're thousands of miles away!" Her voice cracked. "I thought I could count on you."

Lee jumped to his feet. "A lousy school! Why the hell are you getting all worked up about a lousy school?"

Min gestured for Lee to sit down. "Now, now. Let's stay calm and think about it."

"Yes," Yang chimed in. "Let's think about it and discuss it at the next meeting. Anything to eat in the house, Haesu?"

"What?"

"Eat, eat." Lee shoveled imaginary food into his mouth.

"No, there's nothing to eat," she lied.

"Well, I know there's coffee," Kim said.

Haesu gasped and ran to the kitchen. Too late, the water had boiled away.

—9—

Haesu retraced the bus route to Highland Avenue. At the Sarah Mills Uniform Shop, she asked to see the uniforms for the Edwards Military Academy. The clerk smiled. "Your boy will be going to a fine school," she said.

Haesu held up two fingers. "Two boys. Size twelve and size ten. Jackets, hats, pants. No shoes," she said.

She remained composed while the clerk gathered everything together and began adding up the items. She pretended the total cost was no surprise to her.

The clerk was goggle-eyed when she saw Haesu take a hundred dollar bill from her purse. "Would you like them delivered to your home or, if you prefer, we can take them right over to the school," the clerk said.

"No, I take with me."

"They're quite heavy."

"I can carry. I take with me," Haesu repeated.

"Of course. Would you like them in boxes or bags?"

"Box."

When Harold complained that his uniform was a little large, Haesu said, "It's fine. You can wear it longer." John's fitted perfectly. "That's good," she said. "You'll have Harold's to grow into." They looked so handsome that she decided to have their portraits taken.

On Saturday, with Harold and John in full uniform Haesu marched the children to a photography studio. Faye wore a blue chiffon party dress. The photographer took their pictures in several different poses and in various combinations. Haesu's favorite was the one of them standing behind one another, their sides and faces toward the camera, forming a human stairway.

When she showed Chun the pictures, she assured him that the boys looked more handsome than the cadet pictured on the billboard. She thought of sending a photograph to Colonel Leland but Chun told her, "Don't waste your money."

She gave away copies of the final print to Clara, kept several for herself and mailed the rest to her family in Korea. "Mama," she wrote, "here's a picture of the children. We're thinking of returning to Korea. Please write and tell me how things are."

Two months later, she received Mama's reply. She and Chun read the letter together.

"She wrote as soon as she received my letter," Haesu noted. Then, with a sigh of satisfaction, she said, "Mama says we should come home."

"Read it again," Chun suggested. "She says it's every mother's wish to have her family near her *but* Fate doesn't always follow a mother's wish. Listen." He held up the limp rice paper and read the passage, emphasizing the word 'but'.

"She says things are better now," Haesu said.

"She says they're better than they were when we left Korea." Following the vertical path of the lettering with his finger, Chun showed Haesu the words to which he referred.

"I can read it as well as you can," Haesu said. "Probably better. She's my mother."

"Then read it." He tossed the page at her. The tissue thin paper sailed into the air and floated to the floor.

"If she didn't want us to come, she would have said so. If it wasn't safe, she would have warned us," Haesu insisted, not bothering to pick up the letter.

"Maybe she can't. Maybe the letters are read by the Japanese police. We'd have to be fools to trust those bastards. You'd better know what you're doing before you pack up and leave."

But Haesu had already made up her mind. Someone told Yun and Yun told her that the Japanese had formed a new policy toward Koreans. They wanted the world to think they were benevolent rulers. Persecution and torture would impair that image, Haesu told herself. She was convinced that the situation could be no worse for her children than it was in the United States. At least, in Korea, they would not be treated differently than others. She set about making the necessary preparations.

At every step of the way, Chun put up resistance. He complained when he learned that she had bought two steamer trunks at one of the finest department stores in Los Angeles.

"Hartmann trunks," she told him. "The salesman said they were the best money could buy."

"Two hundred dollars just to carry stuff in?" he said in disbelief.

"Two hundred and twenty five," she corrected him. "You don't understand. You never understand. How would it look if we showed up in Korea with cheap luggage?"

"Who's going to notice?"

"Everyone. Everyone's going to be there to meet us. If we show up with cheap luggage, they'll think we had to go back because we failed here."

"Not likely with us traveling in a first class liner."

"We'll be in second class B."

"That's a lot better than the dark belly of the ship we came to America in."

She could not deny that. She had poured over the folders of the N.Y.K. line, studying the floor plans, and was impressed by the photographs of the luxurious accommodations. She had settled on a room with a private bath for her and Faye and a cabin for the boys.

Chun then brought up the issue of closing his business. "It's going to take time. I can't just close the door and leave." On another occasion he said, "What if we decide to come back? How will I make a living?"

Finally, they agreed on a plan: she would go first with the children, assess the situation, then let him know if it was time to return to Korea. That was his idea. Regardless of her findings, he was to follow, bringing enough money to buy land in Korea. She wanted the land in anticipation of their permanent return to Korea, be it this trip or later. That was her idea.

They both agreed on the advantages of his staying behind to reap the profits of another harvest.

"But before I agree to anything," Chun told her, "you have to get a Return Permit for us." Charlie Bancroft had made the suggestion to him.

With the help of Mrs. Thayer, Haesu learned the purpose of a

Return Permit and submitted an application to immigration. She booked passage on the Taiyo Maru and prayed the permit would be granted in time for her scheduled departure in July.

—10—

Haesu carefully pulled the straw cloche over her black marcelled hair, placing the cluster of artificial blue-forget-me-nots behind her left ear. On the dressing table was a real flower. Faye had brought it in from the garden. Excitedly, she had shown Haesu a dahlia that had opened its petals. They were late this year, but the heat of this July day had begun to force the buds open.

At San Pedro Harbor there was always an ocean breeze. She picked up her coat from the bed. As she cast a backward glance in the mirror to see if her slip was showing, she stole a look at her face. She laughed when Clara first told her that she looked like Claudette Colbert, but she had come to see the resemblance. She walked quickly to the porch, not wanting to linger in the house.

"Pull down the lever on the right. NOT TOO MUCH!" Chun was in front of the truck turning the starter crank. He was yelling to Harold who sat attentively in the driver's seat, working his eyes and hands left and right of the steering wheel, struggling to keep up with his father's command.

The engine gave a promising sputter. Chun hurried to the driver's seat to take charge as Harold scrambled across the seat to give his father room. The engine coughed, released puffs of smoke to indicate it was making an effort before dying out. Chun and Harold began all over again until the engine finally settle down to the putt-putt of an idling Model T.

Haesu shouted above the rattling engine. "Harold! Where's John? It's time to go."

Harold cupped his hands around his mouth and called at the top of his lungs. "JO-OHN!"

Don't yell, she was about to tell him, but Chun said it first. Harold ran to fetch his younger brother. He scampered across lawns, jumped over low hedges, and ignored the sidewalk. He was making a bad impression, she thought. She has told him many times, "use the sidewalk, don't jump over the hedges, don't trample the neighbors' lawn, don't knock over the flowers, don't upset the neighbors." She must have told him a thousand time, but today would be the last.

A week and a half ago, the Return Permit arrived in the mail. The trunks were already packed and friends had begun to call or drop in to wish her a safe journey. Several people had left packages for her to deliver in Korea. Almost everyone had asked if she weren't afraid to go back and face the Japanese authorities. She had assured them that she would not leave unless she was granted a Return Permit.

Haesu looked to see if the trunks were on the back of the truck. The bulk of the cargo was hidden behind the sign, "Chun's Wholesale Produce", but glints of brass rivets flashing between the worn wooden stakes told her the two steamer trunks were there. "Were you careful with the trunks?" She said it loud enough to be heard over the engine.

Chun nodded.

Faye had been watching Chun and Harold. She was still sitting on the patch of green between the sidewalk and the curb. "Yah. Faye-yah!" Haesu called. "Go to the bathroom. It's a long drive to San Pedro." Faye brushed the grass from her skirt as she skipped up the narrow walk into the house.

Haesu was about to ask Chun if he had secured the trunks with a rope when Clara and Scully pulled up in a baby-blue Plymouth coupe.

"*Onni!* I'll bet you were worried we would be late. I was all thumbs getting ready." Clara lowered the window as she spoke. She had suffered the heat to keep from mussing her hair.

"I wasn't worried. You wouldn't be late today of all days." Haesu gave a nod to the driver of the car. "Hello, Robert."

"Hello, Mrs. Chun." Scully turned off the ignition as he said it.

Clara had insisted she be the one to escort Haesu to the pier. Haesu had consented, she only wished Scully wasn't driving the car that would carry her out of America.

Harold and John came running down the street and scrambled into the cab of the truck. A word from Chun and they tumbled out again, racing each other into the house, almost knocking Faye over as she came out the screendoor.

Haesu beckoned to her daughter. "You'll have to sit on my lap."

Chun leaned his head out the cab and shouted to Scully, "You follow," then gunned the motor to hurry the boys. Harold was the first to run out of the house. "Bitchin' car, Mr. Scully," he yelled.

That word. Haesu never liked the sound of it. She had mentioned it to Chun but he had brushed the matter aside. "If they say
it when they like something, it must have a good meaning," was his
reasoning.

Scully seemed to know the meaning of the word. He waved his
thanks then ran his hands fondly over the steering wheel.

John came out the screendoor empty-handed. Haesu shouted,
"Your jackets! You forgot your jackets!" John mumbled something
then went back into the house. He came running out with the khaki
bundle in his arms. He almost tripped over the leather strap that
slipped through his hands. It was still dangling when he climbed
into the truck.

The Model T moved forward with a jerk. Scully turned on his
ignition and followed the truck down the street.

"Such pretty curls, Faye. Just like Shirley Temple." Clara ran her
hand gently over Faye's hair.

"That's what Momma says. She burned my neck. It hurt." Faye
said, pouting.

"You don't sit still. If you would just sit still you wouldn't get
burned." Haesu had used those exact words earlier that morning.

"You made my hair stink," Faye complained.

"It's the iron," Haesu explained to Clara. "Heating it on the gas
burner. I can never get it just right. I should get an electric one."

"No, Momma. I don't want you to curl my hair." Faye declared.

"You want to look like Shirley Temple, don't you?" Clara asked.

Faye nodded. "But I don't want Momma to curl my hair."

Her ironic retort made the women smile at one another. Haesu
drew Faye to her. "You were a good girl to let Momma curl your
hair. Now try to get some sleep. It's going to be a long ride." As Faye
nestled into her arms, Haesu said, "Clara, when I get to Korea, I'm
going to look up some of our old friends. I was thinking of Kim Tae
Mook and Wang Kyung Cho, boys who were crazy about you.
Maybe they're not married yet. You used to be lucky with men. Not
like me."

Clara patted Haesu's hand. "Don't bother, *Onni*. They're probably married. It's been almost thirteen years since I've seen them."

"We'll see, we'll see. They were such nice boys. Except there was
that one . . . what was his name? We called him Fisheye."

Clara laughed. "I know who you mean. You called him a 'bathless frog'. He was crazy about you."

Haesu screwed up her face. "My luck with men. He was oblivious to his own repulsiveness."

Clara laughed again. She turned to Scully. "We're talking about our childhood friends."

Scully nodded.

The interjection of English words broke the flow of their conversation, abruptly bringing the subject to a close.

The landscape was flat; they had left the city of stucco buildings and wood-frame houses behind. Isolated gray shacks jutted above the rows of low-growing lettuce. Furrowed fields in geometric precision stretched as far as the eyes could see.

"Chun will be lonely," Clara said wistfully.

"Only for a few weeks," Haesu said.

"I'll miss you. But you'll be so busy you won't have a chance to think about me."

"I'll be thinking about you all the time," Haesu assured her.

"Just think of seeing old friends again. They'll all be there to meet you. You'll be treated like a celebrity—a native daughter returning home." Clara turned to Scully and translated into English what she had said.

"Think she's going to like it there?" Scully asked, nodding toward Faye.

"Why wouldn't she?" Haesu asked.

He shrugged. "You know how kids are. They get used to things."

"She'll get used to Korea." Haesu said.

"You people sure think a lot of your country."

"Aren't you patriotic?"

"Sure, but not night and day."

"You don't know . . ." Haesu began.

Clara broke in. "Koreans have been through a lot."

"I guess you must have," Scully said.

"He'll never understand," Haesu said to Clara in Korean.

Clara nodded but said nothing.

Haesu shifted in her seat. Faye's head lay warm and heavy in her arms; she was fast asleep. Dampness formed where their bodies touched, wrinkling Haesu's dress and straightening Faye's curls. Haesu twisted a strand of Faye's hair around her finger. It was all coming undone.

The air began to smell of sea and oil. Patches of fog brought relief from the sun's hot rays. They were nearing the ocean. Skeletons of steel towers, housing giant oil wells, nested in the hills of sand. Soon they were in the midst of the monstrous pumps. A blue and yellow sign, visible for miles around, claimed it was the property of the Richfield Oil Company. All Haesu knew about the Richfield Oil Company was that they sold gasoline and sponsored the ten o'clock news.

A seagull caught a free ride in the wind and soared above the sign.

Haesu's heart quickened as gigantic sea-going vessels came into view. The ocean lay beyond, its edge merging with the sky. She was startled by Clara's shriek. "There! N.Y.K. Line. You can see it on the smokestack!".

Faye bolted up, her damp hair clinging to her flushed cheeks. "Are we there?"

"We're here," Haesu told her. "See, there's a sign that says N.Y.K. Line." She pointed to a wooden board that hung from a post. English lettering and the curls of Japanese script had been written side by side:

July 12, 1931—Taiyo Maru
Destination: Honolulu, Yokohama, Shanghai, Hongkong, Manila.

The names of the distant cities brought a lump to Haesu's throat. She swallowed hard. "We get off at Yokohama," she said to no one in particular, a quaver in her voice.

As she got out of the car, a crowd of her friends came to greet her. Over thirty compatriots had made the long drive to San Pedro to see her safely off. She began thanking each and every one when Chun came to her side and reached for Faye. "We'd better go aboard," he said. He gave Harold and John permission to run on ahead. "Be in Momma's room before the ship leaves," he ordered.

"Two dash three two seven," Haesu shouted after them.

Without a break in their conversations, her friends followed one another up the gangplank, bumping gently against one another with a familiarity that comes from having shared difficult times, setting aside the bickering and gossip indulged in on an ordinary day, exulting in being Korean as one of their own was about to leave for their homeland on this magnificent ship. They speculated on

how long it would be before they would be passengers on a similar
ship, wondering aloud how much money they would need, then
silently calculating how long it would take them to save that
amount. They told each other how much they wanted to see their
friends and relatives in Korea, expressing what was in their hearts
with guileless candor. Haesu wished she could take everyone with
her.

"Please, your attention for one moment." Min raised his hands
and beckoned all to gather around him. He was standing in front of
a ventilating shaft. The mouth of the large exhaust tube formed a
nimbus about his head, prompting someone to say, "Shh! Buddha
wishes to speak. See the halo around his head?" This brought
laughter. Smiling, Min said, "In memory of this occasion," and
presented a scroll to Haesu.

As she untied the red ribbon, the paper unfurled to reveal a
mixture of Korean and Chinese writing. She recognized the poem
that had won her the prize at the annual church picnic. The black
ink gave nobility to words she had scrawled in pencil on a scrap of
brown paper.

"Read it, read it!" several in the group urged.

Haesu cleared her throat and read:

> The scene at Sycamore Park:
> Autumn hues come uninvited.
> On the trees, few leaves remain.
> Even the crowd is thinning.

Next to her poem, Min had written one of his own. She read:

> The scene at Peiyang Pukto:
> Spring colors come as summoned.
> Pregnant *mugungwha* blossoms.
> Even the crowd grows larger.

The group stirred. Tongues clacked. The sound of air being
drawn in through clenched teeth rippled among them. A few
reached for their handkerchiefs and dabbed away their tears.

"Now, now," Min said to the crowd. "Isn't this supposed to be a
happy occasion?"

His remark drew a laugh and Haesu invited everyone to visit her
room.

"It's a beautiful ship," someone exclaimed, complimenting Haesu
as if the Taiyo Maru belonged to her. "Where is your room?"

"Two dash three two seven," Haesu replied.

"Seven's a lucky number."

As if that were a signal, the group set out to look for Room 2-327. They were ready to descend into the heart of the ship when a steward stopped them. He told them there would not be room for all of them. They closed in around Haesu to discuss what they should do. In the end it was agreed that Clara and Chun would go with Haesu to inspect the room. Clara would have to go if the rest were to learn what the room was like.

"Go! Go! Don't waste time!" the group ordered. Everyone was laughing again.

The corridors were jammed with passengers and their visitors. As the crowd pressed in, champagne glasses were held close to one's chest or high above one's head. One spilled over onto Haesu's dress. A red-haired woman began to apologize but took one look at Haesu and returned to her friends as if nothing had happened. Haesu shared a look of disgust with Clara as she brushed off her dress, brushed aside the offense, and continued down the stairs. Three flights down they came to the sign. "Second-Class-Steerage".

"Steerage? What's that?" Haesu wondered aloud. Her passage was for Second Class. She had insisted on it.

"How should I know?" Chun asked.

They followed the signs to her cabin. Haesu opened the door and ran into the trunks. She squeezed around them to make room for the others. The walls radiated heat from the motors they heard whirring in the next room. It was stuffy and hot. "I'm not going to take this room." Haesu declared.

"Someone has to take this room and it's been assigned to you," Chun stated.

"It's too small. I can't breathe. And that noise. We won't be able to sleep," Haesu glanced around the room. "It's no better than the *China*," she said, recalling the ship that had brought her to America. From Shanghai to Angel Island, she had been seasick and cramped in miserable quarters. The memory of it made her nauseous.

"Oh, it's much nicer, Haesu," Clara tried to sound convincing.

"ALL ASHORE THAT'S GOING ASHORE," a voice bellowed.

"I'll get sick if I stay in here," Haesu said. "We'd better go up. I'll take care of changing the room later."

"Momma! Papa!" The boys ran up panting. "Our room is

bitchin', just like a jail cell. One of the bunk's broken so we're going to take turns sleeping in it. Want to see it?" John tugged at Haesu.

"There's no time," Chun said. He put Faye down. There would be no hugging and kissing; there never was.

"We have to go up to say goodbye to everyone," Haesu said, taking Faye by the hand.

They hurried up the stairs. Haesu was puffing as she told Clara, "Anytime you want to come to Korea, just say so. We'll help you." She turned to Chun. "Don't forget, you're not to do anything about the house until you hear from me." The thought had come from nowhere.

"ALL ASHORE THAT'S GOING ASHORE".

"Mind your mother," Chun instructed the boys. "Come on, Clara," he said as he made for the gangplank.

Everyone was on deck for the departure, first class and steerage passengers alike. Pressed against the railing, waving frantically, those about to set sail clung to thin paper streamers that bridged them to someone on shore. The boys wedged an opening for Haesu and Faye.

"*Yobo!* Haesu! Here!"

She followed the sound of the voices until she found her friends. They were sobbing unashamedly. A deafening blast from the ship's horn drowned out her reply. The pier creaked and groaned as the ship moved to free itself. One by one, the ribbons of paper broke, snapping apart as Haesu fought back her tears.

"Where's Papa?" Harold asked.

They scanned the pier until John shouted. "There he is!"

Haesu looked where John pointed and saw Chun standing alone far behind the crowd. "Look, Faye, over there," she said, lifting her up. "Wave goodbye to Papa." She took Faye's hand in hers and waved.

Chun lifted his chin and gave them a nod. He had seen them.

Standing alone, he looked as if he had been abandoned. Suddenly, Haesu wished he was going with them.

TWO

"Mrs. Chun, the rooms are assigned at the main office in Tokyo. I have nothing to say about it." Dazzling in his white uniform, his bronze skin glowing under his gold-braided cap, Captain Yamamoto shrugged off any responsibility.

There was something about him. It was impossible but Haesu felt she had seen him before. His face was not unusual; broad across the cheeks, a square jaw, eyes shaped like laurel leaves, a pleasant face despite the numerous pock-marks. That did not bother her; while growing up in Korea she had seen many faces scarred by epidemics of chicken pox.

"Captain Yamamoto, do not try to tell me that every room on this ship is filled. I will not stay in this suffocating cell. If necessary, my children and I will sleep on the deck." The despised Japanese language fell from her determined lips.

The Captain sighed. Stalling for time, he reached out to pat Faye on the head. She drew away, repudiating his touch, withdrawing into an armor of suspicion. Her response was like that of the pet turtle in his cabin—a souvenir he had picked up in San Francisco for his daughter in Japan. Whenever he moved toward the creature it would draw in its head, leaving him with an inevitable sense of embarrassment.

The Captain lifted his suspended hand and took off his cap, as if that was what he meant to do all along. "I, I uh . . . have a daughter

68

about the same age as yours," he said, a momentary lapse in formality. Raising a closed hand to his lips, he cleared his throat. "Mrs. Chun," his voice and stance now erect, "what if everyone came to me and demanded another stateroom? The situation would be impossible." His voice had resumed an official tone but Haesu sensed a weakening in his resolve that served to strenghtened her own.

"The fact is, I am the only one who has been assigned this miserable room. I refuse to accept it. It would not surprise me at all if I was given this room because I am Korean." She had no idea why she said that but it obviously had an effect. The Captain's face began to redden, turning the hues of maple leaves stricken by autumn frost. Aware of her advantage without understanding how she had achieved it, she sardonically added, "There's no need to deny it. We both know the Japanese attitude toward Koreans."

Flustered, he turned away from her accusing eyes only to see Faye peering at him from behind her mother's skirt the way a child peers at an unsightly person, head down because she was told it was not nice to stare and eyes up because she could not help herself.

Suddenly, with precise movements, the Captain snapped on his cap, instinctively adjusting the brim over his brows. "I will try to find more suitable quarters for you and your children," he said. Attempting to make a military turn, he ran into the trunks. He squirmed around them to make his way to the door.

Faye whispered. "He's a *wae nom*, isn't he?" using the derogatory term for 'Japanese' reserved for Korean ears.

The Captain paused at the door. "No." He hesitated before adding, "I am Korean."

Haesu could hardly hear him, he spoke so softly, but the words were distinctly in her language. She was dismayed by the sudden revelation.

"Please do not say anything to anyone," he beseeched her. "The crew is not aware . . ."

"I see. Don't worry. I would never turn anyone over to the Japanese authorities," she assured him.

That 'something about him' no longer tantalized her.

The Captain provided them with two spacious connecting rooms in Class 2A-Tourist with no increase in fare. Haesu dismissed any sense of guilt about having accommodations she had not paid for; the rooms would have remained empty while she and the children suffered in their miserable cells.

Two stewards transferred her things to the new stateroom. Despite the two steamer trunks, the rooms were spacious. Haesu tipped the men generously, prompting them to bob their heads in gratitude as they backed out the door. The taller of the two bowed even lower than the other. "I am to be your steward. My name is Kudara. I am at your service," he said. He bowed again, nearly closing the door on his head. Haesu found his servility irritating.

The children examined the drawers, inspected the closets, and tested the plumbing.

"Bitchin', it's bitchin'," John declared as he threw himself on the bed.

"Don't say that word," Haesu ordered.

"Why not?"

"What does it mean?" she demanded to know.

He shrugged. "I don't know. I guess it means it's real nice."

"Then say *that*," she said.

He giggled. "I'd sound like some kind of sissy," he said as he jumped off the bed.

"You can use good language without being a sissy," she retorted, hoping she had made the same impact on John as Chun's pronouncements had. She was never able to exact compliance from her boys in quite the same way as Chun.

The boys began to shove each other toward the door. "We're going on deck," Harold announced.

"Me too," Faye pleaded.

"I have to talk to you, Faye. You boys wait outside," Haesu told them.

"Oh-oh. Faye," John teased, shutting the door after him.

"I want you to listen very carefully. This is very important," Haesu said solemnly, taking Faye's hands in hers. "If the Japanese find out that the Captain is Korean, they will be very mean to him. They will torture him. They will tie him up and beat him until he passes out. Then they'll pour cold water over him to wake him so they can beat him up again."

Faye's eyes grew wide.

"I mean it. Worse things too." She wanted to impress her daughter with the seriousness of the situation without exaggerating. She had heard of tortures no child would understand. "And if you tell anyone. ANYONE, do you hear, I'll give you a spanking you will never forget."

"I won't tell!" Faye promised.

"Don't forget." She released Faye's hands. "You can go now."

As soon as the door slammed shut, the room fell silent. It was filled with the hollowness of her house in Los Angeles when she was alone. She wondered what she was doing, asking a six-year old to keep a secret. No one asked to be part of the Captain's duplicity, least of all Faye. He had volunteered the information, putting himself in jeopardy.

A chill came over her. She walked to where the sun was streaming through the porthole and looked out to the sky. Perhaps the rooms weren't worth it. It may be true the Captain was now indebted to her, but she hated carrying the burden of secrecy no less than Faye.

She looked around the suite. The boys had left their jackets on their beds. She slipped the Edwards Military Academy jackets onto hangers, admiring them before she hung them in the closet. We belong in the rooms, she told herself. Here or in the cell below, she would have had to commit Faye and herself to silence. The imposition would be at least tolerable in a more comfortable setting. She decided to give the subject no more thought.

There was time for a nap before dinner. She undressed and slipped under the covers. The cold sheets made her shudder. She rubbed her hands gently over her body until a soothing warmth began to spread over her and radiate into the bedding. Her hand glided smoothly over her satin underslip.

"Haesu! Come here!". She could almost hear Chun. The time of day would not matter. The fact that she was not feeling well would not matter. She dreaded it most when the children were home, fearful they might hear or unwittingly open the door. "Never mind," he would say, refusing to be interrupted. It was her duty to comply, but she only did so to avoid fighting in front of the children.

Nestling deeper into the blankets, she closed her eyes to sleep, grateful that Chun was not lying next to her.

It was almost five o'clock when Haesu awoke. She sat up, working her way into a state of wakefulness. Nothing in the room had been touched; the children had not been back. She flipped the covers aside to get out of bed when the children ran in.

"Better hurry. We're in the first seating. Dinner at six. First Class dining room," Harold informed her.

"First class?"

"That's what the Captain said and he ought to know," John said.

Faye jumped onto the bed and cupped her hands around Haesu's ear to whisper into it. "He said we're special."

"Your tickling my ear," Haesu laughed as she pushed her away. "You'd better change your dress."

"Do we have to dress up?" John asked incredulously.

"It's First Class," Haesu said.

"Not the uniforms again," he groaned. "Let's move back down below."

"Pipe down," Harold told John.

"You can save your uniforms for a special occasion," Haesu said.

"Good," John said. "I'll save it for Halloween."

The passengers were on deck to promenade before dinner. Haesu had sent the children on ahead while she had gotten dressed. The Captain was talking to the red-haired woman who had spilled champagne on Haesu before the ship left San Pedro. He saw Haesu and gave her a nod.

"Have you seen the children?" she asked him.

He informed her that Faye was with a new-found friend and the boys were somewhere about. He turned toward the woman and said, "This is Mrs. Chun". To Haesu he said, "This is Mrs. Compton." His accent was heavier than Haesu's.

The woman smiled broadly, as if she had never seen Haesu before in her life. "I'm very pleased to meet you, Mrs. Chun. Are you going to Yokohama? I feel so cheated. I'm getting off in Honolulu and all of you will be continuing on to such exotic places. I've always wanted to visit Japan. They say that Mount Fujiyama is spectacular, absolutely breath-taking. And can you imagine the adventure of traveling to China or India or any of those places?"

"I'm going to Korea." Haesu said.

Mrs. Compton looked puzzled. "Where?"

The Captain quickly explained. "It belongs to Japan."

"Oh? It must be one of their many islands. No wonder I hadn't heard of it. Well, how fascinating. You must tell me about it sometime. I love to hear about strange places."

The Captain smiled weakly. Haesu searched for a response. American women never seemed to have trouble finding something to say. She had enjoyed listening to Mrs. Thayer. Clara's landlady never limited herself to perfunctory greetings, but Haesu never found words to equal hers.

Mrs. Compton looked at her watch. "It's almost time for dinner. I think I'll go freshen up a bit." She excused herself and went up the stairs reserved for first-class passengers.

"She's a very wealthy woman," the Captain informed Haesu. "Her husband owns a sugar plantation in Hawaii."

"She should certainly know about Koreans then. There must be many of them working for her husband."

The Captain's jaw dropped. "Of course! I had forgotten about that."

Haesu gave it more thought. "She could still not know," she said.

They strolled side by side toward the dining room, he with his hands clasped behind him and she with her hands in her pockets. "You've been assigned a table with Mrs. Fernandes and her daughter, Maria," he said. "The girls requested it. The boys did not object to sitting elsewhere. I hope you don't mind." He opened the door to the dining room.

The air was alive with the sounds of animated voices, clinking crystal, and clattering silverware, all tastefully modulated by thick carpets and drapery.

"Momma!" Faye's voice called.

Haesu saw her daughter's hands fluttering in the air. She put her finger to her lips to signal Faye not to call again and left the Captain to weave her way to her table.

"Momma, you look pretty," Faye said proudly.

"Oh, Mrs. Chun! I'm so glad you join us. Sit down, sit down, I'm Elena Fernandes." The petite woman smiled as she pulled out the chair next to hers and patted the seat.

Haesu slipped off her coat and draped it over the chair then sat down. "Mrs. Fernandes, I'm happy to meet you."

"Call me Elena . . . and this is my daughter, Maria."

Haesu smiled at the bronzed-skin girl, admiring her dark deep-set eyes.

"Are you going to Yokohama?" As soon as she asked, Haesu remembered it was what Mrs. Compton had asked her.

"No, we go all the way. We go to Manila. I know where you're going. Faye's been telling us all about her family. Your husband sells fruits and vegetables, right?"

Haesu was momentarily taken aback by Elena's bluntness. "Not like that. Wholesale produce business. He's the boss. What does your husband do?"

"My husband? He works for a movie actor."

"A movie actor?" Haesu pulled her chair closer to the table. "What movie actor?"

"Franchot Tone."

"Really?" She wasn't sure she could believe Elena. "What does he do?"

"Who?" Elena's eyes twinkled, delighting in Haesu's interest.

"Your husband."

"He dresses him." Elena threw back her head and laughed. "We only do that for babies, right? My husband dresses this grown man."

Elena jolted Haesu's sense of propriety, but she was straightforward, a quality Haesu admired and one that she tried to nurture in her children—until the current exception regarding the Captain. "I don't understand," she said.

"He's a valet. A personal valet to Franchot Tone."

"Oh, I see. What is he like?"

"My husband? He's okay."

"No, I mean Franchot Tone. I saw him in . . ." Haesu began to search her memory for the name of the movie.

Elena did not wait. "He's okay too, I guess. Like any other man. Inside his clothes he's like any other man . . . maybe a little better looking."

"I'll say!"

"You like him, eh? Personally, he's not my type. Give me George Raft any day."

"My real favorite is Ronald Colman. He's so dignified."

"In pictures," Elena snorted.

"Do you know him?"

"You don't have to know him." She took Haesu by the wrist and drew her close. "Not just him. Any movie actor. They're different in real life." Leaning even closer, she rasped, "Don't believe all that baloney you read."

Haesu drew her hand away. "Well, you can tell something by their looks. A person's face always reveals his character."

Elena looked astonished, "You believe that? I wouldn't trust any man's face. Not until I feel a man in me do I believe in him."

Haesu looked to see if Faye was listening. She was relieved to find the girls huddled together, giggling over some business of their own. She picked up her salad fork and poked at her cottage cheese.

"Is this your first trip?" Elena asked.

"Second, I sailed from Shanghai to California in 1919."

Elena slapped herself on the forehead. "Of course, what's the matter with me? Faye told me you were born in Korea. I guess you don't care for cottage cheese. Well, don't worry, you'll like other things. This ship has excellent food. I know some of the people in the kitchen. They told me and they are the ones who know." Elena sat back to give the waiter room. He took her plate and she gave him a wink. She moved close to Haesu to whisper, "I'm not supposed to be here. I'm supposed to eat," she pointed her finger downward, "but the maitre d' is my cousin." She was all agrin, gleeful about hoodwinking the ship's authorities.

Haesu widened her eyes to acknowledge the information but said nothing. That takes nerve, she thought, then remembered how she came to be in the same dining room.

—2—

The ship cut its way through the sea toward the far horizon where the darkened water drew a clean line between itself and the brilliant orange sky. As the sun continued to drop, the remaining light illuminated the tips of unending swells, exaggerating the motion of the sea.

Haesu took in deep breaths of air. She hoped it was only the sea that had brought on her nausea. Elena saw what was happening. She promised to look after Faye and sent Haesu out into the night.

Walking briskly along the deck, she was bathed in the ocean mist. Through the windows of the dining room she saw that all the chairs had been turned toward a blank screen. The lights went out and the look of anticipation on the faces of the waiting audience disappeared in the dark. Blurred images jerked about as the projectionist searched for the borders of the screen. The music whined out of synchronization with the film and Haesu turned away, not waiting to see the flawless faces of movie stars come into focus.

It was probably a love story, she thought. It usually was. On countless trips to movie houses she would live the life projected on the screen. For ninety minutes she would laugh and cry over situations that could never happen to her. It would end with a kiss, the kiss that brought her blood to her cheeks and left her blushing. To her, the kiss was an act of utmost intimacy. It took place near one's sense of sight, smell, and taste. 'That thing' took place in the nether regions of the body, in the offensive areas. Except for the ceremonial kiss at their wedding, she had never kissed Chun.

She walked until she was back where she started. The railing was damp but she leaned against it to take in more of the night air, pushing her collar over her throat to keep warm.

"Didn't the movie interest you?" The Captain's face was but a shadow under his cap.

"I'm not used to the sea and the motion of the film . . ." She placed an open palm over her stomach, leaving nothing further to explain.

"I'm sure we have some medicine that would help. I'll see that you get some." He leaned against the railing and faced the sea. "The sky was magnificent, wasn't it? And the sea," he smiled at her, "with all due respect, is generously calm."

"Calm?"

He laughed. "You may find it difficult to believe, but it can be much worse. The sea is deceptive. One has to be on the alert for unexpected moves. That's my job, to be prepared for the unexpected. A rather ironic mission in life, isn't it? Grateful if I am rendered useless."

"No one is useless," Haesu said. "You must miss being on land with your family."

"Yes, my thoughts often turn to my daughter, Momo."

"Momo. 'Peach'. A lovely name." A Japanese name.

"The word is meant to be murmured, is it not?" he said with tenderness. He laughed with embarrassment. "Fathers are foolish about their daughters, helpless in their hands."

"So it seems." She thought of Chun. Despite his inability to express his love for anything, she knew that he loved Faye.

"As for being on land, I hate being on land. Entanglements, unresolvable commitments, a web of illogical complications. Because of what happens on land I am forced to be an impersonator at sea," he said.

"You can blame the Japanese for that," she said. "I blame them for taking our country and making exiles of us, blame them for every atrocity they've committed against our people. I would never pose as one of them."

A lift of his eyebrow acknowledged her comment. The Captain reached into his pocket and pulled out a silver case. He snapped it open. "Cigarette?"

No one had ever offered her one before. She shook her head. "May I?"

She nodded.

He set the tip of his cigarette aglow then dropped the burning match into the sea. "The sea swallows everything. It is impossible to plant a flag on water. Not so on land. Men plant their flags in the ground and begin the battle. We are born to our nationality by fate. Why should one be considered better than another?"

"We did not invade Japan," she reminded him.

"True. But, if they had the opportunity, are not Koreans capable of such acts?"

She resented his reference to Koreans as 'they'. "The fact is, we did not invade Japan, she invaded us. We cannot remain dispassionate or indifferent where our country is involved."

He nodded. "Nor can any national of any country. Those unresolvable commitments again."

"Unresolvable only if one is not free to exercise his nationalism," she insisted.

"Yes, well . . ." he said as he straightened up. "I have a resolvable commitment, your medicine." He tipped his cap and excused himself.

She was taken aback by his abrupt departure. She had not had a chance to thank him for his offer of medication or properly bid him goodnight. Feeling rebuffed, she looked around to see if anyone noticed she had been left alone. Clutching the ends of her collar, she started for her stateroom.

Had he left because she had accused him of being unpatriotic, she wondered. He himself had admitted that he was an impostor. No matter what, she would never pose as a Japanese, she told herself, then remembered she had said that to him.

She turned the corner and saw Kudara come out her stateroom door. He bowed when he saw her. "The beds are ready. You'll find fresh water in the pitcher. If you need anything more, please do not hesitate to let me know." With his closely shaven head and his eyes peering through narrow slits, he looked sinister, belying his obsequious mannerisms.

"That's fine. I won't need you for anything," she said, dismissing him.

While Haesu waited in her stateroom for the Captain to bring her the medication, she examined the drawers and looked into the trunks to see if anything was amiss. She wasn't sure what she was looking for, she only knew that she distrusted Kudara. At the sound of the door opening, she spun around.

"I met the Captain in the hall. He said to give you this." Faye handed over a small envelope.

The instructions were printed in Japanese on the outside of the envelope. Inside, written in Korean and unsigned, was a note. "I hope these do the trick. Thank you for a pleasant chat." She took two of the pills before going to bed. A short while later, she leaped out of bed and raced to the bathroom, reaching it just in time. After she had disgorged her dinner, she threw out the rest of the pills.

Harold and John tip-toed into the room, undressed in the dark, and quickly crawled into bed.

"Harold?"

"It's us, Mom," he replied.

"Where have you been?" she asked sleepily.

"Watching a movie."

"Oh. Go to sleep now."

"Okay Mom."

Unknown to Haesu, the boys had seen a different movie than Faye. They had been down in forecastle, in dim airless quarters, where the men were naked except for a piece of cloth tied over their groins and around their hips, where the men held terse conversations in low husky voices. Flattered to be allowed in the crew's quarters, the boys had tried to act like men as they watched pornographic cartoons, laughing whenever the men laughed. Haesu's boys did not understand Japanese words and had been left to guess their meanings. They had guessed the words were wicked.

The air had smelled of fish and soysauce. Holding rice bowls to their lips, the men had shoveled sweet salty meats and wet rice into their mouths with bamboo chopsticks. Harold and John had watched with mouths watering as they were reminded of their mother's cooking.

Then Kudara had spoiled it all. He had come down late and when he saw the boys, he had said, "Go now. Your mother in stateroom"

"She knows we're okay," Harold had said.

"If she know you here, she be mad."

"She's never going to know," John had said. "No ladies allowed here."

The men then told Kudara to leave the boys alone. Kudara had ignored them.

"Go now. Only crew allowed here," he had said as he led the boys to the stairs.

"You should be over it by now," Elena declared, impatient that Haesu never seemed fully herself.

"I'm getting better. I even have an appetite," Haesu said. She was encouraged by the improvement in her health. In a few days they would be in Honolulu and she looked forward to going ashore and visiting with relatives of Clara.

The two women continued to stroll arm-in-arm along the deck, leaning against one another, thrown by the roll of the ship into a zigzag course.

"Let's not talk about me," Haesu said. "Tell me more about movie stars."

"What's there to tell? They're handsome and rich." Elena rolled her eyes up. "God, are they rich. Can you believe they wear their clothes once or twice then give them away? My husband brings home what he gets and I fix them to fit him. Boy, did that get him into trouble in Manila. He wears such fine clothes that all our relatives think he is rich. Everybody wants money from him. 'No, no,' he tells them. 'I get these for nothing'. But they think he lies. Nobody believes him and everybody hates his guts so he doesn't like to visit his home anymore. He just sends Maria and me." Elena smiled broadly. "It's lucky for Maria and me."

"That's one thing I won't have to worry about. My family in Korea are well-to-do," Haesu told Elena.

"Some people have all the luck."

"Well, Koreans haven't been all that lucky."

"Yes, I know. You told me all about the Japanese. Frankly, I'm not so crazy about them myself. Clever but sneaky, right?" she said, as if that should satisfy her friend.

"You'd be surprised how few people know what happened. I'll bet you've never heard about the young girl who led a demonstration and for that the Japanese police gathered together fifteen members of her family, massacred them in front of her eyes, then killed her."

"Sheesh! Sons of bitches! Men are crazy. Fuck them all!"

"Elena!"

"What else can you say?"

"Well, you don't have to say *that.*"

"Scums. Some crazy somebody. It never changes. One rotten one goes down and another one pops up, like you know what." She used her thumb to demonstrate.

"Oh, Elena," Haesu scolded.

"Like bamboo. That's what I meant. Like trying to get rid of bamboo." Elena led Haesu toward the lounge where they had been going to play cards. "I have to ask you something. It's been bothering me. All those things you say about the Japanese. Why do you want to go back to Korea? I don't get it."

"We've heard the Japanese have a new policy in Korea now."

"Leopards don't change their spots."

"And politics for Koreans in America is useless, just theory and talk."

"Gave up, eh?"

"And I was tired of being a foreigner. America is a beautiful country but it's not my home."

"I know what you mean."

They had reached the lounge. Elena held the door open for Haesu then followed her in.

"Do you know what I've been thinking?" Elena sounded as innocent as a child.

"What?" Haesu got a pack or cards from the cabinet where the games were stored.

"I have a good eye for these things, a kind of intuition." Elena sat where she usually sat, facing the door. "I've been watching. You're a very attractive woman. I don't know what you think, but I think the Captain's hot on you."

Haesu dropped into the chair opposite Elena. "What?" She shook her head. "You have such an imagination," she said then began shuffling the cards.

"Okay, okay, you think I'm making it up. But you don't seem so excited about your husband. So what the heck if the Captain is Japanese? I say a man's a man. Where it matters, it doesn't matter where he's from."

"Elena!"

"Okay, okay. I shut up now."

"Good. I can concentrate on my cards." A rare ebullience came over Haesu; she felt lucky.

Elena kept her eyes on her cards, busily rearranging the order. "You know, Haesu, nature didn't make us this way for nothing."

"What do you mean?" Haesu deliberately kept her tone flat to avoid tipping Elena off to her remarkably good hand.

"I don't know how to tell you this."

"Why don't you just say it?" Haesu took a mental count of the potential points she held in her hand.

"Sex is nothing to be afraid of," Elena said as she quickly laid her card on the table.

Haesu held her cards against her chest and looked at Elena. "Who's afraid of it?" She pulled out a card and threw it down.

"You." Elena shoved the cards toward Haesu; they were hers.

Haesu gave a little laugh. "Afraid of that stupid thing?" She gathered the cards. "Watch the game, Elena, I'm going to beat you. I feel lucky."

The game became so engrossing that the women were oblivious to time as it passed and to the Captain as he entered the lounge. His presence at their table took both of them by surprise.

"I didn't see you come in the door," Elena said.

"Your mind must have been on the game," the Captain said. He perused the numbers Elena had scribbled on a piece of paper. "Very close scores. What is the prize for the winner?"

"Have you any suggestions?" Elena asked.

Haesu hastily said. "We play for fun."

"Perhaps the winner will honor me by having dinner at my table this evening," the Captain suggested.

"That would be Haesu," Elena said.

"The game isn't over," Haesu reminded her.

"Why don't you both join me?" he suggested.

"Thank you, but I guarantee it. Haesu will be the winner," Elena insisted.

"I shall be honored," he said then took his leave.

Haesu gave Elena a reproving look.

"For goodness sake, Haesu, have a little fun. What have you got to lose?" Before Haesu could say anything, she added, "Okay, okay. I shut up now."

"Wear your uniforms, 'formal dress requested'. Didn't you read the bulletin?" Haesu asked her sons. She dipped a comb in a glass of water then ran it through Faye's hair. "I wish I had your curling iron here. These stray hairs . . ."

"Ugh! Not me," Faye declared.

"What's all the fuss about? Same old table, same old room, same old people, same old food," Harold muttered. He matched the ends of his necktie, pulled an extra length on one of them, then proceeded to tie the knot.

"Momma's sitting at the Captain's table tonight. She beat Mrs. Fernandes at Rummy," Faye announced.

"Everybody gets asked to sit at the Captain's table," John said, glum about having to wear his uniform.

"That's not the reason," Haesu insisted. "'Formal dress requested', that means everyone."

"We're just kids, they don't mean us," John whined.

"I say it means everyone," Haesu said with finality.

Fidgeting while her mother fussed with the bow of her blue chiffon dress, Faye announced, "Momma's going to wear her velvet dress."

"That dress? I thought you were saving that for a wedding or funeral, Mom," John said.

"Your funeral if you don't keep quiet," Harold warned, tossing a khaki jacket to his younger brother.

"There's going to be dancing later," Haesu informed them.

A smile came to John's face. "That lets us out. It's down below for us," he said with undisguised glee.

"Pipe down," Harold ordered.

"Mrs. Fernandes is going to look after Faye. Harold, you look after John."

"I know, Mom. Don't worry about us."

Satisfied with the appearance of her children, Haesu sent them out then began on herself. As she went through every phase of getting dressed, an inexplicable excitement came over her. The Captain was unlike any man she had ever met. There was a certain daring to his duality, she had to admit. Her fingers trembled as she applied her makeup. Elena had said he was "hot on you". Haesu's lipstick went askew. She laughed and thought, that Elena! Wiping off the smeared red grease, she redid her lips. Of course, there was nothing wrong with having a little fun, as long as she didn't shirk her duties as mother and wife. One thing after another seemed to keep her from thinking of herself. With steadier hands, Haesu smoothed the clinging fabric of her dress over the contours of her body. She wondered what it was like to have a romantic affair as she pushed and repushed the waves in her marcelled hair, softening the curves to suggest an air of carelessness. She looked over her bottles of perfume and decided against the lighter fragrance of crepe de Chine for the heavier scent of Coty's Emeraude.

Everyone at the Captain's table had dressed with care. The elderly Japanese couple, who ordinarily shared their table with Haesu's boys, wore silk kimonos; a change from their usual drab cotton ones. Mrs. Compton wore a green taffeta gown. She was seated at the Captain's right and Haesu was at his left. In his formal black uniform, the Captain was an imposing buffer between them. Although Haesu was spared having to carry on a conversation with the woman, she was unable to shut out the rustling of the taffeta dress. In her silent burgundy velvet, Haesu felt regal.

"You have such fine boys, good-looking, well-mannered." The Japanese woman's voice crackled from across the table.

"Thank you. They enjoy sitting with you." Haesu replied in the elderly woman's language. The boys had amused Haesu with examples of the single-worded conversations they held with the old couple: "like?", "good?", but there was never any indication of disrespect in their mimicry.

The old woman smacked her lips as she began to tell Haesu how impatient her own grandchildren were with her. She turned each word in her mouth, coupling it with breath from the upper reaches of her nasal passage or the lower depths of her throat as she explained that she and her husband had gone to live with their son and his family in America but had decided to return to Japan. "It was all right in the beginning. My son and daughter-in-law drove us everywhere to see the sights. But, in time, the normal pattern of life must be resumed. There was no place in theirs for us. 'We are useless here,' my husband said. So we decided to return home." She quickly added. "But America is a fantastic country, water from metal, blue cooking fire in an instant. "She shook her head. "Unbelievable."

The old woman's husband gently patted his wife's hand. "He's promised to come visit us. He is young, the journey will not be so difficult for him. We made the right decision, Mama," he reassured her.

"I know you have," Haesu concurred. She was glad she would never have to face that decision. No ocean will ever separate her from her children.

After the last dish was removed from the tables, the waiters cleared the floor for dancing. Elena motioned from across the room that she was leaving with Faye and Maria and threw a kiss. Haesu smiled to herself. She knew what mischievous thoughts filled Elena's head.

Music announced the beginning of the dance.

"I'm not very good, but if you are willing to risk it, I would like to have this dance with you." The Captain sounded like a schoolboy.

At Haesu's consent, he led her to the dancefloor then leaned awkwardly toward her, holding her gingerly, apologetically. His palms were moist. She discovered that his candor was no exaggeration. It was impossible to follow his uncertain, unrhythmic steps. It could be partly her fault. Her experience was limited to practicing with Clara in her parlor.

"The things a captain is expected to do," he lamented.

She was amused. "Dancing is supposed to be enjoyable."

"This is not dancing. This is a mortal struggle. My job is to steer ships, not women."

"I haven't had much experience," she explained.

"It isn't you. No matter how much I try, I cannot master the art."

"There's no need to suffer. Why don't we take a stroll instead?"

He heaved a sigh of relief. "An excellent suggestion," he said.

They stepped into the night. She revelled in its brilliance. The sea was aglitter under the golden moon. The silver cigarette case flashed fleetingly as the Captain took it from his pocket. With a wave of her hand, Haesu refused even before he offered her one. His face glowed serenely as he lit his cigarette.

"I cannot stay away long and ignore my other guests. It's all part of my duty." He shook out the match. "Does the sea still bother you?"

"Not at all. It's beautiful."

They leaned on the rail, their shoulders touching, and faced the void. "We still have a few days at sea. A stop in Honolulu, then on to Yokohama. That will be quite an event for you. My homecoming is quite an ordinary occurrence, like any man coming home from work. Although lately, with Momo growing so rapidly, it has become an extraordinary event for me. Each time I return, I scarcely recognize her." He shook his head as he gave a little laugh. "To think, I almost became a Buddhist monk. What would I come home to then? I lived in a monastery for a year, the Diamond Mountains. I was very young and quite happy. Peace and tranquility, isn't that what we all seek?"

"I've never been to the Diamond Mountains."

He looked aghast. "But that's impossible! It is the most spectacular sight in Korea. Every Korean has been there." His unabashed response dissolved any distance between them.

"I left home when I was quite young," she explained.

"Well, you must not miss it this time. You're the first Korean I have met who has not been to the Diamond Mountains." He drew smoke from his cigarette and slowly blew it out. "It all came to an end when my father took us to Japan."

"Who was your father?"

He hesitated before replying. "He wanted me to forget his name, commanded me to forget. Do you know that one cannot help remembering what one has been told to forget? Park Chon Tak . .

How strange to hear it aloud. Park Chon Tak. It doesn't matter anymore. He's 'returned' now," he said, using the euphemistic term for 'dead'.

"I'm sorry," she said, and wondered if he had died at the hands of the Japanese.

The Captain accepted her sympathy then shook his head. "He was a tormented man. After he gave up his name, he seemed never at peace."

Haesu clacked her tongue sympathetically. "Even a swallow flying skyward . . ."

"Has a place to return," the Captain said, completing the line of a well-known Korean poem.

She was pleasantly surprised. His knowledge of poetry indicated a refinement undisclosed in his capacity as a captain. "Does your wife enjoy poetry as well?"

"She is familiar with the poetry of her country. She is Japanese."

Haesu wondered if Mrs. Yamamoto knew that she was also Mrs. Park. It was not a question she could ask the Captain. She created Mrs. Yamamoto in her mind, saw her in a kimono of silk threads that had been woven into a garden of flowers, saw her as a woman of delicacy waiting for her husband to return from the sea.

She too should be in silk, airy gauze flowing freely in the night air because Korean skirts are full and unconstrained. Haesu suddenly felt the weight of her burgundy velvet dress as it hung plainly over her. Her arms seemed bound by the long sleeves buttoned tightly at the wrist. The dress resembled one Greta Garbo had worn in a movie. That was the reason Haesu had chosen it. It now struck her that the dress made her no closer to being Garbo than the Captain was to being John Gilbert. Notions of a love affair had suddenly become silly, the stuff of Hollywood films and Elena's fantasies.

The Captain straightened up. "I must not neglect my duties," he said.

Haesu did not want to be left standing alone again. And she had no desire to return to the dining room and face the likes of Mrs. Compton. "I think I'll go to my room. I'm not very fond of ballroom dancing."

He nodded. "I understand. It's not in our blood, is it?"

She hurried through the corridors, stopping suddenly to avoid being seen by Kudara as he left her stateroom. As soon as he disappeared through a door, she scurried into her room. She had meant to discuss Kudara with the Captain but she had no tangible evidence to offer. Her suspicions, thus far, were based on her intuition. As much as she desired it, Kudara provided no reason to support a request for another steward.

Tonight, she felt no impulse to search for evidence against him. She was wrapped up in her own humiliation. How could she have even entertained thoughts of a romantic affair, she wondered. She was born and bred a *yangban*. He was a mere Captain and a traitor, at that. She thanked God she had not led the Captain on and made a fool of herself.

She unbuttoned her sleeves and pulled the dress over her head, mussing the waves in her hair.

Haesu's eyes snapped open to the dark. There was a rapping on the door, so soft that the children slept on undisturbed. She wondered how long she had been asleep. Tense and restless, it had taken her hours to fall asleep. She was slow to collect herself. The tapping stopped and there were sounds of footsteps leading away from the door. She leaped out of bed and opened the door in time to see a fragment of white uniform disappear around the corner. The Captain, she thought. Her cheeks grew hot as she speculated on the purpose of his late visit. Thinking about it kept her in a state of wakefulness until daybreak when sleep finally overcame her. In her dreams, she kissed the Captain.

Elena could not contain herself. She demanded a full report. Haesu knew that if she mentioned the Captain's late visit, Elena would be beside herself.

"Just a dance and chat," Haesu said casually.

"That's all? I can't believe it! I thought with you missing breakfast . . . Didn't he even try anything?" she asked disappointedly. "I don't get it. Something's wrong with him. Maybe what you said about his being interested because Faye is like a daughter to him is true. But that should make you like a wife to him, shouldn't it? Then again, maybe he's not hot on wives. He speaks Korean. Did you know that?"

Haesu had been following Elena's circular logic with amusement and was caught off her guard. "How did you know that?" she blurted out.

"Maria told me. She says when he talks to Faye and she doesn't pay attention, he talks to her in Korean."

"What makes Maria think he's speaking Korean?"

"Faye told her. Awk! I spilled the beans! Maria wasn't supposed to tell me. She promised Faye."

Haesu tried to appear calm as she searched for an explanation. "Well . . . it's not unusual. I mean about his speaking Korean. You see, quite a few Japanese learned to speak Korean. It was necessary for the occupation. And it's useful for business . . . that kind of thing."

"It's okay then?"

"What do you mean?"

"Maria noticed one of the stewards listening. That tall one. Your steward. 'Ku' something or other. He was listening but he didn't let the Captain see him."

"Kudara," Haesu said. She had something to tell the Captain now. As he flashed into her mind, she caught her breath. The Captain had worn his black uniform. Her late night visitor had been in white. Kudara? What would he want with her?

Elena took Haesu by the arm to lead her to the lounge. "It probably wouldn't have worked," she said. "The Captain's not your type."

—3—

The heat in Honolulu was unbearable. Haesu's plan was to take the children to visit the Songs. They were Clara's relatives and Haesu had agreed to deliver a package to them. She knew several Koreans living in Honolulu, but there was only time to visit the Songs.

Haesu had been yearning to be on land and hoped she and the children would be invited to a lunch of cold noodles and *kimchi*. She was tired of the ship's 'international cuisine'.

"Cheez, it's hot. I hope they feed us some *nang mien*." Harold said.

"I was thinking the same thing." Haesu said.

"Me too," Faye said, "and *kimchi*."

John blew in her face. "And stink everybody off the ship," he said.

"Who cares?" Harold wanted to know. "They don't know what they're missing."

"Yeah," John said, "garlic, onions, peppers, and farts."

"What's farts?" Haesu asked. She recognized the other ingredients.

Harold and John fell on each other laughing.

Haesu looked at them reproachfully. "Must be something bad."

"*Pangu.*" John explained, still laughing. "Fart means *pangu.*"

"Then say, *pangu*," Haesu told him.

They walked down the gangplank onto the pier where Haesu located a public telephone and called the Songs. Mrs. Song clacked her tongue and cooed her apology for not meeting them. They had no car, she explained, then began to instruct Haesu on how to get to her house by public transportation. Haesu interrupted her to tell her there would not be enough time. When Mrs. Song said that she was preparing *nang mien* for them, Haesu told her they would come by taxi.

Fifteen minutes later, they were walking under the papaya trees that grew in the Song's front yard. Mrs. Song had set a table in the screened porch. The wooden floor of the white cottage sloped toward the front of the house. Everything on the table was poised to slide toward the red hibiscus growing against the screen. In further defiance of gravity, the table was covered with a slick check-ered oilcloth. The chopsticks had been wrapped in paper napkins to keep them from rolling to the floor.

While Haesu and Mrs. Song exchanged salutations, the children moved restlessly from seat to seat, trying to stay in the path of the small fan mounted on the wall as it turned from side to side.

"I'll bring the food," Mrs. Song said, stepping into the interior of the house.

"Let me help," Haesu offered.

"No, no. You stay here and try to keep cool. I'm used to this weather." Although she was chubby, her movements were quick. "Mr. Song should be here any moment. He had to meet someone," she said, her voice fading as she went deeper into her house.

"Is there somewhere we can wash our hands?" Haesu asked loudly.

Mrs. Song was already returning to the porch. "I'll show you." She put a bowl of *kimchi* and a platter of cold sliced meat on the table and opened the screendoor to lead them to a faucet outside.

Haesu marvelled at the woman's energy. All she wanted to do was take off her clothes and sit in front of the fan.

As she unhooked a basin from the side of the house, Mrs. Song suggested Faye take off her dress. "You can put it back on before you leave."

Faye's eyes brightened. When Haesu nodded her consent, Faye could not get out of her dress fast enough.

"How about us?" John asked, his hands on his belt buckle.

"You can take off your shirts," Haesu said.

"When do you have to be back?" Mrs. Song asked, on her way back to the kitchen.

"Three thirty," Haesu shouted.

"You'd better go ahead and eat. I don't know what's holding Mr. Song up."

She was back, carrying a tray with four bowls of noodles on it. Ice floated in the broth.

"What about you?" Haesu asked, feeling uncomfortable about eating without the host or hostess.

"I have all the time in the world to eat. I'll wait for Mr. Song," she said, and sat on the cane settee to open the gift Haesu had brought from Clara. She untied the bow and rewound the ribbon neatly around her hand before setting it aside for future use. As she unwrapped the tissue paper, she folded each sheet carefully. By the time she was ready to open the box, Harold and John had eaten half their noodles.

"Oh, how beautiful!" she said as she lifted a glass candy dish from the box. She unwrapped the lid and placed it on top of the dish. "I can use it to serve *kimchi*. Keep it covered until we're ready for it. You know how the smell attracts flies." She put the dish and lid back into the box. "I'll write Clara. It was so considerate of her to think of us." She stood up. "I have the water boiling for more noodles. Eat plenty," she called, on her way to the kitchen.

Haesu and the children topped the mound of noodles with *kimchi* and meat. Some spilled down the sides into the juice. Almost in unison, they raised the noodles with their chopsticks to draw the meat and *kimchi* into the folds of the slippery strands, churning the mixture until everything was saturated with broth. Lifting a white cascade of noodles to their mouth, they began to slurp, pausing to bite into crisp *kimchi* or chew on an unyielding piece of meat. They didn't notice Mr. Song until the screendoor squeaked open.

"I have company. It must be my birthday!" he said, popping his eyes open.

The children laughed, scurrying to their feet at a signal from Haesu. She was about to stand too as he was at least ten years her senior.

"Sit down, sit down," he said as he waved everyone down. "Eat or your *nang mien* will get warm." He tossed his straw hat onto the settee and sat down next to Haesu. "I'm sorry to be late. I had to meet with a fellow partiot. He's going to be here for only a few hours. He had much to report. Our underground work now stretches across the ocean."

Haesu explained that she would never have started eating before he arrived but the Taiyo Maru was only in port for several hours.

"Yes, I know. That's why I'm late. The person I met with is from the ship."

Mrs. Song interrupted him as she carried in two more bowls. "I thought I heard you." She placed a bowl in front of him. "Eat, eat, or everything will get soggy." She took Harold's and John's empty bowls. "I'll get more for you," she said, and marched back to the kitchen.

"Someone from the ship?" Haesu asked.

"Yes. We now have agents on almost every ship that goes from Japan to the United States. It's how we keep Koreans at home and abroad informed. It has become the only dependable source of information between Koreans on both sides of the ocean. The link has been invaluable to our movement."

A huge belch escaped from John's lips.

"Wonderful!" Mr. Song exclaimed. "The *nang mien* was a success!"

The children laughed and Harold held his hand over his mouth to release a series of burps.

"No, no. Don't hide it." Mr. Song reached over and took Harold's hand away from his face. "Loud and full like the Korean national anthem." He waved his arms like a conductor of an orchestra.

In the midst of the laughter, Haesu looked at her watch. "*Aigoo*," I'm afraid we have to make our way back to the ship.

The children groaned.

"Let the boys finish their second bowl," Mrs. Song said, handing a full bowl to each of them.

"We can't be late." She looked at her watch again. "I guess we'll have time. Put on your clothes as soon as you've finished," she instructed the children. Turning to Mr. Song, she said, "Is there anything I can do to help? Can I take a message to Korea for you . . . a package or anything?"

"It's all been taken care of," he replied.

"Would it be of any use for me to know who your contact is on the Taiyo Maru?"

"I don't think so. We cannot risk revealing his identity."

"I'm sorry we have to rush off." She stood up to leave. "You haven't even had a chance to eat."

"Never mind," he said, waving her concern aside. "I have all the time in the world to eat." He stood up to escort her to the curb where Mrs. Song had hailed down a cab. "I'm only sorry we did not have more time to talk. How is Clara?"

"She's fine," Haesu said as she climbed into the cab.

The children thanked Mrs. Song for the 'dee-li-shush' lunch. As the taxi started off, Faye stuck her head out the window and yelled, "Happy Birthday, Mr. Song!"

In the balmy twilight, the Taiyo Maru pulled out of Honolulu and set out to sea. The passengers resumed their activities aboard ship. Haesu was taking a stroll when she ran into the Captain. After they agreed it had been miserably hot on shore, she told him of Kudara's eavesdropping exactly as Elena had told her.

The Captain sighed. "I should use more caution. But he is a mindless man and of no consequence. I would not worry about him. There will be a new crew in Yokohama." He smiled wistfully. "It is there that you and I and Kudara will come to a parting of the way." Then suddenly remembering, he said, "Mrs. Compton wanted me to say goodbye for her."

"Mrs. Compton? To me?"

"Yes. She said that she would always remember you because you are the first and only Korean she has ever met."

It took only a moment, but a smile came to their lips simultaneously. They burst into laughter. Strollers turned to look at them and wondered what it was that had so amused the Captain and 'that lovely Korean woman'.

The second time that Harold and John had gone down to the crew's quarters, they saw some of the cartoons they had already seen and a few new ones. Although Kudara was not around to dampen their enjoyment, the thrill of their initial visit was wearing off. They left before the ending of a cartoon they had seen before and went above to play shuffleboard.

John began to pester Harold about the number of days left before they were to reach Yokohama.

"Six. I told you yesterday it was seven. Keep your own calendar," Harold told him. "You can count."

On Movie Night the ship was showing "Mammy" with Al Jolson. The boys had already seen it twice.

"We might as well go down below," Harold said.

The men in the crew's quarters noticed the boys' lackluster inter-

est and animatedly teased them, encouraging them to enjoy themselves. One finally suggested a game of cards, casually inquiring if
the boys had any money to bet. John emptied his pocket of some
odd change left from his fifty cent allowance. Harold had saved a
dollar. He put it on the floor beside him.

"You know poker?" the crewman asked.

John shook his head while Harold gave a hesitant nod.

The crewman began to deal the cards. "I teach first. Play for
money later." He dealt the cards face up so that he could explain
the value of each one.

Kudara came below and saw what was happening. He stormed
into the middle of the huddled group and cursed at the men. He
told the boys, "They're taking advantage of you. Take your money
and get out of here!" The men gaped at him with bewildered
expressions on their faces. Harold and John picked up their money
and started for the stairs. As they scrambled onto the deck, Harold
reached for John's arm and pulled him close. "He was talking
Korean," he said.

John's mouth dropped open. "Yeah. How come?"

Harold drew John next to him against a smokestack where no
one would over hear them.

"I'll bet he's the one." Harold said.

"Which one?"

"The one Mr. Song told Mom about. I'll bet Kudara's the one he
talked to when he was late."

"About what?"

"You weren't listening. You never hear anything because you've
always got your mouth going."

"I was eating. You going to tell Mom?"

"I can't. She'll wonder what we were doing in the crew's quarters.
She'll get mad if she finds out we were gambling. I can't tell her
without making up some cock 'n bull story."

"You're not going to tell her?"

Harold shook his head. "She doesn't have to know." He took John
by the shoulder. "You tell her and I'll knock your teeth out!"

John pulled away. "I'm no snitch."

THREE

Sixteen days after its departure from San Pedro, the Taiyo Maru entered Yokohama harbor. Short sharp commands cut through the darkening sky, bringing everyone on deck. The passengers watched as practiced men worked in choreographed movements to bring the ship safely to rest. Silhouetted in the fading light, sentries of towering ships stood by.

"Be sure to look me up if you get back to L.A.," Elena said.

"Of course I will," Haesu promised.

The women embraced. Elena smiled through her tears. She and Maria waved vigorously as Haesu and the children went down the gangplank. Neither woman had thought to give the other her address.

On the firm motionless ground, Haesu's gait was unsteady as she rushed to keep up with the crowd. Standing in line, her legs still imagined the sea.

"How long do you plan to stay in Japan?" Sitting behind a glass panel, the customs officer began the usual questioning.

She leaned forward to hear him better. His eyes were on the passports, leaving her to face his mound of crew cut hair. "Just traveling through. We're staying in Yokohama overnight," she answered.

"What are your plans while in Japan?"

"Just traveling through," she repeated.

"Your husband is not with you?"

"He's joining us later." She saw that some of the other passengers were already through; she had picked the wrong line.

His face remained hidden as he continued the questioning. When he inquired about Chun, she wondered if he knew that Chun had to leave Korea to avoid arrest. He paused between questions to flip the pages of the passport or tap his pen against the desk, stalling, detaining her for reasons known only to him.

"Your Japanese is excellent. Do your children speak it?" he asked.

"No." She vowed to herself to use as little of his language as possible.

"Korean?"

"What?"

He looked up from his desk and at her for the first time. "Do your children speak Korean?" His words were measured. He appeared exasperated at having to repeat himself.

"Of course."

"Better teach them Japanese." He stamped the passports hard then stood up, displaying his blue uniform in full before walking out. She was the last one to get through customs.

Angrily, she gathered up the documents and put them in her purse. Instructing Harold on what Japanese words to use, she sent him and the children to secure a taxi while she looked after the trunks.

"Mrs. Chun!" Kudara was running to catch up with her. He took her by the elbow and drew her aside. She pulled her arm away. "As you know, the Captain has been posing as a Japanese," he said in Korean.

"And you? A Japanese posing as a Korean?" she said sarcastically.

"No, no" he protested. "I too am Korean. The purpose of our pretense, however, differs. The Captain for his own benefit and I for my country."

She backed away, about to excuse herself. He took a firm grip of her arm and spoke rapidly but quietly. He told her that he was a member of a certain leftist group. "I planned to tell you while we were at sea. Mr. Song was afraid for me and advised me to take no risks. Then last week, I almost gave myself away. I would have aroused further suspicion if anyone saw me talking to you. I can tell you now, we have our man."

She had long admired the work of the organization to which Kudara belonged. It had been so disruptive to the Japanese that the organization was outlawed and forced underground. But Kudara's revelation did not allay her dislike for him. "What do you mean?" she demanded to know.

"Park is a traitor to his people. He is worse than a Japanese. He will not be allowed to get away with it."

"But he has a family and . . ." She was about to add that the Captain was a very nice man but it seemed inappropriate. Nothing she thought of seemed appropriate. She had never been in a situation of real espionage to know what the appropriate response should be.

He snickered. "That doesn't stop the Japanese from torturing and killing Koreans," he reminded her.

"Torture and killing? But you say you're Korean. He is Korean too." She was desperate for the right words to save the Captain.

"He wants to be Japanese. We will treat him accordingly. I wanted to thank you. You have been most helpful." He tried to form a camaraderie with her, to share the unexpected bounty of uncovering a traitor. "Be careful while you are in Japan and Korea," he warned. "You have been away and do not know the situation here. It takes little, very little, to put your family and friends in danger."

She wanted to explain that she had not intentionally sought the Captain's identity and should be given no credit for exposing him. But Kudara left before she could say anything.

She felt numb, mechanically found her way to the baggage center and made the necessary arrangements for the trunks, her mind in a stupor.

"Mom! Where have you been? We have to hurry. I got us a cab." Harold's voice came sweetly to her, calling her back to a reality she understood. She placed her hands around his shoulders and followed him through the crowd.

John and Faye were waiting where Harold had left them.

"Momma, look! The Captain just went by and gave me this." Faye lifted the lid to the small wooden box she held in her hands. Inside, a brightly painted turtle pulled in its head.

"The Captain? Was he alone?" Haesu eagerly asked.

"He was with Kudara and another man. Never saw him before." Faye held the box higher so Haesu would notice.

Absent-mindedly, Haesu closed the lid of the box. She motioned the children into the cab. "Let's get out of here," she said.

The floor of her room in the Yokohama Hotel was cold. She couldn't sleep. Haesu was no longer accustomed to sleeping on the floor and discovered that she missed the rocking of the ship. Her wakeful hours were filled with fears for the Captain. The following day, she helplessly dozed on the train while riding northward to where she and the children caught a boat to cross the Straits of Korea, renamed the Straits of Japan. The last one hundred and twenty miles lay before them.

"John says the turtle's dead." Faye whimpered.

Haesu shuddered. "I guess we'd better get rid of it."

"No, please. I want to keep it," Faye pleaded.

"Give it a burial at sea," John taunted her. "Just throw it overboard."

"No! It'll drown!"

"Dummy, it's already dead."

"That's enough, John," Haesu admonished.

"You probably forgot to feed it," John accused Faye.

"I didn't forget." She began to bawl.

"You don't know anything, John," Harold said. "Everyone thinks pet turtles die because they're starved. They can live days without food. It's probably the paint. Maybe the chemicals or maybe it binds the shell."

"Where'd you hear that?" John asked with some skepticism.

"I read it."

"Then why do they paint them?"

"Sells better, I guess." Harold took the box from Faye. "Might as well throw it away. You can always get another one," he told her as he hurled it into the ocean.

They were rid of it. But as the box disappeared into the sea, a shiver ran through Haesu.

"Will you buy me another one?" Faye asked.

"We'll see," Haesu said, not promising anything.

The thin dark line that had been lying motionless in the distance slowly grew into a confusion of shapes. Land formed a baffle, amplifying the steady hum of the boat. Haesu's heart quickened at the clamorous confirmation they had reached Korea.

"Put on your jackets. Be sure you put the leather straps through the shoulder loop. Looks so sloppy when it hangs over your arms.

Someone may be here to meet us," Haesu said as she gathered their things together. When they stepped off the gangplank onto the pier, she said, "We're home, children."

"Is this Sunchoun?" Harold asked.

"No, I mean Korea. This is Pusan." she replied.

"I don't know this place," John declared. "L.A.'s my home." He held his nose. "It stinks here."

Haesu slapped his hands away from his face. "Don't do that! It's not nice." She looked for someone to step forward and ask for her. No one did.

"Where's Sunchoun? I want to go home," Faye whined.

"We have to take a train. From here to Seoul. Then tomorrow, from Seoul to Sunchoun," Haesu said, still scanning the crowd.

Faye groaned. "Will it stink there? I don't like it here." She noticed people staring at her and buried her face in Haesu's skirt.

"Don't do that," Haesu said, pushing her away. "It's not their fault." She wanted her children to feel neither pity nor scorn for her people . . . their people. She also realized that it wasn't her children's fault that they were accustomed to paved streets, cement sidewalks, and flush toilets. "It isn't anyone's fault. You'll get used to it," she assured her children, softening her tone.

Suddenly, they were surrounded by infant and pubescent beggars. Outstretched hands extending from undernourished limbs fluttered in front of Haesu's face. The tattered rags hanging from the children's arms shook under the insistent gesticulation, waving the banners of deprivation. Haesu dropped a few coins into their hands, avoiding their dirt-caked ulcerated skin.

"Go away now. That's all I'm going to give you," she sternly told them.

The eyes of one of the young boys grew wide. "She speaks Korean! She speaks Korean!, he chanted. It was a clarion call. Dozens of waifs appeared from nowhere.

Haesu had never seen such a ragged bunch of undernourished children. Even as she shooed the youngsters away and slapped at the hands that tugged at her clothes, her sympathy went out to them. As she and the children walked to the depot, the child-beggars hung on.

"Cheez, what's wrong with them?" John said as he threatened them all with his fist.

John's belligerence disturbed Haesu. He showed no compassion for the children, no concern for their deprivation, no awareness that he was of the same ancestry as they. "Give them your jackets," she said suddenly.

The boys looked at one another. "You don't mean our uniforms?" John could not conceal the smile that came to his lips."

"They cost a lot of money," Harold reminded her as she had reminded him countless times.

"Do as I say," she ordered. "They'll need something warm when winter comes."

The young paupers had followed them all the way to the railroad station. A voice blared over the loudspeaker instructing the passengers to board the train.

The boys had taken off their jackets. "Shall I just throw them into the crowd?" Harold asked. "They might tear them apart."

"We have to hurry." Haesu pointed to a boy who had been lingering behind the others, too shy to beg. "Give them to him and get on the train." She lifted Faye onto the train and climbed up the stairs. John scrambled in after them. Harold hurriedly handed the dumbfounded boy the jackets and quickly boarded the train.

When they found their seats, Faye pointed out the window at the trail of children disappearing into the distance, the young boy cradling the jackets in the lead.

"He acts like he's carrying a bomb," John said, bursting into laughter.

Harolds' face broke into a grin. Even Haesu laughed as an unexpected sense of relief came over her.

She was beginning to find uniforms distasteful. The Captain's black uniform and gold buttons, Kudara's white uniform and plain buttons, the blue uniform of the customs officer had all been parading across her mind. Seductive uniforms, she thought, shielding duplicity and sedition. She felt no loss at having the boys shed their Academy jackets. And she was satisfied that the Edwards Military Academy had been put to noble use.

The train picked up speed, unfurling a sepia landscape that had run through Haesu's memory repeatedly; stark stretches of continuous rice fields dotted with huddles of thatched huts. The earth's monotone was relieved by brilliant silk *hanboks* worn by women carrying baskets on their heads. Backs straight and taking broad strides, they seemed to glide over the rough fields.

Korean women are strong. Haesu thought, their steps are energetic and sure.

Rising incongruously from the flat land, sections of unploughed earth bulged to form a scattering of mounds, often near a grove of pine trees. In one of the fields, a handful of people moved in procession carrying a long pine box. Mourners dressed in virgin white were led by a man who wore a brightly colored silk robe. He carried a tall bamboo pole. Scrolls of white paper emblazoned with Chinese ideographs were tied to the supple shaft. The tenuous paper tangled with solid silk banners and trembled in the breeze. Beams of golden light reflected off metal cymbals as the instruments were struck against each other.

The train moved too fast; the writings were blurred. Haesu remembered they were usually messages from obedient wives, dutiful sons, and loyal friends. The engine was too loud, silencing the prayerful chants and clanging cymbals.

"A funeral," Haesu explained. "The mounds are graves," she told her children. She was pleased to be able to show them the customs of her land . . . their land. Her heritage was an anachronism in the United States; it had been a struggle to pass it on to her children. "Sit back and use your eyes. You can learn a lot looking out windows of trains."

"There's not much out there," Harold said.

"Maybe not like L.A., but different things."

Faye put her head on Haesu's lap to sleep.

"When you wake up, we'll be near Seoul. There'll be people at the station to meet us," Haesu promised.

The Seoul station was noisy and filled with people, but no one was there to meet Haesu. She delivered the messages, money, and goods entrusted to her by Koreans in Los Angeles, but "some other time" was her answer to the numerous invitations. A quiet dinner at the hotel was what she and her weary children preferred on the last night of their journey.

"I can't understand it. No one, not a single person," Haesu said, shaking her head.

"Do they know we're coming?" Harold asked.

"Of course." Haesu got ready for bed. "Tomorrow, my cousin, Moonja, and her family will be at the Pyongyang station. It's just a brief stop before we go on to Sunchoun."

The boys stood up to go to their room. "I sure hope *Halmoni* will meet us in Sunchoun," John said.

"Of course. Do you think your grandmother will let anything keep her from meeting grandchildren she will be seeing for the first time?"

John shrugged his shoulders. "I don't know," he said as he left the room.

The next day in Pyongyang, Haesu got off the train to look for Moonja. She looked everywhere. Disappointed and puzzled, she returned to the train. "That's strange. They're family," she told the children.

"Maybe they had something to do," Harold said.

"No, no. They would have dropped everything to meet us," she said.

"Maybe they don't know we're here," John said.

"Of course they know. That's not it," she said.

"Maybe they're all going to be in Sunchoun just like everybody was in San Pedro," Faye said.

Haesu brightened up. "Maybe," she said.

The last stretch of the train ride seemed the longest. The children were disagreeable and Haesu was running out of patience. When the train suddenly jerked and reduced its speed, they perked up. At the first sound of screeching wheels, followed by the acrid smell of hot metal, Haesu said, "We're here." She pulled up Faye's sagging bobby socks then neatly folded the tops down, lining up the pink bordered yellow daisies. Tucking in Harold's shirttail with one hand and smoothing down John's cowlick with the other, she instructed Harold to tie his shoe laces. Seeing her reflection in the window, she straightened her hat.

The platform was lined with craning people who peered into the windows of the train, eagerly looking for a familiar face. Their gaze lingered on Haesu.

What were they gaping at, she wondered, then remembered her straw cloche. She looked beyond the staring faces to scan the station, fearful that no one would be looking for her.

She saw a heavy-set woman examining each window, working her way from the front of the train to the back. It was her mother. She had on a white turban that added inches to her height, but Haesu remembered her taller. The curved sleeves of her silk gauze blouse broke through the sleeveless gray vest like the wings of a wasp. Her

long full skirt matched her vest. Under her skirt peeked the up-
turned toes of her rubber shoes. Some of the other women in the
crowd wore shorter skirts that revealed lisle stockings and leather
shoes. Mama was in traditional dress from head to toe.

She saw Haesu and broke into a broad smile.

"She's here, children. *Halmoni's* here," Haesu said.

John pressed his face against the window to look. Haesu told him
his grandmother was the one wearing the white turban. "You've
always told us she was beautiful," he said, sounding disappointed.

Haesu rushed her children off the train. Mama reached out and
engulfed Haesu in a staggering embrace. "*Aigoo, aigoo,* it's good to
lay eyes on you again. And, at last, I can actually touch my grandchildren." She gathered the children together in a single encom-
passing hug. John, in the middle, was caught in the voluminous
folds of her skirt. "Hey, I can't breathe," he complained.

"What?" Mama tucked her hand under his chin and lifted his
face. "You'll have to speak Korean for me to understand you," she
told him.

John gave Harold a wily look then cast his eyes downward.
"Nothing, I didn't say anything."

Mama tousled his hair. "You speak Korean well. And have a
pretty face too."

That brought a titter from Harold which, in turn, brought a look
of warning from Haesu.

"Isn't Papa here?" Haesu asked as she looked around. The crowd
was rapidly dispursing. "Where is everybody?"

"I'll explain later. Let's look after your baggage." Mama suggested and led the way.

Haesu was disappointed. A smile from her mild-mannered father would have returned her to the folds of his family. As head of
the clan, his words of welcome would have confirmed the cor-
rectness of her returning. But he had not come to the station. Her
irascible but affectionate Uncle Ansik would have waited impatiently for his brother to complete the formalities, eager to sweep
Haesu and her children into his arms and march everyone home.
He too had not come to the station. She should have been surrounded by her numerous cousins, pressing in, rivaling with one
another to welcome her back, giddily scolding each other for not
giving everyone a chance. Her cousins were like brothers and
sisters to her. They were grown now and married, spread out in

Peiyang Pukto raising their families. She had traveled half the world to come back. The least they could have done was come to the station.

"Momma?" Faye tugged at Haesu's hand. "Maybe everyone's waiting at the house."

"Maybe," Haesu said, but she had her doubts.

—2—

A motley pile of baggage had been heaped onto the platform. Some were bundles wrapped in woven hemp and others were barely held together by frayed rope.

"Those must be yours," Mama said, indicating the two steamer trunks. She clacked her tongue and shook her head.

"What's the matter?" Haesu asked.

Mama quietly asked herself, "Should we take them with us or should we leave them here?"

Following her lead, Haesu lowered her voice to say, "Leave them here? They're Hartmann trunks. The best money can buy."

"That's the problem. They'll attract attention." She drew air between her teeth and continued debating with herself. "Is it safer to take them now or have them picked up later?"

"Everything we have is in there," Haesu informed her.

Mama threw her hands in the air. "Then we had better take them with us." She looked around and saw a man with a cart. "Here! Can you handle these trunks?"

He scurried over. "Those two?" he rasped in a gravelly voice. He scratched his head as he pondered then shook his head. "It will take at least two men." He shouted at once to an equally disheveled crony and beckoned him to come. His friend rushed over with his cart, stirring up a cloud of dust. "Those two royal-looking trunks," the first porter said, giving his associate a wink.

"Bring them. And you had better be careful," Mama warned. She stood over the men as they loaded the trunks onto their unsteady carts. Grunting and groaning, they made much ado about the weight of the trunks. "Do you want the job or don't you?" Mama demanded to know.

Haesu wished her mother wasn't so overbearing.

"We are doing it. We are doing it. There's no law against complaining is there?" the porter said. He then put a woebegone expression on his face. "*Halmoni*, don't we have enough laws without taking away our right to moan and groan." With a smile, he added, "Don't worry, we'll get these burdensome trunks to their destination." He patted the wardrobe trunk with assurance.

With Haesu and the children laughing, Mama smiled begrudgingly.

It was the rainy season, but the sun was hotter than the Fourth of July. Whether or not John dragged his feet or Harold trotted along, every step kicked up dried mud that parched their lips and put grit between their teeth. The stream in the middle of the road offered no relief, only a rush of brown water from an earlier rain. They passed makeshift stalls that were too small to contain the merchandise that cascaded onto the road. Sharp-eyed merchants shifted their watchful gaze from their wares to the strange collection of people that passed before them; a woman dressed in western-style clothes with similarly dressed children followed by two ragged peasants pulling two grand steamer trunks on their rickety carts, all being led by a townswoman familiar to everyone. There was no way Haesu could undo the procession; she had to follow Mama.

John pursed his lips to blow an imaginary trumpet and tooted, "Hoorah for the Red, White, and Blue" as if he were in a real parade. "This is bitchin'. I mean, this is real nice. I like it here, Mom."

"Really, John?" His unsolicited declaration took her by surprise.

"You're just kidding," Harold accused.

"No, I'm not. I like it. It's different." With that, John ran ahead to catch up with Mama.

Haesu wasn't sure what she felt. The dust that covered her shoes, the flies that shared her thirst, the air laden with unclean smells had brought Scully to her mind. She was relieved he was not there to witness any of it, to question her decision to bring her children to Korea. But John's enthusiasm lifted her spirit. She put Scully out of her mind.

Stopping in front of a newly varnished gate, Mama announced, "We're here."

Everything inside the gate was hidden from the street. Secluded, Haesu thought, close to everything but secluded. Korean seclusion was intended to keep precious possessions hidden. As a young girl, she had been hidden from view, required to cover her face whenever she went outside the walls. As her sexuality increased, the greater was her concealment. The higher the woman's rank, the more she was sequestered, and hers was of the upper class. Her country had fought for its own seclusion, struggling against the penetration of eastern invaders and western ideology. A futile struggle, she thought. Korean walls were made of clay, crumbling under repeated blows, leaving nothing as it was before. Chun had wanted a wall around their house in Los Angeles, she remembered, and she had ridiculed him.

She stepped over the freshly painted threshold. "A wooden wall, Mama?

"It's much easier to put up and repair than stone and clay walls," she said. She waved her hand toward the house. "How do you like it? The carpenter and I studied pictures of American houses."

The brick and stucco exterior easily held aloft the shingled roof. Like those leading to temples, four massive stone steps led to the front door. Shaped by a stonecutter's hand, each step was unlike any other. Above the entry, on top of the overhang, perched a miniature replica of a pagoda, a vestige of a Buddhist past.

Haesu had imagined herself returning to the house of her memories, bare wood beams and papered sliding doors. "It's very impressive, Mama," she said.

The porters wandered into the yard and gaped at the house, starting at the foundation and working their eyes to the roof, their mouths wide open as they calculated the cost. Mama looked at them with exasperation. "Just what do you think you're doing? Bring in the trunks!"

The porter made some feeble excuse about not being able to pull the carts through the gate and Mama told him in no uncertain terms that they were to carry the trunks into the house. "Let's go in," she said to Haesu, "or they'll find excuses to exact more money from us."

"Should I take off my shoes?" Haesu asked, confused by the architectural mix.

"Inside. Go inside first," Mama instructed, then led the way.

They entered through the double doors into a narrow entry. An empty wooden rack sat on the floor and unoccupied coat hooks hung on the wall. To the right and left of the short corridor was a door. The children ran in, crowding into the small room. The rack was soon covered with their shoes. Mama sent the boys to the door on the left and sprung at Faye when she began to follow them. "No, you go this way," she said, guiding Faye to the opposite door.

Haesu slipped off her shoes and stepped into the room designated for female occupants. She caught herself from falling as her silk stockings slid on the polished floor.

"Yah! Be careful!" Mama warned, using a tone reserved for children and porters.

Haesu winced. She had not been spoken to in that manner since she left Korea. But she refrained from saying anything and began to explore the new home. She faced four bare walls. Round knobs, spaced as evenly as a row of buttons on a captain's uniform, broke the monotony of the room. The knobs were on cabinet doors that concealed the furnishings: silk cushions, lacquered tables, pads, and quilts. All to be brought out at ·proper times for proper use, whether it be while sitting alone or at a gathering of friends, when dining or sleeping, or doing whatever Haesu would be doing while living in this house. The custom confirmed how few one's needs are. But Haesu found it barren.

She looked through the door that led out of the room. At ground level, between the male and female quarters, was the kitchen. A massive stove, punctured with deep cooking wells, stood with its back to the core of the house. The heat from its fires would warm the floors. She remembered that on bitter cold days, she had hugged the *ondol* floors.

The design of the house followed an ancient plan. Centuries of life had produced little reason to change it. But Haesu found it austere.

When the porters brought in the trunks and placed one in each room, Haesu and the children had moved in.

The men bobbed their heads in gratitude as Haesu gave them twice the amount Mama had suggested. "With money one can command a ghost," the porter said. His associate nodded vigorously in agreement.

Haesu laughed. She was sorry to see them go and saw them to the gate. Walking back to the house, she wondered what there was about shared humor that drew people together. The porter had made her feel at home; a feeling that was long in coming. In America, in the dark of the theatre, she had laughed freely at the antics of Charlie Chaplin and Buster Keaton. In her home, alone with the radio, she never understood what was funny about Fred Allen. The cutting remarks of W.C. Fields invariably drew a blank from her. Chun used to say, "You know you're a foreigner when everyone's laughing but you."

Mama was lying down resting when Haesu entered the room. "You had a lot to do, Mama," Haesu acknowledged.

"What is a lot?" Mama brushed it aside as if it were nothing. "Everyone wanted to meet you at the station but it would have attracted too much attention." She smacked her lips. "I probably should have sent for the trunks later but they looked too valuable to leave behind. Once we decided that, it was better to carry them brazenly in the open than try to hide them. The police are less apt to be suspicious at what is done in front of their eyes." She gave a wave of her hand. "Well, it's done now."

"Do they watch people that closely?"

"If the whole clan gathers at one time, the police will come to find out what we're up to. There's no point in going out of our way to ask for trouble."

"I can't believe that Papa would have attracted anyone's attention."

"He's not here. He's overseeing the harvest in Chulsang."

"How is he?"

"All right. A landowner's work is not difficult."

Haesu waited for more news but none was forthcoming. "No one was at the station in Pyongyang either," she said.

"Your cousin, Moonja, plans to visit you here," Mama explained.

Harold knocked then peeked in the door. "Oh, you don't have anything in your room either."

"Everything is in the cabinets. You can pull out whatever you need," Haesu told him.

I guess we stay over there, right?" he said. Anticipating the answer, he shrugged his shoulders, shut the door, and returned to his quarters.

Mama chuckled. "The children have a great deal to learn."

They learned quickly. They learned that wearing *hanboks*, Korean clothes, made them less conspicuous so they put away their western clothes. They learned to speak Korean to everyone but used English when they wanted the information confined to themselves.

They learned to use the outhouse, passing each other on their frequent trips to the co-educational *twikan*. They learned that the water made them ill.

Between bouts of upset stomachs, the children made friends and learned the games of their new neighborhood. In return, they taught their friends to play kick-the-can. Finding a tin can was not easy. John poured the evaporated milk into a jar to empty the only one he could find. Haesu put a stop to that when she later discovered flies floating in the yellowed milk. The players kicked the one tin can until it was battered beyond recognition, but it remained the most prized possession in the neighborhood.

No one would let Haesu forget America. Everyone she met asked about the country she had left behind. She gave in to their persistent inquiries and told them about the running water and flush toilets, about department stores and their bountiful goods, about paved streets and automobiles, about the varieties of food and opportunities to make money. Whatever they asked, she answered. It sounded like paradise to them, but she said, "There's no place like home."

These were the days she had been waiting for: hours of shopping or visiting, evenings of amusing conversation and mahjong. She was a returning member of the leisure class, a *yangban*.

Mama and Haesu were alone. The children had been sent to spend a few days with Chun's older brother.

"Dinner was quite good," Mama said. She had come to evaluate the new maid she had hired for Haesu. "Good maids are scarce. Most of them are lazy and will steal anything that strikes their fancy. Juna seems honest, but one can never tell."

Haesu fidgeted with her cushion, trying to get into a comfortable position."I think I'll visit the carpenter tomorrow and see about having some furniture made."

"Be firm with Juna. Don't let her get away with anything. Call attention to every mistake she makes as soon as you discover them or she'll develop bad habits."

Haesu went to the cupboard for a second cushion. "It's odd, isn't it? When I first went to America, I wasn't comfortable unless I was sitting on the floor."

"Don't forget what I've said. Keep the upper hand with Juna."

There was a knock on the door.

"I'll get it," Haesu said.

"Let Juna answer it," Mama said.

"No, I can get it," Haesu insisted. She welcomed the excuse to avoid discussing maids with Mama. She never had the heart to tell her about Mrs. Randolph and her own demeaning role as a maid.

There was a second knock.

"Impatient, whoever it is," Mama noted.

Haesu hurried. Stepping into the entry, she closed the door behind her as she went to open the front door. With only the dim light of the entry to see by, she asked, "Yes? What do you want?"

A slight man of middle-age, his eyes magnified through thick lenses, his flat lips failing to cover his protruding teeth, stepped forward. He wore a black uniform. "Are you Mrs. Chun?" he asked in a sinuous voice.

"Yes."

"We are the police. We wish to ask you a few questions."

As her eyes adjusted to the darkness, the face of a second officer became visible. His black uniform merged with the night, above it floated a round golden face. His hands disappeared into his pocket and pulled out a pad and pencil. He wasn't much older than Harold, she thought.

"Well, what do you want to know?" she asked unceremoniously.

"Please respond in Japanese," he requested politely. He stretched his lips over his teeth then opened them with a smack. "Do you know Kim Taeyul?"

"No."

"You were seen talking to him."

"I'm sure there's been a mistake. I've never heard of the man," she said with impatience.

"Mrs. Chun, it should not be necessary to remind you that you are still a citizen of Korea and under Japanese jurisdiction."

She bit her lip and said nothing.

"Perhaps you will remember him as the steward on the Taiyo Maru. He called himself Kudara."

"Oh, him. Why didn't you say so. The man spoke to me only once."

"What about?" he quickly asked.

"I don't recall. After all, he is only a steward." She cautioned herself to refrain from volunteering any information.

"A pretense. He is actively engaged in espionage. You knew that he was Korean, did you not?"

"Sometimes it is difficult to tell," she said, conveying annoyance to remind him of her station in life. "Would you mind telling me what this has to do with me?"

"Your associations raise questions as to the purpose of your visit. You have not declared your intentions. Is yours a temporary or permanent stay?"

The manner in which he asked the question alerted her. He gave it greater significance than she thought was warranted. She searched for the right answer. "My visa has not expired," she said.

"An evasive answer," he correctly guessed. "This is going to take longer than I had hoped." He craned his neck to look in the door as if to suggest they continue their discussion inside.

"My mother is visiting," she said.

"Ah. Perhaps we would all be more comfortable at the station," he said.

His fellow officer nodded.

"I know nothing," she insisted.

"You will have to come to the station." He looked at his watch, holding it toward the light to get a clearer view. "A little late to do it now. Tomorrow morning at ten o'clock. We'll finish the matter then." He was about to leave but paused to tell her. "By the way, we were too late to save Captain Yamamoto. Someone will have to pay for that. We expect your cooperation." He motioned to his companion and disappeared into the darkness.

Mama was wrapping her turban around her head. She had grown tired of waiting and was getting ready to leave. "Well, that took long enough. What was it about?"

"I don't know." Haesu ran her moist hands down the side of her skirt. Her chest tightened. She swallowed hard as she felt her pulse beating against her throat. Did they know the Captain was Korean? It will be hard on his wife and Momo if they know. "An example," Kudara had said. The Captain was to be used as an example and now Kudara was in trouble.

"Who was it?" Mama asked. Alarmed by the detached expression on Haesu's face, she said "What's wrong?"

"It was the police. I haven't done anything."

"Then there's no need to worry. Probably just routine."

"I had no idea it would be like this," Haesu's face glistened with perspiration.

"You've been away. You'll get used to it . . ." She got up from the floor.

"Stay Mama. Spend the night. They want me to be at the police station in the morning."

"Why?"

"More questions, I guess."

"That's strange." Mama looked troubled. "You haven't been here long enough to raise suspicion. You've been socializing openly . . . What could they want with you?"

"Not here. On the boat. I mean . . . They think that . . ." she hesitated. Perhaps it would be safer for Mama if she knew nothing. "It isn't something that I did."

Mama began unwinding the length of raw silk from her head.

Relieved that her mother would stay with her, Haesu said, "I thought the situation was supposed to be better."

"It was, for awhile. It gets better then it gets worse," Mama said. She shouted to the maid. "Juna! Come prepare the beds!"

"I have nothing to hide," Haesu began, but Mama signaled her to be quiet when the maid entered the room.

Haesu started to undress. She watched as Mama began to remove the pins from her hair. As a child, she had been entranced by the movement of the thick black strands as they fell to form a screen across her mother's back. The ritual had signaled the close of a day, mother and daughter drawn together for a night of sleep. She longed for the comfort a child derives from believing in her mother, to feel safe in the intimacy of their sharing the women's quarters.

Later, in the darkened room, they sensed each other's wakefulness.

"Haesu, be careful. You accomplish nothing by expressing your feelings. You could endanger everyone." Mama's voice came to her from the void.

"I can't believe there's no freedom at all."

"It's so easy to talk about freedom. What is freedom but to feed your stomach and stay alive?"

Haesu had no desire to argue; she needed her mother. She was confused and no longer sure of anything. She struggled to think clearly but nothing fell into place.

"I'd better get some sleep, Mama."

Morning brought the decision to tell the truth. Sleep had cleared her head. She had done nothing wrong, therefore, no one could do anything to her. It was as simple as that. And how could anyone fault her for telling the truth?

She decided to wear her apple-green floral print dress and black patent leather pumps, putting her *hanbok* aside for the moment. Eager to have the matter settled, she arrived at the police station precisely on time.

"Please, sit down." In daylight the officer seemed quite ordinary, not at all sinister. He settled into his chair and began the questioning. "Now you admitted you spoke to Kim, that is, Kudara. Let's simply refer to him as Kim. Did you speak to him in Korean or Japanese?"

"Both," Haesu replied as she reached down to brush the dust from her shoes.

"Did he tell you that he was Korean?"

"Well, that's what he claimed." She slapped the dust from her hands.

"What else did he . . . uh claim?"

"Let me see . . . He said that things have changed since I was last here."

"In what way?"

"Oh, nothing specific. Every place goes through changes." She opened her purse and began to probe its contents.

"Let's try to be specific."

He made telling the truth difficult. "Are you in charge here?" she asked as she took a perfumed handkerchief from her purse.

"I'm in charge of this questioning," he replied.

She snapped her purse shut. "Yes, but are you in charge of this station. Are you the chief?"

"Now really, Mrs. Chun. More delays?" The way he said it made her appear ridiculous.

She stood up. "I wish to speak to the chief." As soon as she said it she regretted it. She did not want to speak to the chief, she knew only that she did not want to speak to her interrogator.

"There's no point in that." He motioned her to sit. "Now, did Kim tell you anything about Captain Yamamoto?"

She remained standing. "I demand to speak to your chief." She raised her voice. "I refuse to answer any more questions. You have not charged me with anything. I have done nothing." Her voice became strident. "I don't have to answer your questions!"

A door flew open and a fat man, his flesh cascading in folds over his body, his white-shirted belly sagging below his black gold-buttoned jacket, announced, "I am in charge here." His eyes bulged as he glared at her. He then ran his gaze over her clothes. "What have we here?"

"I am from America," she said.

He stepped closer. "America? Why, aren't you . . . Don't I know you?"

"Perhaps you know my family. My father's name is Kim Nong-son."

"Of course! Don't you recognize me?" He grabbed her hand and drew her close.

The musty odor of unwashed flesh was reminiscent of someone she knew as a child. She looked at him closely. The smell was unmistakable; he was Fisheye, the 'bathless frog'. "Lee Myungho," she said, putting her handkerchief to her nose.

"Come in, come into my office." He took the papers from the officer's desk. "I'll take care of these," he told him.

In the privacy of his office, Fisheye asked about America. He wanted to know if she liked it there, wanted to know if life was good there, wanted to know how many children she had, wanted to know everything a friend wants to know about a friend. He was delighted to hear that she and Clara still saw one another. He almost forgot to ask about Chun. She hoped he would forget to ask about Kudara.

"Well, well, well. I never thought we would meet again. You haven't changed except," he ran his hands around his bulbous face, "more beautiful." He sighed then began to scan the papers. "Do you know anything about Kim Taeyul's activities?"

"Nothing."

"Then there's no need to detain you. When will you be returning to America? My wife and I would like to have you and your family come to our house for dinner sometime."

"I'm not sure. Mr. Chun's coming next month." His social amenity melted away her anxieties.

"Hmm. October. But you are going back?"

"Well . . ."

"It would be wise, you know."

"Why? I haven't done anything."

Fisheye pulled out a small silver instrument from his pocket and began to pick in his ear. "I accept what you have told me. I am not obligated to do so, but I have." He examined the pick. "However, Kim Taeyul is a dangerous association. Espionage and murder are serious offenses, not to be taken for granted. You will be watched."

"But that's ridiculous!" The absurdity of it brought a smile to her lips.

He saw nothing amusing in it. "Do you have a return permit?"

She nodded.

"I advise you to use it." He blew the pick clean and returned it to his pocket.

"But this is my country," she stated firmly.

"Take my word for it, you'll be better off in America. I may not be in a position to help you the next time."

"Help me? I told you that I am innocent."

"Everyone says he is innocent. The statement is meaningless. We haven't even touched on your visit with Song, Kim's contact in Honolulu."

"We only went to his house for *nang mien!*"

He leaned forward. "My wife makes the best *nang mien.* I'll tell her you're back. You will eat with us, won't you?"

Haesu found the air suffocating. She wanted to bite her tongue as she thanked him for his help. Excusing herself, she left without replying to his invitation. On the way home, she stopped at the telegraph office. "DON'T SELL THE HOUSE STOP" was the message she sent to Chun in California.

Mama was not relieved when she heard what had happened. "He's a terrible man and not given to idle warnings."

Haesu had changed back into her *hanbok.* She took a deck of playing cards from the cabinet and sat down for a game of Solitaire. "He advised me to go back to America," she said, distributing her cards.

Mama heaved a sigh. "Korea is such a difficult homeland. Almost any other country would be easier."

"I didn't do anything; an innocent victim caught in a web of circumstances," she said, using the Captain's own words.

"In my lifetime I have heard promises of trust from China and Japan while they helped themselves to our land. Germans and Frenchmen were on our soil digging out our gold. Americans looked the other way when we asked for recognition, and Russia considered us her legitimate spoil of war." Mama's lips were taut, anger behind her despair. "All we wanted from them was to be left alone."

"What should I do?" Haesu asked as she gathered up the cards.

Mama sighed deeply, as if the weight of history had fallen upon her. The air she drew through her teeth rattled. "I had hoped it would work. A family should be together. But the safety of those living here, your safety, your children's safety, we have to think about that . . . I had hoped it would work."

"You keep saying that. Some word, some indication from you before I left America. Something . . ."

"No one commits anything to writing. It's too dangerous. You must not write anything about this to Chun. This is not America." She looked at Haesu compassionately. "Couldn't you have said something to satisfy him? I don't remember you being so intractable."

The words closed in on Haesu. Her chest ached as she struggled to contain the sound that fought to be released. A silent scream. She threw the cards against the wall. Hearts and diamonds fell like drops of blood on black symbols and meaningless numbers.

Mama clacked her tongue. Then, for the first time since Haesu could remember, her mother cried.

—4—

Haesu's father and her cousin, Moonja, had arrived on the same train.

"Imagine my surprise when I ran into my niece on the train." Papa said. "And then to discover that we were both coming to see Haesu!" Wisps of hair flew up from his whiskers as he aspirated his words. "Well," he looked fondly at Haesu, "you've come, at last."

She bowed respectfully to him, instructing Harold and John to do the same.

Papa laughed at the boys' awkward bow and waved them up. "Not too much formality. We are going to be sleeping companions. Show me to your room so I can unpack my things."

"You're staying here?" Haesu was careful not to sound impolite, but she had expected him to go home with Mama.

"How else can I get acquainted with my grandsons?" he asked, lifting his chin to untie the ribbon that had held his black horsehair hat to his graying hair.

"Mama is with Faye," Haesu said.

"Who?" he asked.

Haesu laughed. "You've forgotten you have a granddaughter."

"Oh, of course! Two boys and one girl. It's hard to remember people one has never seen," he said, his hat in hand as he followed the boys into their room.

Moonja took Haesu into her arms. "It's perfect to have you back. The family never seemed complete without you," she said. She held Haesu at arm's length to examine her, scrutinizing every detail as was her habit. "You look different. Your hair . . . something. You've grown more beautiful, there's no doubt about that."

"Nonsense. It's only makeup," Haesu said, remembering that Moonja was unstinting in her opinion.

"Cosmetics can't hide what's underneath," Moonja said, having the last word.

"Moonja, why is my father staying here?"

"You don't know?"

"About what?"

"That your father lives in Chulsang and your mother stays here in Sunchoun," Moonja said, gliding right into the answer. "Hasn't she said anything to you?"

Haesu shook her head. More information Mama had not committed to writing. "What happens when they see each other?"

"Nothing. They carry on as if nothing is wrong."

"I see." Haesu had agreed with Mama to handle her encounter with the police in precisely the same manner. They had decided not to alarm the family.

Moonja tugged at Haesu's arm. "We'll have such fun. Like the old days. We'll go shopping and I'll tell everyone that you're my cousin from America. And you can tell them about the streets paved with gold."

"I've seen no streets paved with gold. Fairy tales. You mustn't believe everything you hear."

"America is a rich country, isn't it?" Moonja demanded, justifying herself.

"Moonja, where is Uncle Ansik?"

"Hasn't anyone told you anything?"

"I thought, like you and Papa, he would just show up one day."

"No one knows Uncle Ansik's whereabouts." Moonja looked around then dropped her voice. "He's wanted by the police."

"Why?"

Moonja shrugged her shoulders. "I don't know the details. But why is any Korean wanted by the police?"

"Could he be in prison?"

"He was, more than once. We think he's out now."

"Is that all you know?"

Moonja nodded.

"Is that why you were afraid to meet me at the station?"

"Haesuuu . . ." Moonja pouted, looking every bit the repentant child, "don't be angry with me. It's been so many years since you've left. I didn't know what to expect. Think of the attention we might have attracted."

"Just to meet me at the station? You're not involved in anything, are you?"

"Of course not!"

Haesu believed her; it was impossible for Moonja to keep a secret.

Mama's voice came booming from the entry. "Juna! Come get these groceries!"

Haesu and Moonja raced to give her a hand. "Auntie, you shouldn't try to carry so much," Moonja said. When she saw Faye, she grabbed her and gave her a hug. "I know who you are. You're my precious niece."

"I got tired carrying my bag," Faye explained to Haesu.

"You were a big help to your grandmother," Mama said. "Hello, Moonja. I'm happy to see you. Bow to your Aunt Moonja," she told Faye. As she slipped out of her shoes, Mama noticed another pair on the rack. "So your father has arrived. Has he explained why he had not come sooner?"

Before Haesu could answer, Juna came running in, her head bobbing as she bowed to everyone.

"Take these," Mama ordered. "I'll be in the kitchen to give you some instructions. Mr. Kim has a delicate stomach," she said as she stepped into the house.

Mama had helped Juna prepare a delicious meal. Papa was served in the men's quarters with the boys while the women ate in Haesu's room. After dinner, everyone gathered in the female quarter, using it now as a sitting room.

"I'm pleased that the children speak Korean so well," Papa said. "Otherwise, I would be a stranger to my own flesh and blood." He was sitting cross-legged on a silk cushion, unconfined because Korean pants were full and tied only at the waist and ankles to the wearer's liking. There were no binding buttons on his jacket-blouse. His *chokori* was tied loosely over his heart.

"They're turning into real Koreans," Mama was pleased to say.

"That's what they've always been," Haesu said.

"Of course, of course. They just didn't act like it," Mama said with a grin.

Faye went over to Papa and sat in the nest formed by his crossed legs. He put his arms around her and drew her close, displaying his affection for her as he never dared with his own daughter.

"Your maid told me a funny story," Moonja said. "Yesterday, when she served the children their meal, John refused to accept his bowl. 'Two hands! Two hands!' he demanded. When she told me about it, she said, 'I didn't know they had *yangbans* in America'!"

Mama threw back her head to give her laughter room.

John embarrassedly buried his head in his grandfather's arm. Papa tousled his hair. "You did right, you did right," he told the boy.

Everyone laughed but Haesu. She saw nothing amusing in the incident.

But when she looked at her father with her sons on either side of him, reminding her of a Buddhist triptych, and at her mother, who sat with one knee raised, resting an arm casually on it in the Bodhisattva position, Haesu was overcome with sublime happiness.

Papa was fully dressed, his black horsehair hat secured under his chin, his starched white overcoat tied, his walking cane and bundle of clothes in his hands. He looked as he did when he had arrived the day before.

"Only one night, Papa. You've only stayed one night." Haesu was incredulous when he announced that he was leaving.

"You have a houseful. Come to Chulsang with the children and your husband," he said.

The children, sad and silent, had gathered in the entry to see their grandfather.

"Look how disappointed they are," Haesu said.

"If I stay longer, they will feel even worse when I leave," he said. He gave each of the children money to buy themselves presents as they walked him to the gate.

"I shouldn't have been here at the same time," Moonja said when she learned her uncle had left.

Haesu assured her it wasn't her fault, but after a week of shopping and nightly games of mahjong, she was relieved when Moonja's visit came to an end.

"Promise me you and the children will come to Pyongyang. Let me know if there is anything I can do for you," Moonja said.

It was then the thought came to Haesu. "As an assessor, your husband must know when a choice piece of land is available." At Moonja's nod, she went on. "Chun and I are prepared to buy a sizeable holding."

Moonja's face brightened. "Of course, he would be just the person to know. I'll ask him to be your agent." She pressed her cheeks against Haesu's. "It is good to have you back. I can't wait for you to come to Pyongyang."

"Will there be someone at the station to meet us?" Haesu teased.

Moonja sighed. "Will you never forget?"

—5—

Lying in the dark, Haesu listened to the muffled voices. She recognized Harold's chuckle and John's giggle, but she could not identify the third voice. She wondered what time it was, but decided against turning on the light to look at her watch lest she awaken Faye. She felt for her robe, slipped it on, then groped her way to the door. The voices stopped when she tripped over the shoe rack in the entry. She heard the door to the boys' room open.

"Momma, is that you?" Harold whispered.

"Of course it's me," she declared.

"Sshh! Momma." He reached in the dark for her. He found her hand and guided her into the room. She slipped her hand away. "What are you doing?" he asked.

"I'm looking for the light."

"No! Don't do that!"

"Haesu. Haesu, it's me, your Uncle Ansik," a voice in the dark rasped.

"I want to see you," she said, unconvinced.

"No! No lights!" He reached for her and held her. "It's really me," he said softly.

She recognized his voice. "I'm so glad you're safe," she said.

"I've been sitting here in the dark so long that I can almost see your face," he said.

"How long can you stay?" she asked.

"Not much longer. Perhaps before your eyes adjust to the night and you're able to see me."

"He has to leave before it gets light," Harold told his mother.

"Where is the little one?" Uncle Ansik asked.

"She's asleep. I'll go wake her," Haesu said.

"Wait. Better not. There's no point in burdening her with secrets."

No one could see Haesu nod her head in the dark.

Suddenly, Uncle Ansik chuckled. "Now I'm curious. I want to see all of you more clearly."

She heard him rustling. "What are you doing?"

"Finding a match. All right, now everyone huddle close. I hope I don't burn off anyone's nose."

Harold and John giggled. Haesu heard her uncle flick his fingernail against the match several times before it set off a flame and the odor of sulphur. He held the light to her face first, moved it to Harold's and John's, then held it briefly in front of him before blowing out the match. "You're all beautiful," he said. "I only hope my appearance did not shock you."

"No, no," Haesu quickly denied. "It's so dark and it's been such a long time," she said, trying to conceal her shock.

"And I have had my bones broken and my flesh seared," he added.

She had remembered him handsome with deep, dark eyes, and a fine aristocratic nose. "A Korean John Barrymore" she had told her boys. What she saw in the eerie glow of the match was a face deformed with scars and a nose turned to a pulpy mass. She felt his arms in the dark. "You're still strong," she said.

"From living in the woods and running from the police," he said, then added ironically, "It's no longer due to tennis."

Haesu had always thought of Uncle Ansik as the family celebrity, famous for his prowess on the tennis court. "No one knows you're here. Stay with us," Haesu pleaded.

"There's probably someone watching this house at this moment."

"Uncle Ansik," John whispered. "Tell us some more stories."

"Pipe down," Harold ordered.

Uncle Ansik quietly laughed. "I'd better save something for the next time. You rest now while I talk to your mother." He drew Haesu down to the floor to sit beside him.

"Do you really think someone is watching this house?" she asked nervously.

"The last time I was caught was when I had to come home for a family matter. It's that bastard, Lee Myungho."

"Fisheye?"

"What?"

"We used to call him Fisheye."

"Snake would be more like it. No, that would be an insult to snakes. He probably knows that I will try to come and see you. Stay away from him. He's the kind who can inquire about your mother's health while he picks out your eyes."

"Uncle. I'm beginning to see the outline of your face, Haesu said sadly.

"Yes. It's time for me to go. I've accomplished what I had set out to do. Now to get away." He found Haesu's ear in the dark and put his lips to it. "I intend to get Lee before he gets me." He rose to his feet. "I have a job for you, Keeyong."

John's voice shot up at once. "Okay."

"Count up to thirty after I leave. Then turn on your lights. Make a lot of noise like you have a terrible stomach ache. Create a lot of activity. Haesu, take Keeyong to the *twikan*. Use a flashlight."

"Uncle, uncle!" John excitedly sought his attention.

"What is it? Are you afraid?"

"No, not that. Should I count in Korean or English?"

Uncle Ansik had difficulty restraining himself, almost laughing aloud. "Whichever is slowest," he said. He turned serious as he told Haesu, "Tell my sister-in-law I was here. She told me to stay away, knowing that I could not do that. She will be relieved to know that I am still alive."

He embraced Haesu. It was impossible to tell whether the tears on her cheeks belonged to her or Uncle Ansik. When they heard the door shut, John began counting.

"Hana, tul, saet . . ."

Haesu waited until Mama had sent Juna on an errand and Faye was out playing.

"Uncle Ansik was here," she said.

Mama nodded. "I knew he would come. Your father's family seem determined to destroy us all."

"What has Uncle done?"

A smirk came over Mama's face. "I have to admit, he hasn't done anything. It was all a stupid mistake."

"I wish you would tell me about it. I feel as if I've been shut out of everything that goes on in this family."

Seeing no way out of it, Mama began. "You know how easily your uncle gets bored, always looking for some diversion. He used to travel to Manchuria just for a lark. He made friends there then fell in love with a Manchurian woman. His frequent trips across the border drew the attention of the police. Everyone warned Ansik to be careful, but when he discovered that he was being followed, he openly bought gifts for the woman and made certain he was seen entering her house. A childish display of defiance. It turned out that the woman's housekeeper was Korean and hid patriots who were making their escape to China. On his last trip to Manchuria, he discovered that the woman and her housekeeper had disappeared, leaving him no word. When Ansik returned home, he was taken prisoner and beaten. The police thought he was withholding information and tortured him mercilessly."

"Lee Myungho?"

Mama nodded. "Ansik escaped from prison but was recaptured when he came to my house about a family matter."

"You and Papa?"

Mama gave a sigh of exasperation. "It's impossible for Moonja to keep anything to herself."

"I'm your daughter."

"It isn't always best for everyone to know everything."

"Is that the whole story?"

"That's all that I know."

"You don't believe that Uncle was involved politically?"

Mama scoffed. "That playboy? Just a lovable playboy known for his tennis playing."

"Once champion of Korea," Haesu reminded her.

"No one envies him now," Mama said.

"The boys do."

"Let them. They're too young to know the truth."

Despite what her mother said, Haesu found nobility in Uncle Ansik's life as a fugitive. A tragic figure, perhaps, but the enemy of stupidity. She kept her thoughts to herself; Mama would think she was 'too young to know the truth'.

"It never ends," Mama said as she threw up her hands. "First Ansik, now you."

"Me?" Haesu felt as if walls were closing in on her. "What have I done?" she asked, looking for a way out.

"Nothing," Mama said. "Nothing intentional, but trouble just the same."

A false exit, Haesu thought. It seemed that every time she thought she had found a way out, she would run into a stone wall. But she wasn't ready to make a decision to leave Korea. She was all too familiar with the walls that surrounded her in America.

"He got away safely," she told Mama.

"This time."

—6—

The young officer with the moon-face who had accompanied Haesu's 'interrogator' was named Okada. His real name was Yun. Harold had met him on the school grounds playing basketball.

"Don't say anything to him about the family," Haesu warned.

"Aw, Mom, he's a nice guy. He's not going to do anything to us," Harold assured her.

"He works for the Japanese. Don't trust him. Did you tell him anything?"

"All he wants to know about is America. Everyone wants to know about the States. He wanted to know how much money he could make there, what we do for fun, who we know . . ."

"Who we know?"

"Us. Our family. Me, you, Papa. I didn't say anything about Uncle Ansik."

"I never do!" John popped up.

"What did you say?" Haesu continued questioning Harold.

"I told him he wouldn't know any of our friends except maybe Aunt Clara. She's the only one we know from this town."

"You shouldn't have told him anything!" she said, then regretted it. She was reproaching Harold for being straightforward, a quality she had encouraged. "Never mind. You didn't do anything wrong. It's just that we have to think about other members of the family. We have to be careful."

Harold nodded. "I get it."

A week later, Harold came home shocked by what he had seen. "He just shot this kid! This little kid, no bigger than John, called Yun a '*wae nom*', pulled out a Korean flag, and yelled, '*Mansei!* May Korea live ten thousand years! *Mansei!*'. I thought it was funny, this puny little kid hollering at Yun, saying that all Japanese were dogs and that he hoped Japan would sink into the ocean. He told Yun he was worse than a '*wae nom*', a disgrace to his family and to his country. Then he started to run like hell. I was laughing at the whole thing. Yun ordered the kid to stop, then ran after him. They looked like Laurel and Hardy. Then I heard a shot. I couldn't believe it. When Yun got back I asked him. 'Did you hit him? He's just a kid, just fooling around.'"

"Did he kill him?" John wanted to know.

"Said he just grazed him to teach him a lesson. 'You can't shoot someone for that,' I told him. So he said, 'for resisting arrest then'. Cheez, I couldn't believe it. The guy must be nuts."

"Pow, pow!" John was shooting a gun he had made with his fingers.

"John!" Haesu slapped his hand.

"Ow! I didn't do anything," John whined.

If Haesu had wished for a worse scene, it would be Mama's appearance.

"What's going on here? What's wrong, Keeyong?" Mama demanded to know.

John started to cry. Harold was disgusted. "Faker," he accused and dug his elbows into John's ribs.

"Chulyong!" Mama struck Harold across his face.

"Mama!" Haesu protested. "This is none of your business. You have no right to interfere."

"No right? Have you forgotten your place? I am your mother and the grandmother of these children." Mama was scarlet with anger.

"It isn't like that anymore. You can't just order people around because they're your children, or maids, or . . ." She knew she had started on a futile argument. Haesu threw her hands in the air. "What's the use!"

"I don't know what you're talking about." Mama turned her back to Haesu to talk to the boys. "Chulyong, you must never lay a hand on your younger brother. Your duty is to guide him without hurting him. Keeyong, you must always do what your older brother tells you to do. Now run off and play, the both of you." She turned to Haesu. "You're upset and in no mood to visit. I'll come back when you have settled down." She turned on her heels and left without waiting for Haesu to reply.

Haesu was stunned; it had all happened so quickly. Mama took over then left without giving her a chance to say anything. What should she think, Haesu wondered. She needed to be by herself, to sort things out. She went into her sons' room, no one would look for her there, and sat on the floor with her back against one of the steamer trunks. The trunk was still packed with things from California. The floor was cold; the fires from breakfast had long been out. She reached for a cushion and slid it under her.

It was almost ludicrous, she thought. In the midst of the melee, her mother remembered to cite the rules of conduct to the boys. None of the old rules had changed. The new ones only created a pastiche of directions that Haesu found confusing, unrelated rules that said her boys could be thrown in jail for whistling the wrong tune and no wisdom of Confucius could save them.

But she realized it wasn't Mama; Mama hadn't changed. It wasn't Fisheye or that young officer Yun. Fisheye smelled no better before and Yun wasn't even born when she left Korea. It was she. She was out of sorts in her homeland, homesick in Korea without being homesick for America.

When a messenger appeared one day with an invitation for dinner from Fisheye and his wife, thoughts of returning to California entered Haesu's mind.

—7—

Harold, go to the station. Papa is supposed to arrive today," Haesu said. If Chun had followed the original itinerary, he was due in Sunchoun this morning. And none too soon, she thought. A few days ago, Moonja had sent a messenger with the information that a large holding of land in Qwaksan was available. Haesu wanted the land badly. For some reason, the more she thought of returning to California, the more she wanted to own land in Korea.

"Can I go with Harold?" John asked.

"No, it's still too soon for you to be out," Haesu told him.

John sulked back to his room, forgoing his usual vehement claims to feeling well.

His case of mumps had been a godsend, providing her with a legitimate excuse for not having dinner with Fisheye and his wife, an excuse that would be acceptable until John's recovery. She had wrapped the fetid black poultice to John's cheeks herself, insisting upon continuing the treatment beyond the time prescribed by the doctor. "We want to be sure that you're completely well," she had told John. But her purpose was to stave off another invitation from Fisheye.

Haesu sent Faye to the front door several times to see if anyone was at the gate. When at last she heard Faye scream, "Papa!" the muscles around Haesu's shoulders relaxed and she began to breathe deeply. Chun walked in carrying Faye and a worn leather valise Haesu had never seen before. The only indication he gave that this was an unusual event was that he wore a suit. He slipped off his shoes in the entry.

"So you've come," Haesu said.

"I never realized it was so far," he said. "Where's my room? I have to get out of this suit."

She nodded toward the door where John was waiting. Chun put Faye down and began unbuttoning his coat as he went into the room.

"Where did you find him?" Haesu asked Harold.

"He was waiting at the station. He said he knew someone would come."

After a pause, she nodded and said, "Yes, of course."

Mama arrived. "Is he here?" she asked quietly.

"Yes. He's changing his clothes," Haesu told her.

"He knows how to travel in Korea. I wouldn't be surprised if no one knew he was here. I don't think he will be interested in seeing anyone today. After dinner, have Juna bring Faye to me," she instructed then left.

Haesu had learned that Mama never dwelled on disputes or harbored grudges. And now she had seen to it that Haesu and Chun would have the room to themselves tonight.

It was after dinner. The boys were in their room and Faye was at Mama's. Haesu and Chun were alone. He changed into his robe and tied it loosely about him.

"That was a good meal. I haven't eaten like that since you left," Chun said as he lit a cigarette.

"We have a chance to buy land in Qwaksan. Moonja's husband is acting as our agent. Our money will be safe there." She pulled two sleeping pads from the cabinet and dropped them on the floor.

"Good." He looked for an ashtray. "How have the children been?"

"All right," she said. She tucked the ends of the sheets under the pads, wrapping the two as one.

"Shouldn't the maid be doing that?" Chun caught the ashes in his hand.

Haesu handed him a porcelain saucer. "I'm capable of doing it," she replied.

He took a deep draw of his cigarette before snuffing it out on the dish, smearing charcoal on the blue undulating dragon. "This is a nice house," he said.

"Style's a little mixed up. There's something wrong with the water. We keep getting sick. Medicine's no help. Nothing is." She smoothed the quilt then tossed the pillows to the head of the bed.

"It's probably the well. That can be fixed." He took off his robe and slipped under the quilt. "I'm more tired than I thought."

Haesu put out the light and undressed in the dark. "What did you do about the business?" she asked as she groped her way into bed.

"There's several men who want to buy me out anytime I give the word. Charlie will sell the house whenever he hears from me."

"You didn't do anything about the furniture, did you?"

"I left everything alone. Just locked the door and left. After your telegram, I didn't know what you wanted me to do. Clara said she would take care of everything for us."

"But that's so much for her to do."

"She offered. I guess she feels she owes it to us."

"There's no need for her to feel that way."

Chun yawned. "She borrowed some money from me." He turned over and pulled the quilt over his shoulders.

"To come to Korea?" She was going to let Clara know a few things before she let that happen.

"No, not that," he said sleepily.

"Well? Tell me. What did she do with the money?" It was always a struggle to get information from him. "Tell me," she said impatiently.

"I shouldn't have brought it up. You won't like what she did. An operation. Peeled her skin; made her eyes and nose bigger."

"What?" She was shocked. "You gave her money to do that?"

"She asked for the money. No business of mine what she does with it."

"But to do that to her face. Is she more beautiful?"

"She shouldn't have done it. Something went wrong. They burned her skin. It looks bruised. She'll never come to Korea now."

"Oh, poor Clara. What made her do it? I'll bet it was that Scully. She lost her head completely over him."

"Forget Scully. He's gone."

"Gone? After what she did for him? I knew I was right about him. I should be with Clara. She needs me."

A snore escaped Chun. Haesu shook him. He muttered. "That's all I know."

Haesu folded her hands over the quilt then ran her fingers over the swirls of Chinese ideographs woven into the silk, words of filial piety. She wondered how the aubergine cover would look on her bed in Los Angeles.

"Yobo, we'll need money for the land."

He stirred. "I've got it. Let's talk about it tomorrow."

"How much did you bring?"

Suddenly, he threw the blanket aside and sat up. She heard the crackle of cellophane as he pulled out a cigarette. When he lit the match, she caught a glimpse of him sitting cross-legged on the pad naked.

"It's been four months since I left Los Angeles. Naturally, I have many questions to ask you," she said defensively.

"Ask away," he said, "but after that, sleep."

"How much did you bring?"

"Five thousand."

"Where did you get that much without selling the business or the house?" Before he could say anything, the answer came to her. "You got it gambling."

"I won almost half of it on the ship," he said, boasting. "There wasn't anything to do but play cards. Can I help it if poker isn't everybody's game?" He sounded amused.

It occurred to Haesu that if the money had come from the sale of the house and business, they would have nothing to go back to. "Most of it will go for the land," she said, justifying their having the money.

Chun put out his cigarette.

"Better cover yourself," she said, handing him an edge of the quilt.

He slipped under the cover and turned toward her, dropping his arm over her waist.

"We could use some of the money to visit the Diamond Mountains. Every Korean should visit the Diamond Mountains," she said.

His hand found her breasts and he caressed them gently.

"We'll have to stay at least five months, until the children finish the school year," she said.

He wrapped his leg over her thigh and drew her closer to him.

"We can't stay," she said sadly. "It isn't safe for the children. It isn't safe for any of us."

As he groped under the quilt, she guided his hand. The unyielding *ondol* floor held her firmly against him. There was no soft mattress to recede into, no squeaking springs to betray them. Her movements were eager. He wanted to prolong the pleasure she now shared with him, but she was too eager. His murmurings ended abruptly and, with low uneven moans, he fell against her. She wanted him to go on, but he couldn't. He raised his head to brush his lips across her face. She turned away. "No," she said, denying him her lips.

Chun fell to his side of the bed. He turned his back to her and was soon fast asleep. The rattle of his rasps filled the darkness.

Haesu lay awake, wishing for something; she knew not what. She grew cold and pulled the quilt over her and waited for sleep to come.

They should see the Diamond Mountains before the snow or after the thaw, she told herself. They would not be in Korea for the dry season.

PART TWO

CHUN

FOUR

As soon as Chun and the family returned to California, he telephoned Charlie Bancroft.

"Chun! It's good to hear you. How'd it go?" Charlie asked.

"Good. We had a good time. Back now. Back to work. How's the business?"

Chun had wired Charlie from Korea he would be back in five months. Although Charlie was no longer a partner, he agreed to run the business until Chun returned.

"Not bad, not bad. We-ell, there is a little problem. Let's meet at the market."

"Problem? Bad?"

"Not too bad and not too good."

"Meet when?"

"Tonight. The sooner the better. I still can't take the hours."

Chun laughed. "Same old Charlie."

It was Saturday night and the market was closed. A couple of trucks and Charlie's pickup were parked alongside the loading dock. Chun's truck made the only noise in the compound.

Charlie met him at the door to the office. He extended his large hands to Chun. When he shook them, his jowls shook as well. He had always struck Chun as being a giant of a man, but Charlie was an American of average height who had large-boned ancestors. Chun knew he could be trusted because of his "clear and honest" dark brown eyes.

133

"Tell me bad news," Chun said, taking off his cap as he sat at the desk.

Charlie rubbed his round stomach. "There wasn't anything anyone could do about it," he said.

"Okay. Nobody's fault."

"Except Matheson."

"He wanted more?"

Charlie shook his head. "Not that. You know how he got your contract in the first place?"

Chun nodded. "Politics."

He remembered when Matheson had come to the market dangling the contract as bait, a government contract that would enable the signer to supply produce to all the Navy bases in southern California. All Matheson asked for was a little whiskey, free produce, and a little kickback. None of that had bothered Chun. He figured that's the way government business was done. He remembered feeling lucky that day. He had just become the father of a baby girl.

Charlie ran his hand over his thinning brown hair. "Well, the guy Matheson worked for was kicked out of office. All of his contracts got thrown out with him, including Matheson's, including yours."

"Why? I gave them best produce, fair prices, good service. Matheson can go, but my business is still the same."

"It doesn't work that way. The new guy will give out his own contracts. Matheson and his deals are out." Charlie sliced the air with the side of his hand.

Chun sank into his chair. "That's seventy five percent of my business."

Charlie was about to grasp Chun on the shoulder, but remembered how Chun hated anyone to do that. He clasped his hands together. "You'll make it all right. You've got a good reputation. The books are up-to-date. They don't look too bad."

"I know they're okay, Charlie. Did you pay yourself?"

"Yep, just like we agreed." He slapped the cover of the ledger. "It's all in there."

"What did Matheson's man do?" Chun asked, unable to get over it.

"Probably what everybody does, only he got caught. They call it graft . . . uh, getting ahead illegally. You probably don't have anything like that in Korea."

Chun looked at Charlie earnestly. "We have worse. Came back because we have worse."

"Yeah? Is that so?"

Chun nodded. "That's so." He didn't elaborate. He knew Charlie would not understand false arrest and torture.

After Charlie left, Chun looked for the abacus. He always kept it at his fingertips, but Charlie must have put it away to make room for the adding machine. He looked in every drawer and finally found it in the file cabinet under "A".

Chun worked the beads of the abacus, calculating and adjusting the quantity of produce he would now need. Charlie was right; things weren't so bad. They just weren't as good as they used to be. Chun made a list of the farmers and packing houses he would have to call to cancel standing orders. They weren't going to like it. Some will even be angry, blaming him for their getting stuck with unsold produce, perhaps holding him responsible for their financial loss. He wondered how he could keep his contract and save everyone, trying with all his might to come up with a plan and discovering he had no idea where to begin.

He rubbed his eyes to stay awake. He had become used to sleeping at night. Standing up to stretch, he exercised by throwing his hands out and bringing them back against his chest. "Breathe in deep and empty your thoughts," his father used to say. "Give play to your feelings and everything will fall into place." Chun would sit quietly gazing at the ploughed fields until a sense of peace came over him.

He had taken Harold and John to gaze over the same fields, hiking all day to retrace the steps of his past with his sons. His older brother had greeted them, opening the doors to the house in which Chun was born. They had gone to the gravesite of Chun's mother and father. Years ago, he was saddened when the news of their death had reached him in Los Angeles; his mind had been on Haesu who was on her way to him from Shanghai. Five months ago, standing over their graves, he had wept.

Chun sat down and stared blankly at the list he had made. Then he put his head on the desk, resting it in his folded arms . . .

Five lis for the younger brother and ten for the older one. Chun's father never said it, but that was the way it turned out. There wasn't enough land for all three sons.

"We'll send you to school, but after that you will be on your own," is what Chun's father told him.

The American missionaries had been to their village and Chun's family had become Presbyterians. His mother insisted Chun prove himself devout. "So we don't anger the new God," she explained. That was why he was at church when he received the news. He ran home calling his father.

"*Aboji! Aboji!* It's all arranged. Bishop Lee said I am to attend Sunchoun High School."

"Good. Good. He said he would see to it. Now, we'll have to manage the rest. Losing a hand on the farm, school expenses . . ."

"No no, it's going to be all right. I'm to work for the president of the school. Reverend McNeil. All my expenses will be taken care of."

"Oooh, then it can be done." His father slapped his thigh with delight. "Good. Good. Well now, we'll have a son with an education. Of course, you'll prepare for a practical vocation. Your grandfather would not have approved a tradesman in the family but look how the Japanese have prospered. Why should we not do the same? This is our country. Why should they reap all the benefits?" But *Aboji*'s enthusiasm was forced. He gave it up and sighed. "Too bad, my son, our land is too small for all of us. Three sons! Our plot was never meant to support three families."

His father's apology embarrassed Chun. "I'll have an education that will help all of us," he promised.

He had had nothing to do with the decision but once it was made, Chun was eager to get on with it. He was also scared, wondering how it was going to turn out.

As far back as he could recall, his life had been regulated by the seasons. During the rains, mud oozed between his toes as he fought with the clawing earth, struggling to keep from being swallowed by the undisciplined furrows. The dry season found him grappling with the hand plough to penetrate the unyielding earth. Life for him had been a duel with nature. He had been born into farming. All that was now coming to an end.

He awakened to the rat-a-tat-tat of the hand-honed cleaver striking against a wooden board, too rapid for his heart to beat in time. The scent of sesame oil, beansprouts, and boiled meat merged, forming a fragrance that filled him with contentment. The sound of his mother's activities stirred him with excitement. This was to be no ordinary day; it was to be his last at home.

Across the room, his brothers continued to sleep, sprawled in a tangled heap of padding and quilt, their mouths agape. Three stacks of clothing stood inside the sliding door, free of soil and beaten flat with wooden sticks, perhaps the last time *Omoni*, his ever-toiling mother, would prepare his clothes for him.

His eyes took in the rest of the room; empty of furnishings except for an ancient chest made of Paulownia wood. The surface, cut and filled with mother-of-pearl, was alive with entwining tendrils and jewelled grapes, ornamentation evolved from aristocracy and a tribal sense of beauty.

Chun lifted the lid and pulled out a muslin loin cloth. He tied the loin cloth securely around his hips then picked up his clothes. His fingers followed the narrow band along the neck of the *chokori*. It was newly stitched. With each washing, the band had to be removed and replaced. He buried his face in the homespun cloth and drew in its fresh smell.

"*Omoni*, I'm going to the stream," he announced as he paused at the kitchen door. The cleaver chattered against the wooden board without interruption. His mother nodded to indicate she had heard.

Steam rose from the earth as sunlight struck the morning dew. His eyes scanned the soil that had been worked and re-worked over the centuries, the flat furrows broken only by mounds of earth where lay buried generations of his ancestors. Beyond that were the mountains surrounding Sunchoun. From there he would be able to see the tips of his family's burial mound and the edge of his father's land.

He walked until he reached a grove of pine trees. Beyond the trees he came to a place where rocks formed a barrier around a small inlet. On the same flat stone he had used everytime before, he placed his clothes.

The first step was the most dreaded one; it was always colder than he expected. He crossed his arms over his chest, shielding his fatless ribs. His teeth began to click against each other. He plunged into the icy water, quickly rubbed his head and body hard then scrambled out. Not until he was dry and dressed in his clothes did his teeth stop chattering. He felt exhilarated and told himself he truly enjoyed his bath.

Droplets of water dotted his clothes as he ran his hands through his hair. The stream of water he wrung out of his loin cloth splattered dust onto his feet. He spread the cloth over a bush to dry. Warmed by the advancing sun, the pine needles began to release their pungence. A song about an evergreen tree, blue skies, a rabbit on a hill and a boat sailing southward came to him. He whistled it softly to himself and lolled on the riverbank.

DUMdee DUMdee ta-ra-dee Dum. The distant beat of the *changu* sent shivers up his spine; the harvest festival had begun. He grabbed the loin cloth and trotted home, kicking up the dirt until his feet were shod in ochre dust. His black hair shimmered in the sunlight.

The songbird voices of women and the husky laughter of men turned the morning into a holiday. The women hovered over the food, serving with one hand and waving away the flies with the other, possessively managing what they had carefully prepared.

His mother had made the *mandu*. She handled the distribution of the dumplings with an authority Chun found reassuring.

DUMdee DUMdee ta-ra-dee Dum. Farmers turned dancers and lifted and dropped their shoulders in short rhythmical movements. They shuffled their feet with masculine confidence and moved their arms and hands with feminine grace.

Chota! Spontaneous shouts of approval broke loose from the crowd.

Chun imagined himself in the center of the dancers, singing in a voice craggy and provocative. He saw himself break into a dance, moving with such elegance that the girls would find him irresistable.

Munching on a piece of fire-broiled meat, he stood behind the crowd and imagined it.

Chota!

He couldn't help it. He ran home and behind the house where no one could see him, he heard the drums and he danced.

His muscles jerked suddenly and Chun sat up. He turned his head from side to side to loosen the kink in his neck. Sliding the abacus to its place, he carefully folded the paper with the list of names and put it in his pocket. He would come back tomorrow to call everyone, when they would most likely be home from church.

He couldn't call from home; he wasn't ready to tell Haesu about his losing the contract.

—2—

Chun had been able to keep the news from Haesu for several months. He continued to give her the same amount of 'house money' each month, drawing it from the safe where he kept all his money. He kept his cash where he could see it and count it whenever he wanted; no bank run by perfect strangers was going to handle his money. Haesu had draped a silk shawl over the black steel safe making it more acceptable as part of the dining room furniture. Chun never told her how much it contained, nor did he tell her the combination to the safe. Only he knew that their reserve was dwindling.

"I saw a piano today. A hundred and fifty dollars. I can't remember the make, but it's one of the best," Haesu said, knocking the rice paddle against the pot to shake off the remaining kernels.

Chun had been arguing with himself about going back to the market to join a poker game that had been going on for two nights, indecisive because he did not feel lucky. "Piano? Who said anything about a piano?" he asked.

"I did. I want the children to learn to play. I'm going to take lessons too."

"We can't afford a piano," he said flatly.

Haesu laughed as if she thought he must be joking. "It's not one of the expensive ones, but the salesman told me it has an unusually good tone."

"It doesn't matter how good it sounds. We can't afford it."

"I can get it for a good price because the person who ordered it changed his mind. His deposit makes the price cheap to me." She frowned at him. "Why do I have to argue with you about it?"

Chun opened his mouth to speak then closed it.

She went on. "We can have it delivered, but if you want to save five dollars, you and Sam or Karl can pick it up."

"Have you put a deposit on it?" he wanted to know.

Haesu picked up the corner of her apron to wipe her hands. "I had to. He wanted more but I told him I would only leave ten dollars until I talked to you. Tomorrow, I have to give him twenty five dollars to hold it until it's delivered."

"A man can make a fortune on one piano." Chun said with irony.

"It's really a good one. I listened to several and this one has the best sound."

"I didn't know you could tell one piano from another."

"You have to listen carefully."

Where would he get the money, he wondered. He'd better face up to it; sooner or later he would have to tell her. "We can't buy the piano because I don't have a contract with Matheson anymore."

"What do you mean?"

"When we were in Korea, my contract was thrown out." He went on to explain political graft and how contracts were made and revoked without warning.

"You didn't do anything wrong. A contract's a contract. Make the government stick to it," she said matter-of-factly.

"Who is the government?" he asked smiling, mocking her suggestion.

"You call Matheson. He's the one who made you sign the paper," she said adamantly.

Chun stood up. "There's no one to call, Haesu. You'll have to give up the piano." He got his cap and walked out the door.

He felt miserable as he drove down 37th Place, the motor chugging and the exhaust popping. It would be nice to come home to music, he thought. Who knows? The children may have a talent for it.

The engine coughed as if it was trying to spit out air. Chun pulled out the choke.

It would be nice to satisfy Haesu—money or no money, he thought.

The sudden blast of a horn startled him. The driver of a car coming from the right shook his fist at Chun. His face red with anger, he pointed to a stop sign.

Chun felt foolish, but he had gone too far to back up. He stepped on the gas and sped out of the man's way . . .

"Watch out!"

The bowl of rice teetered on the edge of the table. Chun caught it just in time. The near mishap set the girls giggling. They had been invited to Sunchoun High School for a rally and Chun was waiting on their table.

Round and pink with adolescent flesh, Haesu's deep dark eyes disappeared as she laughed. "Haven't you heard? Only dogs eat off the floor," she teased.

Her remark drew laughter from her friends, turning Chun's cheek crimson with embarrassment. He could think of nothing to say but, from that moment on, his mind was filled with thoughts of her.

Casually and discreetly, to avoid arousing suspicion, he asked his friends about her. "Breathe easily, Chun. She's not promised to anyone," a perceptive friend informed him.

Chun was relieved and decided to act immediately. Stammering while beads of perspiration popped out on his nose, he mixed pidgin Korean with pidgin English to present his request to his employer and president of the school, Reverend McNeil.

"*Naega* . . . I . . . uh . . . Kim Haesu *yakhun* . . ." Chun clasped his hands together then pointed to the Reverend. "You, please, *chungme hae chuse yo.*"

Reverend McNeil had been following each word closely, but his vocabulary of Korean words were mostly derived from the Bible. "You, Kim Haesu. Me, what? *Chungme, chungme* . . ." the Reverend repeated, as if that would bring the meaning to him.

Chun tried again. "Me. Kim Haesu," he linked his little fingers. "You talk Mr. and Mrs. Kim Nongson."

"Aah," the Reverend said, throwing back his head. He pointed to himself. "Matchmaker?"

Chun sighed. "Yes."

"Of course, my son. I would be honored to speak on your behalf. Mrs. Kim is a devout Christian. Her daughter must be a fine young lady."

Chun knew that the social status of his family would not enhance his chances. Haesu's parents would want to marry her off to a *yangban*, not to a farmer's son like himself. Having an esteemed American missionary represent him would work to his advantage. He could not eat or sleep until the Reverend had set out on his mission and returned with the answer.

"*Dwet da,*" he told Chun. "It is settled, my boy."

Chun was speechless. He could not believe that his greatest

desire had been achieved so easily.

"I told them what a fine boy you are, obedient and trustworthy," the Reverend said. He grasped Chun by the shoulders. "You're betrothed, my son."

"Thank you," Chun said in genuine gratitude. He slouched out of the Reverend's grip. He felt uncomfortable when anyone laid a hand on him, considered it an infringement no matter how indebted he was to the person touching him.

Ecstatic beyond belief, Chun visualized his life with Haesu. She would obey his commands, serve his needs, and mother his children. At night they would be bedded together, pressed against each other on the warm *ondol* floor, night after night, forever in Sunchoun.

The truck was running smoothly now. Chun pushed in the choke.

He had no idea that Haesu had protested. The marriage contract was made with such ease that he had assumed she wanted him. He learned after they were married that she had no love for him. What can a man do with news like that, he asked himself. He had wanted to be the source of her happiness and was told he was the source of her misery. She tried to make him feel unworthy of her, but he was determined not to grovel for her love. It would just be a matter of time, he had told himself. He thought the time had come when he returned to Korea, but came to realize that Haesu's change of heart had less to do with him and more to do with her disappointments in Korea. He was still waiting.

He bounced over the curb into the market lot, parked the truck in front of his office, and walked a block to a room behind the Hangchow Restaurant. He was nervous. The stakes would be high; the players were Chinese businessmen from Shanghai. He didn't plan on staying long. As soon as he won a hundred and fifty dollars, he was going to pull out.

The smell of cooking oil from the kitchen squeezed through a crack in the wall and spread over the room. The five players looked disheveled, their shoulders sagging from sleeplessness. Chun took off his cap and stuffed it into his pocket. He wished he could leave the door open and let the rancid air out.

He pointed to the poker table. "Room for me?"

The dealer gestured for him to shut the door and pull up a chair. As Chun took a fifty dollar bill from his wallet, the dealer waved it aside. "You want in? One hundred dollars," he said. Chun hesitated then drew out fifty dollars more.

Tapping his knuckle on the table, the dealer said. "Dollar ante."

"Chips?" Chun asked.

"No chips," the man said. "Use money."

Chun smiled to himself and thought, a Chinese never gives anyone a chance to cheat him.

Two hours later, it was over. The men exchanged a few words and agreed to end the game. One of them held up three fingers to Chun. "Three days, no sleep. We quit."

Chun never had a hundred and fifty dollars in his hands to quit first. He had lost over two hundred dollars and the game was pulled out from under him. He felt sick. He could have bought the piano for Haesu and still be fifty dollars to the good.

The men stood up and, cupping one hand over the other, held their hands up to one another; a gesture of grace. Playing with cash, no one owed anyone anything. Free and unencumbered, they had remained friends.

"You have a good time?" one of the men asked Chun.

"Sure," he replied, not wanting to appear a sore loser.

The man smiled. "Good."

Driving back home, Chun blamed himself. He should have followed his instincts; he hadn't felt lucky. He brought his remorse to an end by reminding himself of one immutable fact; luck always changes.

Half way home, Chun noticed the gas gauge registered empty. He decided to take a chance and try to make it to Bill Chang's gas station and made a turn toward Temple Street. A few blocks before the station, at the top of a hill, he shifted into neutral, turned off the ignition and coasted into Chang's, putting on the brakes behind a dark blue Lincoln Continental. His heart began to pound when he recognized the car. His first impulse was to shift into reverse and drive away, but his tank was empty.

He was relieved to see that no one was in the Lincoln. He jumped out of his truck to go to the restroom. Walking with one hand in his pocket and the other holding the brim of his cap low, he hurried.

"So you're back. I had heard you were." Loretta's lilting voice sent a shiver through him. She had been in the ladies' room.

"Hello, Loretta," Chun said, continuing on his way.

"I thought you were going to stay in Korea," she said disdainfully.

"Changed our plans," he said, arriving at the door to the men's room.

"I'll just think of you as still being there," she said through her teeth.

"Whatever you like. Pretend I don't exist," he said as he went in the door. Once inside, he took off his cap and fanned himself with it.

He let sufficient time pass before he looked out the door to see if she was gone. Bill Chang had moved the truck to where the Lincoln had been standing and was filling the tank.

"Loretta Lyu backed into your truck. Didn't hurt anything," Bill assured Chun. "She was in a hurry. Probably on her way to a meeting. Great lady. Always doing something for the community."

Chun nodded.

"When are you going to get a new truck, Chun?" Bill hung up the nozzle on the side of the pump. "This one's ready for the museum."

"It still runs good," Chun said, digging into his pocket for change.

When he was back on the road toward home, he shook his head. He should have stayed in bed today, he thought. First the gamblers from Shanghai and now Loretta. He had been dreading the prospects of running into her. Just his luck, he grumbled to himself. Before their little affair, he would never run into her unless he had to attend church for someone's wedding or funeral where she would be warbling a solo with that professionally-trained voice of hers. Haesu's only comment about Loretta was, "She only comes to church to show off." It wasn't easy to fault a woman who attended church regularly, led the choir, worked for charitable causes, raised a family, and spoke perfect English. But Chun thought her mannerisms affected and her singing hard on his ears.

She had appeared at his door, one day, doing her do-gooding work, dressed 'fit-to-kill', with a jar of *kimchi* in her arms . . .

"I wondered if you had heard from Haesu," she said. "She was to deliver a letter and a gift to my aunt." She said "aunt" with a broad 'a'.

Chun covered a yawn with his free hand. He had thrown a robe over his shoulders and held it closed with the other hand.

"I hope I didn't wake you," she said.

He opened the screendoor for her. "Come on in. I have to get up pretty soon." Since Haesu left for Korea, he had been getting up an hour earlier to have his dinner at Hank's Cafe. "I haven't heard from her but I'm sure she took care of it."

"I've brought you some *kimchi*. I thought with you're being alone and all." She handed him the jar of pickled cabbage.

He held it in his free arm. "That's very nice of you."

She reached for the jar. "Here, let me take that and put it in the kitchen." She caught the edge of his robe with her diamond ring.

Chun quickly retrieved the lap of the robe, slipped his arms through the sleeves, and tied his belt; he had nothing on underneath.

Loretta Lyu walked into the kitchen as if it were her own. At the sound of the icebox door closing, Chun pulled his robe tighter about him and waited to hold the front door open for Loretta. He was waking up now. She returned to the parlor and sat in the blue mohair chair. Crossing her slim ankles, she settled back.

There was nothing for Chun to do but sit on the sofa. He carefully closed his robe over his knees. He was wide awake now. "How's Gil?" he asked. It was all he could think of to say.

"Fine, I guess. He's been traveling. The last I heard from him was from Monte Carlo." She undid her ankles and crossed her knees. "I'm a gambler's widow," she said.

Along with the whole community, Chun thought them an incongruous pair. But the gambler and his church-going wife carried on as if their alliance was beyond their power; each bearing the cross of being married to the other.

"How does he get into those places?" A mixture of curiosity and admiration entered Chun's tone.

"They think he's a rich Chinaman from Shanghai."

Chun laughed then searched for something more to say. He thought of getting up for a cigarette but was afraid that would encourage her to stay until he finished smoking it. He didn't know how the thought occurred to him but the purpose of her visit was beginning to dawn on him.

She saw it happening and smiled.

With Haesu gone he had been aching for a woman but Loretta Lyu was the last person he had in mind.

He stopped searching for something to say when she was beside him and untieing his robe. She took his hand and slipped it under her dress. He saw no reason to resist her. She took off her clothes carefully and draped them over the chair so as not to wrinkle them. She drew Chun to the floor, giving him no chance to invite her to his bed. As she made love to him, she uttered no words of English. All her utterances were in Korean, low words of the lower class.

Chun had never experienced anything like it. He now knew what Haesu meant when she accused him of raping her. For him, it was ecstatic.

When it was over, Loretta found the bathroom and filled the tub with steaming hot water. In perfect English, she called to him and ordered him into the tub. He was dumbfounded but too satisfied to resist. The stinging heat of the water caused him to draw air between his teeth. Clutching the sides of the tub, he slowly slipped in, giving himself time to adjust to the temperature. Loretta saturated a washcloth with soap then began to bathe him.

Having his back scrubbed sent Chun into new raptures. With sure hands, she washed him until he felt love for his own body. He wished she would never stop but he discovered pleasure of a different sort when she rubbed him dry with a towel.

"Now it's my turn," she said, drawing new water.

He was awkward at first, never having bathed anyone, but spreading lather across her rounded back and over her firm nipples rid him of any maladroitness. As he slid his hands over her shimmering body, he lost all timidity.

When she was dressed, she said, "I'll be here next Thursday."

He nodded.

The bath was good, almost the best part, he remembered. He had once suggested they begin with the bath but Loretta had refused. Then, out of courtesy, he had offered to bathe her first, but she rejected the suggestion, saying that in his eagerness to have his turn in the tub he would skimp on her. He had denied it, but decided it was not worth an argument.

He never got her to his bed. She wanted him everywhere but there. He did not mind; it was as if the sanctity of his marriage had been preserved.

Because of Loretta, he might have been persuaded to stay in Korea. He wasn't afraid Haesu would learn of his 'affair' because he was certain she would not be jealous. She would turn it into justification for her opinion of his unseemly sexual appetite. It would be for Loretta's sake and his. He was uncomfortable being the reminder of her insatiable lust.

It was no wonder she was upset at his returning. She had never expected to see him again.

As he pulled up to the curb, Chun laughed to himself. He knew he would never tell her, but he speculated on Haesu's response if she were to learn the truth about Loretta. He was smiling when he walked into the house.

"What's there to smile about?" Haesu wanted to know. "I've been trying to think of ways to make the government stick to its agreement. A contract's a contract."

"Are you still on that?" Chun asked.

"You have to do something," she insisted.

"It's too late. We're lucky we had the contract as long as we did."

—3—

"The man called about the piano again. He's already given me an extra week to pay him the twenty five dollars." Haesu said.

Chun had just finished dressing. He was ready to have dinner before going to the market. "For the last time, tell him you're not going to buy it and ask for your ten dollars," he said, sitting down at the table. It was about the tenth time he had said that to her.

"Are we going to get a piano?" Faye asked, reaching for the broiled meat.

"Eat a lot, Faye," Chun said. He regretted seeing her lose her baby fat. Her limbs were beginning to string out.

"What's the piano for?" Harold inquired.

"No piano for anything," Chun said, annoyed with Haesu for bringing it up in front of the children.

"So we can all learn to play," Haesu said.

"Not me," John said. "No sissy piano playing for me."

"Would you rather play the violin?" Haesu suggested.

"Violin? That's worse!" John exclaimed.

"You have nothing to worry about, John," Chun assured him.

"Why can't we get a piano for me?" Faye asked, pulling the meat from the bone with her teeth.

Before Chun could say anything, Haesu replied, "Your Papa says we can't afford it."

"Must be expensive," Harold noted.

Chun gave Haesu a look of warning, but she ignored him. "I'm sure Papa has enough money in his safe," she said.

"No more talk of piano," Chun said sternly.

"Okay by me," John said, slurping up his bowl of soup.

"Don't make so much noise with your soup!" Haesu said sharply.

Harold took a piece of meat from the platter. The chunk of meat slipped from his chopsticks, hitting the edge of his plate before dropping to the floor. "Shit," he muttered, then gasped as he realized what he had said. "Sorry," he added quickly.

"Where did you learn that kind of language?" Haesu demanded to know.

"Leave him alone. He said he was sorry," Chun said.

"You're the one who won't allow anyone to use bad language," Haesu reminded him.

Chun was silent for a moment then told Harold, "That's the last time I want to hear you say that in this house."

"Maybe if the boys were home practicing on the piano instead of playing in the streets, they wouldn't use such language," Haesu pointed out.

The heat rose to Chun's face. "That's the last time I want to hear you say anything about that piano."

"You'd find a hundred and fifty dollars fast enough for a game of poker." She swept her hand toward the safe. "It's all in there."

Chun stood up, knocking over his bowl of soup. "There's no money for a piano!" he shouted.

Faye began to cry. "I don't want a piano," she sobbed.

"I'm sorry I swore, Papa." Harold said solemnly.

"Let's talk about something else," John pleaded.

Haesu stood up to face Chun. "There would be enough money if you went to see Matheson," she said, her voice modulated and steady.

Chun stormed out of the house. He cranked his truck hard—too hard. Pulling down the accelerator lever once too often, he flooded the engine. He threw the crank to the ground and sat on the curb, waiting until it was time to try to start the engine again.

What the hell does she know, he angrily asked himself. While she sleeps, I'm at Ninth and San Pedro dealing with muscle-bound, foul-mouthed men, fighting with them over pears and potatoes until one of them gives in to a battle-worn price. "Hey!" they say, "Fifty cents a lug don't pay for my fuckin' gas." I tell them, "Don't give me that bullshit. You'll make a hundred percent profit and more. You bleed the farmers and you sure as hell would bleed me if I let you. Take it or leave it."

What the hell does she know, he asked himself again. While she sleeps, truckers pull into the market, hauling their load from packing houses up and down California, driving their bull-headed trucks on narrow two-lane roads, a thin white line separating them from oncoming trucks; a ribbon of paint to save them from becoming a pile of shattered glass and mangled flesh, of torn steel and splintered bones. They fight to stay awake while she sleeps.

Chun reached alongside of him and pulled out a handful of grass then threw it down. She doesn't know anything, he told himself. While she dreams, at the first light of day come the retailers, not so muscle-bound or foul-mouthed. They handle the fruit, examine the greens, holding up the defective ones to lower the price, to start the argument. They barter with me in words thick with accent: Greeks, Italians, a few Chinese, but mostly Japanese. When I finally close my stall and call it a night, the retailers have already begun to polish the fruit and wash the mud off the greens, getting them ready to sell for twice the price they objected to paying me. She'll just be getting up then, grudgingly fixing breakfast for me. I'd come home hungry and tired from saying words and doing things I wouldn't want to teach my children.

Chun walked to the driver's seat and reset the levers on the steering wheel. He picked up the crank. When he had inserted it into the engine and given it a turn, the motor started right up. He threw the crank into the passenger seat, climbed in, and drove off.

She doesn't know anything, he thought to himself. She's never even stepped foot in the market.

By the time Chun reached the market, he had cooled down considerably. Samsung was waiting in the office with a thermos of coffee.

"Things are slow tonight. I thought we would have our coffee early," he explained to Chun. He shared his coffee with Chun every night.

"Good idea, Sam. I could use it right now," Chun said. He

reached up to take off his cap then discovered that he did not have it on. "I must be losing my mind."

"Everything all right?" Samsung asked, putting a cup of coffee in Chun's hand.

"Nothing money wouldn't cure."

"Everyone's complaining. No one's making any money except Yun. His packing house is sending stuff all over the state."

"Yeah," Chun said, sipping his coffee.

"He's going back and forth between here and Reedley keeping an eye on his business. I wonder when he sleeps," Samsung said, squatting on his heels.

"Probably doesn't," Chun answered, pulling out his chair to sit down.

"Timing. In this business timing is the secret to success. Yun had enough capital to buy out the Shin brothers the year there was a bumper crop of peaches."

"Yeah, timing makes the difference," Chun agreed. No one ever produced any proof, but Chun suspected that Yun had accumulated his 'capital' from the donations he collected for the Korean independence movement. Some of that was his money.

"Yun told Karl he would never make any money loading trucks," Samsung said.

"He did? Did he suggest stealing it?"

Samsung laughed. "Karl didn't stay around long enough to find out. He told Yun he didn't have time to talk with him; he was too busy making money."

Chun laughed. "Karl can always come up with something."

Samsung finished his coffee. He stood up and set his cup next to the thermos. "Back to work for me. I'll be back later to pick up the thermos." He opened the door and went out to the loading dock.

Chun leaned back in his chair and pulled out the desk drawer. He took out a black address book and ran his fingers down the tabs until he reached the letter "M". He knew Matheson's number by heart, but he wanted to be sure. He disliked calling a wrong number and bothering a stranger. He's been through the motions countless times, never able to complete a call, hanging up before the phone would ring, afraid Matheson with think him a fool. . .

"Did you hear that?" *Omoni's* eyes were round with amazement. "They leave their shoes on inside the house!"

Aboji took his long-stemmed pipe from his mouth to smile.

Continuing with the account of his responsibilities as Reverend McNeil's houseboy, Chun said, "As a consequence, I have to sweep the floors every day." He tried to make his experiences away from home sound interesting, searching for words that would transport his parents into a world rich with imagination and fascinating information. "You should see how the missionaries fill their rooms with chairs to sit on, tables to eat from, beds to lie in. All out and in place whether or not they are in use. My job is to wipe the dust off and put away objects that have been misplaced. Sometimes I repair broken objects."

"They pay you to do that?" *Omoni* said with disbelief. "They wouldn't have to pay anyone to do any of that if they lived the way we do."

"I also run errands. I've been all over Sunchoun and have seen everthing," he added.

Aboji laid his pipe across his lap. "What about your studies?"

"Oh, that's coming along." Chun hardly paused for a breath before going on. "It is truly amazing. They talk about everything. I don't know where they find the words. The weather, their feelings, their thoughts, everything. They put everything into words. I'm slowly learning their language, but I'll never be able to use it the way they do.

Aboji picked up his pipe. "They have their language and we have ours. You'd better spend more time on your studies." He sucked hard to set his pipe burning again.

Chun had discovered that working for the Reverend was easier than working in the fields, but he found his studies to be the most difficult. Pictures revealed a world beyond his imagination, but the words were baffling. When dusting the library, he often became absorbed with the photographs in books. One day, he failed to notice the Reverend approaching.

"Ah, Chun. Insects. We call those insects. Very interesting," the Reverend said.

Chun quickly closed the book. "Sorry."

"It's all right. No sorry. It's all right." He reassured Chun with a pat on the shoulder. "Reading is good."

Chun was relieved at the Reverend's kindness.

The library offered another temptation. Chun had resisted the impulse many times but, one day, when he saw no sign of anyone, he sat in the Reverend's tapestry covered wing-chair. His feet barely touched the floor. Running his hands over the upholstered arms, he thought about how he would describe the feeling he experienced to his parents. Words like 'royal' and 'authority' came to his mind, but not 'comfort'. When he leaned back, the chair forced him to keep his back straight and his head erect. He studied the paisley pattern on the fabric, noticing its similarity to the intricate designs on the oriental carpet. He became so engrossed that he did not hear Reverend McNeil enter. The Reverend was in his stocking-feet, having left his muddy shoes outside.

Chun would never be able to describe the rage on the Reverend's face nor would he be able to repeat his words. The Reverend yanked Chun from the chair, led him to the courtyard, broke off a twig from the plum tree and, still shoeless, gave Chun a switching, the first Chun had received in his life.

He never told his parents of the incident.

Chun threw the black book into the drawer and pushed the drawer shut. He would not call Matheson, not until he was sure of what he wanted to say.

The next morning, as soon as Chun walked in the door, Haesu asked, "What did he say?"

He hung up his sweater in the back porch where the air would dissipate the musty odor of the market. He took off his shoes and slipped his feet into his leather scuffs.

"What did he say? she asked again.

"I didn't call him," Chun replied as he walked into the bathroom. When he came out, Haesu confronted him with, "Why not?"

"I didn't have anything to say to him. Is the food ready?"

Chun's place at the table was in front of the phony marble hearth that formed a niche for a gas heater, facing the parlor and the front door. On cold mornings, he would sit at the table with his back to the row of gas jets, inviting the orange-blue flames to take the chill from his body. The heater was not on this morning.

As Haesu walked out of the kitchen she said, "You ask him how he can sign a contract and . . ."

Chun slapped his hand on the table. "I'm hungry. Let's have the food."

Haesu put the bowl of rice and platter of meat and vegetables in front of him " . . . break it." she said, completing her sentence. "Tell him . . ."

"*Kimchi*," Chun said, beating his finger on the table where he wanted her to set the pickled vegetables.

"It's there," she said, pointing to a covered bowl. "Take off the cover."

Chun fumbled and dropped the cover in a saucer of soysauce. "Shit!" he said.

Haesu rushed to get a dishrag and wipe up the dark amber liquid. "The stain will never come out," she said.

Chun picked up his bowl of rice and stomped to the kitchen. He poured hot water from the kettle over his rice then looked for a soupspoon. He yanked out the drawer, causing the silverware to clatter. Rummaging around until he found a soupspoon, he slammed the drawer shut and stomped back to the dining room.

He sat with his left hand on his thigh, fingers turned inward and elbows bent, immobilizing that hand and using the other as if he had been born with one arm. He spooned up his water-rice to his mouth, alternating it with chopstickful of meat and vegetables then *kimchi*. Whenever he sensed Haesu was about to say something, he laid down his chopsticks and noisely slurped up the water from the bowl.

He heard the boys stirring in their room and Faye paddling to the bathroom in her slippers. Chun stopped chewing to tell Haesu, "Not another word. You're losing your control. Don't say another word in front of the children."

"I'm losing my control? You're the one who shouted and walked out of the house."

"Don't provoke me, Haesu," he said, putting the bowl to his lips.

Lowering her voice, she said, "Why shouldn't they know? If you won't do anything for my sake, maybe you'll do it for theirs. Why are you so afraid to call Matheson?"

Harold was the first to dress and come to the table. "Good morning," he said cheerfully.

Chun grunted.

Harold looked at his mother expectantly then said, "Never mind. I'll get my breakfast," and went to the kitchen.

John and Faye tried to enter simultaneously, jamming each other in the doorway. John extended his upper arms to lock Faye in place. "Ouch!" she yelped.

Carrying a bowl of cereal to the dining room, Harold tried to send his brother a look of warning, but John wasn't paying attention. Chun got up from the table, walked over and grabbed John by his belt and yanked him through the doorway, terrifying John.

"How many times do you have to be told to look after your sister?" Chun's voice was deep and measured. "You treat her worse than anyone."

John was trembling. "I was just playing with her."

"You hurt my shoulders," Faye told him.

Haesu shot her a look that commanded her to be quiet.

"You go out and find a switch," Chun ordered John.

After John went out to find the instrument for his punishment, Haesu told Chun, "You're too severe on him. You can't deal with Matheson so you take it out on John."

Chen flew into a rage. He picked up the bowl and threw it against the wall.

"You're making everyone miserable!" Haesu said, her voice beginning to break.

Tears came to Harold's eyes. He quickly wiped them away and went back into the kitchen. Faye ran up to Chun. "Please, Papa. Please don't hurt anyone," she pleaded.

When he realized what he had done, Chun wanted to cut off his hands. He wished he could turn time backwards and undo what he had done. "Don't be scared," he told Faye, his voice quavering. John walked in with a small branch he had broken off the plum tree. "Get rid of it," Chun told him hoarsely.

Chun walked to his room and shut the door. He began to undress. It was an effort to get out of his clothes; his arms were like lead. Every ounce of energy had been drained from him. His remorse was overwhelming. He wished he could take his children into his arms and beg their forgiveness but he told himself that doing so would embarrass everyone and undermine his authority. As he lay in bed, he heard Haesu pick up the broken pieces of china. He pulled the blanket over his head and waited for sleep to come. . .

"Be quiet, my boy, I'll get rid of the police." Reverend McNeil lifted the edge of the bedspread as Chun fell to the floor and scurried through.

At the drop of the cover, Chun was enveloped in darkness. He now blessed the peculiar foreign custom of leaving one's bed standing. He listened for signs of danger, trying to still his throbbing heart, chewing on the tie of his *chokori* to silence his chattering teeth.

"We have the evidence here." The policeman rattled a piece of paper in the air. "We'll be back. Do not make the mistake of harboring a traitor. This matter is in our jurisdiction not yours."

It was a mistake. Chun wanted to shout it out. His name did not belong on the list. He's never been involved with politics.

"I've told you, I sent the boy on an errand to the Presbyterian mission in Pyongyang. He's not due back for several days." The Reverend's voice was steady. "I gave him permission to visit his uncle on the way. I have no idea where his uncle lives. I do know that you have made a mistake. Youngjune could not have possibly participated in the demonstration."

"We'll be back for him," the policeman promised.

Chun waited for the Reverend to lift the cover and light his hiding place; it seemed an eternity.

"They're gone. I waited to be sure. You cannot stay here. Not stay here," the Reverend whispered, motioning Chun to come out. "There's no place safe for you as long as you are wanted by the police. Not safe. Must go."

"But I did not do it. Not guilty," Chun said, his voice quavering.

"I know, I know. You must leave. Go to America." The Reverend went to his desk and unlocked the drawer. "Take money. Go to Shanghai then to America." He handed Chun bills totaling three hundred dollars, but Chun tried to hand them back. The Reverend closed Chun's fist around the money. "No worry, Haesu's mother pay back."

"Haesu. I marry Haesu," Chun said desperately.

"She'll follow you. Go America later." The Reverend went to the closet and pulled out a sweater and a pair of black worsted pants. "Here. Wear in China, wear on boat. Go. Hurry." He gave Chun a push toward the door.

Chun moved quickly, hugging the deepest shadows as he made his way home. There was only time to bid his parents farewell and gather a few belongings.

"The police found a list of student protestors," he explained as he grabbed his things. He had no idea what he would need, but he knew he could not slow his flight with a heavy pack. He spread his loin cloth on the floor and placed the pants and sweater the Reverend had given him in the center, stuffing a few toilet articles into the folds before tieing the corners of the cloth. "I have to go to America."

"America? Why must you go so far away?" His mother clutched at his *chokori*.

"My name was on the list. The police will arrest me." Chun rasped, still short of breath.

"Jail? You cannot stay," his father said.

"It was a mistake." Chun shook his head in disbelief, unable to get over his bad luck.

"Then not America," his mother pleaded.

His father drew air between his teeth and shook his head sadly. "If he has been accused, he cannot stay."

Omoni began to moan. Chun was in a panic, not wanting to leave but anxious to get away. He broke away from his mother's grasp. "I will send a message as soon as I am safe."

In the days that followed, he found refuge with sympathizers, cast from one Korean patriot to another until he reached China. Even there he was in constant fear of his life. Posing as a Chinese, he was fearful that he would forget the warnings of his countrymen and turn his head at the shout of *"Yobo!"*, a trick the Japanese secret police used to single out Koreans.

He felt a measure of relief when he boarded the ship to America. Not until he stepped onto California soil did he feel safe.

—4—

"Olly, Olly, oxen free!"

Chun woke up and heard the metal hit the pavement then rattle as it rolled to a stop.

Harold's voice rose above the noise. "Run!" he shouted to the captives he had freed. His command sent footsteps scattering in all directions, over asphalt streets, along cement sidewalks, and across green lawns. The one who was 'it' ran to retrieve the can, garbled his count to ten, then yelled, "Here I come, ready or not!" It was the voice of Yukio Watashi.

His penetrating voice could bring down the Diamond Mountain,

Chun thought. Harold's voice of authority had pleased him. Chun wanted his sons to command the respect of their playmates. The game provided good training, he thought. It encouraged the boys to develop confidence and kowtow to no one.

He heard a couple of boys chuckle as they raced to the tin can. "One, two, three for John!" Yukio yelled. The sharp crack of shoe leather hitting metal followed. "Olly, Olly, oxen free!" John shouted. Chun smiled to himself; John had outrun Yukio.

Chun liked waking to the sound of children playing and witnessing the pleasures of his sons' boyhood. They were the sounds of delight in the New World. His playground had been the silent earth.

He got out of bed. Remembering his earlier fit of rage turned his mood sour. He dreaded facing the family.

No one uttered a word throughout dinner. As soon as the boys finished eating, they asked to be excused. Chun waved them out then, shortly afterwards, went out to sit on the porch steps and smoke a cigarette. It was beginning to turn dark. It would be pitch black at this hour in winter, he thought, but summer days seemed to stretch themselves out for the benefit of the children.

Suddenly, hanging high from the wires where 37th Place met Dalton Avenue, the street lights went on. A pallid amber glow fell over what moments before had faded into the darkness. The lights went on every night at the same time, but the children looked at one another as if they were experiencing a miracle. "Bitchin'! Ain't that just bitchin'!" They exclaimed. They smiled uncontrollably as the battered tin can was placed under the light, the misshapen twist of metal spot-lighted on the black macadam.

Chun wished he could stay and watch, but he had to get to the market and call Matheson.

When he got to his office, he wasted no time. Without consulting the black address book, Chun dialed the number. He cleared his throat several times while the phone rang at the other end. When he heard Matheson's voice, Chun managed a deep and confident, "Hello Matheson, this is Chun."

"Who?"

"Chun. You know, Chun's Wholesale Produce?"

"I don't know who you are, but if it's money you want, I ain't got any."

"No, not that."

"Well, what then? I'm a busy man."

"We had contract . . ." Chun began.

"Yeah? I'm not bound to any contract I know of."

"I handled produce for Navy."

There was a pause. "Oh yeah, yeah . . . I remember you. Good produce."

"I still have good produce but no contract."

"I'm damn sorry, but it's out of my hands. The government threw out all the contracts I had. There's nothing I can do about it. Sorry," he said and hung up.

Chun looked at the receiver, blaming it for the message it carried. He told Haesu it would be a waste of time, he thought, blaming her for the futility of his call.

Later, when he and Samsung were having coffee, he confided in his friend. "Business is bad. I'm going broke." It was the first time he had put it into words.

"You? Broke? Everyone's complaining but I thought you were doing okay."

"I'm thinking about selling half the business, form a partnership," Chun said. The thought had just occurred to him.

"I wish I had the money, but I don't even have enough saved to get married. Yun's the only one I know who has enough to buy into any business."

"That robber? I wouldn't sell my ghost to him," Chun declared.

Samsung laughed then shrugged his shoulders. "I'll ask around."

"No, don't do that. I'll handle it." Chun walked to the window to raise the blinds. "Maybe I ought to sell out, go into something else."

"What else? I can't see you waiting on tables," Samsung said.

"I can't either, but I'd better think of something."

Samsung ran his hand through his hair. "It's like running and getting nowhere. Working extra at a produce stand during the day only cuts down my energy to load trucks at night. Karl said I should get married and let my wife work. I couldn't do that."

"Neither can he. It's just talk. He's not the kind of man to let his wife work," Chun said, knowing that he wasn't either.

Samsung stood up. "Meanwhile, it's back to work for me." As Samsung went out the door, Chun shouted after him, "Luck always changes, Sam."

Strangely, despite his failure with Matheson, Chun was not despondent. The acknowledgement of his failing business to Samsung seemed to have relieved him of his burden. He could not understand it but he felt unencumbered and free. He felt lucky.

After he had sold the last lug of apricots, Chun locked the door and pulled the shade. "Chun's Wholesale Produce", painted in block letters on the window, cast a shadow of itself on the blind. The market closed at noon on Saturdays. It was payday. Most of the drivers headed back to the San Joaquin Valley in their empty trucks. Some of them hung around to 'blow' their money in town. L.A. had a lot to offer: first-run movies, pool halls, and women.

As usual, a few truckers and some local hands hung around Chun's office. They waited while Chun threw an old Army blanket on the floor and, as was his habit, slipped off his shoes.

Chun began to shake a pair of dice in his hands; the click of the ivory quickened his pulse. He blew through the crack between his hands to warm the dice. One last hot breath then he squatted to give the dice a short sharp throw across the blanket.

The men kneeled for a closer look as the cubes bounced about like a pair of decapitated heads, waiting for them to come to a stop, first one and then the other. "Nine!" the men called out in a chorus. It was the number Chun was to repeat if he wanted to win.

"Nine," Chun whispered into his hands as he shook the dice. When finally six dots on one cube and three on the other made him a winner, his heart was filled with joy.

Putting his money where everyone could see it was a player's declaration that he was in the game. Green bills were spread like peacock feathers in some hands, neatly folded and woven between the fingers in one and, in Samsung's case, crumpled and seen through the chinks of his tightly closed fist.

"For Christ's sake, Sam, why can't you hold your money nice? Goddamn wrinkes don't come out," Bill Chang complained. He had left his brother in charge of the gas station so that he could join the game.

Karl butt in before Samsung could say anything. "I was just going to ask you if you was a basketweaver, Bill, the way you knit your money in and out of your fingers like that." He turned to Samsung. "If he doesn't want your money, don't give it to him."

"Fuck you, Karl," Bill snapped.

The men laughed, but Chun winced. He could never get used to that word.

Not more than a dozen throws of the dice later, Gilbert Lyu tapped at the window. Peeking in the narrow slit between the drawn shade and the window sash, he gestured to be let in. The men could not believe it; Gilbert Lyu, the gambler, wanted in.

"He must be lost," Karl joked.

Chun went to open the door. "Hello, Gil. What can I do for you?'

"Mind if I come in? I was in the neighborhood."

"C'mon in. We've got a little game going. I don't suppose you would be interested."

"Why not? I've got time to kill."

A knowing wink passed between some of the men as they reached into their pockets to add a few more bills to the ones they already displayed. Gilbert Lyu reached inside his coat, pulled out a brown leather billfold, and set it on the seat of the chair. His heavy-set frame prevented him from squatting on his heels like the other men. "How the hell do you boys do it?" he said after he tried several times to get down with the other players.

"Sit in the chair, Gil," Chun suggested. "Might as well be comfortable." He knew that Gil gambled at fancy places in Reno and Monte Carlo. Loretta had told him.

"No thanks. I'll stand. It'll give me a bird's eye-view of everything," he said, laughing by himself. When it was his turn to throw the dice, he crouched awkwardly and threw the dice haphazardly.

One of these days I'm going to have to get a new blanket, Chun told himself.

The Saturday craps game usually lasted a couple of hours, breaking up when men with families had to get home. Gil's presence gave stature to this game; no one wanted to be a piker so they played a little longer and bet a little more than usual.

Chun looked for Gil's response. He discovered that Gil was not above congratulating the winners or beneath smiling sympathetically at the losers. He took his own losses philosophically. Chun felt an esteem developing for Gil.

At every roll of the dice, the accuracy of Chun's instincts was confirmed. He was winning handily. Gil, on the other hand, could not seem to get his numbers to work for him.

"Jesus, Chun, did you load them dice?" Bill Chang teased.

Chun laughed. "They sure act like it, don't they?"

"When you're hot, you're hot," Karl said.

"There must be a knack to it," Gil said. "Which I don't seem to have."

"What's your game?" Karl asked.

"Poker, I guess. I stay away from the craps table in Monte Carlo," Gil informed him.

Bill whistled. "Monte Carlo?"

Gil smiled as he gave Chang a friendly pat on the back. "It's nothing great. Maybe bigger tables, fancier clothes," he nodded toward the bare light bulb hanging from the ceiling, "crystal lights. But the money's the same."

"More of it, I'll bet," Chang said.

Gil shrugged. "Win more, lose more."

While the two were talking, Samsung showed Chun the money he had won. They smiled at each other. As the afternoon wore on, Gil won less and lost more. Chun found himself feeling sorry for him, but was satisfied he had won Gil's money honestly. When he felt his stomach growl, he suggested they send out for some Chinese food.

"I can't," Karl said. "I promised the wife I'd be home." He looked at his watch. "Oh, oh. Late already. Well . . ." he smoothed out the money in his hands and slipped the bills into his wallet. "Better late than never." He stood up. "Sorry to break it up."

"Gil's out some money. He ought to have a chance to win some of it back," Chun said.

Gil quickly brushed aside any concern over his losses. "Hell, Chun, that's the name of the game."

"Tell you what. Why don't all of you come over to my place later and we'll get a game going? Poker," Chun suggested. He had won most of the five hundred Gil had lost.

The men were for it. Bill Chang couldn't make it, but the others would be there.

Chun sped his way home. He couldn't wait to tell Haesu. Good news for a change.

Chun pulled up to the curb and leaped out of the truck. "Yobo!" he called as he walked in the screendoor. He found Haesu in the kitchen. "Look at this!" He pulled the bills from his pocket and waved the money in the air. "Almost five hundred dollars!"

"You've been gambling again," Haesu said, continuing to rinse out the rice.

"I knew my luck was going to change. Yesterday I dreamt about killing a snake and today I won all this money. Not only that. I won it from Gilbert Lyu."

"Gilbert Lyu? What are you doing playing with him? He's a professional gambler." Haesu began to take notice.

"He's nothing great, only a man just like me." Chun pointed to himself then beat his finger against his chest. "He has to lose sometimes too." He sighed with satisfaction. "I feel good." He paused before adding, "He's coming over later for some poker."

Haesu turned to look Chun squarely in the eyes. "Have you lost your mind? Play poker with Gilbert Lyu? He's too smart for you. You can't beat him."

"Why do you think Gil came to the market? 'Time to kill,'" he said. Fat chance. Big-time gamblers don't play to kill time. He's down. Otherwise, why would he come to the market to take on a bunch of loaders and truck drivers? Too smart? Smart has nothing to do with it. No one can win without the right numbers."

Haesu picked up the pot of rice and put it on the stove. "You don't know when to quit," she said.

Chun put the money away in his pocket; he was going to need it for the game. He was convinced she was trying to erode his joy of anticipation, constricting him because she did not believe in his instincts. He sat at the small table in front of the window facing the backyard where the dahlias grew.

Haesu went on cooking. He saw that, as far as she was concerned, he might as well not be there. She yanked a cabinet door open and pulled out a deep kettle, then held it under the tap, turning the faucet on full. The water resounded hollowly. Carrying the heavy pot to the stove, she scraped its botton on the grate of the gas burner.

Chun cringed at the abrasive sound. He felt that her line of thinking went against his grain as well. She wanted him to make events happen, events over which he had no control. Was it his fault that no one was dangling a new contract under his nose, he asked himself.

Haesu paused before smashing a clove of garlic with the side of the cleaver. "You don't seem to realize that you have to make good luck happen," she said. She brought the knife down and the garlic's pungent fragrance wafted through the kitchen.

Chun felt the muscles of his temple tighten. She was asking him to abandon the tenets of his ancestors. He believed that to 'not-contend' required the highest level of human behavior and the deepest understanding of life. "Haesu, you know that if you want muddy water to become clear, you have to lie still." He stood up and as he left the kitchen, he said, "Since when did you advocate dog eat dog?"

Throughout dinner, Chun said nothing. His mind was on the game and he wanted no one to dampen his boundless expectations. The intensity of his silence hushed the children.

Finally, Haesu spoke. "Faye, after dinner we're going to the movies. You'll need a sweater."

"Can't I watch the boys play kick-the-can?" Faye asked.

"Papa's friends are coming over to play cards. We'll be in the way." A puzzled look came over Haesu's face. "I thought you liked to go to the movies."

"I want to play kick-the-can but Harold and John won't let me," Faye complained.

"We let you watch," John said.

Almost simultaneously Harold said, "You might get hurt."

"Don't you like the movies?" Haesu asked.

"My bottom gets sore," Faye replied.

Chun laughed. "What you need is a girl to play with. You should have had a sister."

"It's supposed to be a good movie," Haesu said. "Ronald Colman is in it."

Chun reached into his pocket for some change. He rummaged through the coins in his hands and gave Faye a fifty-cent piece. "Buy yourself some ice cream and candy at the show."

John leaped out of his seat. "I'll go with you, Momma."

Faye held out the coin to him. "I'll give you this if you let me play kick-the-can," she said.

"Faye goes with Momma. You boys stay here and give me a hand," Chun said, putting an end to the discussion.

Haesu did not bring up the game until she was ready to leave. "Quit if you start to win," she said.

A smile came over Chun's face. "You mean, quit if you start to lose," he chuckled.

She paused a moment to think about what he had said then replied, "What's the use, you won't quit either way." She followed Faye out the door, slamming the screendoor behind her.

—5—

The lily white mattress pad smelled of sun-dried laundry. Years of rubbing against coiled-spring beds and wooden washboards had unraveled the stitches, leaving the cotton padding free to gather in uneven lumps under tangled loops of broken thread.

Chun and Harold placed the mattress pad over the round Duncan Phyfe mahoghany table, not a genuine antique but a copy that was Haesu's pride. Their practiced movements, measured and cautious to avoid marring the table, required no exchange of words between them. Picking up the rose colored blanket from the chair, Chun handed an edge of it to Harold. It unfolded as Harold walked to the opposite end of the table. They raised it high, bringing it down slowly to avoid disturbing the pad underneath. The nap was worn. Carelessly placed cigarettes and ignored ashes had left a scattering of scorched blemishes. At one corner, a label hung by a thread. "Gotham-100% virgin wool," it said. Chun yanked it off.

The telephone rang. "I'll get it. You can go now," Chun told Harold, then walked to the hall to answer it. "Chun here," he said.

"Chun! This is Yun! How are you?"

Yun's forceful greeting caused Chun to move the receiver away from his ear. "Okay. What's up? he asked, bringing the receiver to his ear again.

"Chun! I hear you're looking for someone to buy you out."

"You heard wrong," Chun said.

"How could that be?" Yun asked.

"You know how people like to blow things up," Chun said. Samsung wouldn't have told Yun; he must have told Karl and Yun got it from him.

"You're not in trouble?"

"What kind of trouble?"

"Money trouble."

Chun laughed it off. "No such luck. By the way, we're having a game at my house tonight. Poker. Why don't you join us? Gilbert Lyu's going to be here."

"Gilbert Lyu?"

The thought of including Yun to 'sweeten the pot' appealed to Chun. "Big stakes, Yun. It'll be worth your while," he said.

"Sounds good. I'll be there. Mind if I bring Koh? You know, Koh Kwang Yong from Reedley. Works for my company. He's in town on business."

"Sure. The more the merrier."

Chun was smiling when he hung up the receiver. Having Yun call up was a stroke of luck. He was being given the chance to get back the money Haesu had handed to Yun for Korean independence.

Fitting six chairs around the table crowded the room. An ebony rocker stood in the path of the front door. Chun picked it up and looked for a place to set it. He turned half circle then back again. He wondered where Haesu would put a piano. He suddenly felt obliged to win the money for a piano so that she could figure that one out. He opened the door to the boys' room and set the rocker in the middle of the floor then closed the door.

Cluttered rooms still got on his nerves. There wasn't a piece of furniture in the house he would miss. Except the safe. He needed the safe. It was almost empty, but he intended to fill it again. A single stack of bills had been left intact, money intended for Haesu in case anything happened to him. He vowed he would never touch it. He refused to buy insurance, thinking it unsavory to offer someone a windfall in the event of a loved one's death.

"Hey Chun! Can we come in?"

Karl and Samsung had arrived. They had changed into clean workpants and short-sleeved shirts. Karl's wife had ordered their clothes from the same mail-order catalogue. The item number of their shirts differed by one digit.

"I didn't hear you drive up," Chun said.

"I guess we're early. Who's coming?" Karl wanted to know.

"Yun and Koh are coming. I told Yun about the game. I guess he wants to play with a big-time gambler."

Chun's reference to Gil as a big-time gambler brought a grin to the men's faces. "Word gets around fast," Samsung said. "There may be a mob here."

"Think they'd like to shoot craps? Poker's not my game," Karl confessed.

"Craps or poker, what's the difference?" Chun asked then proceeded to answer himself. "The only difference is that craps is like jumping off the edge of a cliff. Before you have time to shit in your pants, you know whether you'll live or die. Poker is slower. Poker is like stepping into quicksand; no hurry, plenty of time to sit in your shit."

The men laughed. Chun did not allow profanity in his home, but words unacceptable to him in English sounded amusingly coarse in Korean.

Chun looked at the clock. "Maybe I'll have time to get cleaned up. I won't be long. Let the men in when they come," he said. He hated to rush. A leisurely bath would have calmed his nerves. Bathing quickly, he changed his clothes and returned to the parlor, filling it with the smell of Palmolive soap.

Two men in a coupe pulled up to the curb. The color of the Dodge was barely discernible under the amber streetlight.

"Looks like Yun's car. Koh must be with him," Karl said, looking out as he stood at the screendoor.

Chun heard the sound of the '34 Lincoln swing into the driveway. He did not have to see the car to know that it was Loretta's. He looked out the window, anyway. Only the circles of the white sidewalled tires were visible. No one could miss Gil as he emerged from the dark blue car, a thick ghostly figure in his off-white sharkskin suit.

A suit on a night like this. Chun thought it ridiculous. What he wore made more sense to him: a white cotton shirt with the sleeves rolled up to his elbows, gray corduroy pants—aged soft to his liking—and brown felt slippers. It takes a remarkable event to get him into a suit. The impeding cut of stiff fabric, the tie that restricted his 'Adam's apple' were counter to his anatomy, denying him any comfort.

"Well, we meet again. Poker this time, eh?" Gil said as he entered.

"Poker or craps, what's the difference?" Karl said.

Gil gave a nod of his head in greeting to the others. No introductions were necessary.

"No point in wasting time," Chun said as he waved everyone toward the table.

Gil walked to the front of the mantel and pulled out Chun's chair.

"Why don't you take the chair on the other side, Gil?" Chun suggested. It was his seat. He never sat anywhere else.

"Whatever you say," Gil said as he moved on to the chair opposite Chun. He took off his coat and carefully draped it over the back of the chair, adjusting the shoulders so that they extended evenly on either side. Silver "GL" cuff-links closed the sleeves of his navy blue shirt. The swirls of maroon and royal blue on his yellow tie were hard to ignore. He loosened the silk cravat and unbuttoned his collar. His neck remained hidden behind his jowls. He was as thick as Chun was lean.

Chun wondered if Gil was equal to Loretta's acrobatics. He doubted it; the man could barely stoop to shoot craps. Chun's cheeks suddenly turned warm. The audacity of his speculation embarrassed him. The image of Loretta and Gil making love had never entered his head before.

Koh and Yun had taken the seats on either side of Gil, leaving Samsung and Karl to flank Chun.

"What'll be the limit?" Chun brought the chips over from the mantel.

"Let's start easy. Fifty cents opens and five bucks the limit," Gil suggested.

The craps shooters went for it, the poker players were agreeable, but Chun though it was a little low. "That's all?" he asked.

"That's enough," Karl quickly replied. "Do you want to wipe us out before the game starts?" He wore a silly grin as he looked to the men for accord.

"Yeah," Gil said, "plenty of time for that."

Chun shrugged. "Okay. How much do you want?" He was the host, that made him the banker.

Sam and Karl bought fifty dollars worth. Yun asked for two hundred and fifty, Koh asked for the same.

"I'll take five hundred," Gil said as he counted the money from his wallet. "I don't like to bother the banker."

Chun doled out the chips then counted five hundred dollars worth for himself.

Hell, he thought. I won almost that much from Gil. Beat him with his own money.

The irony of it amused him. He felt he was equal to the match.

It was not often that Chun found something to admire in a man, nor was he prone to be critical or envious. A man was what he was and that's the way Chun took him. But the manner in which Gil used his hands impressed him.

Gil's thick but nimble fingers kept the cards under perfect control as he divided the stack and interlaced the corners in machine gun rhythm. He repeated the movements with equal precision until he was satisfied that none of the cards fell into any fixed order. Snapping the cards down in front of Yun, his hands hovered over the deck while the 'cut' was made. He slapped the two halves together and began to toss the cards in the carefree manner of a farmer sowing his seeds, dropping each one precisely where he wanted.

"Five-card stud," Gil announced. They had agreed the games were to be dealer's choice.

Karl and Samsung preferred Deuces Wild and Seven-card stud games that increased the possibility for a winning combination of cards. They ignored the fact that it also added the chances for other players to win. Draw poker and Five-card stud were the experienced players' choices, games that required carefully calculated risks. Chun had no preference. He played every game with equal enthusiasm.

Chun was sure that Gil had a strategy; professional gamblers could not afford to be capricious. He resolved to formulate one of his own, play the game smart, forgo the delight he experienced in having winning cards fall into his hands no matter how he played the game. He studied Gil's moves and noticed that Gil stayed in the game whether or not he had a good hand, challenging his opponents, building the pot so that the winner won big.

The players took turns at winning. The even distribution of the pot suited Chun. He never liked to win too much too soon. It made him nervous. He wondered if that was part of Gil's tactics.

"Are you in, Chun?" Gil asked. He was dealing his sixth round of Five-card stud.

Chun peeked another look at his bottom card. He had four and five of spades back-to-back. "Sure," he said, tossing in the required amount of chips, sealing his eligibility.

Samsung turned his cards face down, rejecting them in disgust. "I'm out," he said.

Yun threw in his chips. "The only way to make any money nowadays is to expand. Take my company, for instance. We get the profits from the ground up, from the seed to the mouth. You, Chun, you should expand. Keep growing. No one can afford to stand still. I'm thinking about getting into canning. Why should I break my back to grow crops then let a bunch of middlemen make all the profits?"

"I've got enough to handle. My business is big enough. Any bigger and the headaches grow," Chun said. He wished Yun would put his mind to the game.

The next card made Chun sit up; a seven of spades opened the possibility of a straight flush. A slim chance, he knew that, but a possibility nonetheless.

"I could have used that seven," Yun said, taking another look at his bottom card. "You can't make it on farming alone. You can't make it on wholesaling alone. You can't make it on retailing alone. You have to get in on all of it. Use that old Yankee know-how."

"When in Rome," Koh added.

"What's Yankee know-how have to do with it?" Chun asked. "Farming has nothing to do with profits. You're born into it. It's not even a question of liking it. It's a matter of learning how to do it." He gave a lift of his chin toward Yun. "What's your bid?"

Gil had dealt Yun an eight giving him a pair showing. Yun shrugged. "What the hell, make it the limit."

"I'll keep you company," Gil said and threw in his share.

Koh gathered up his cards. "No potential," he announced, dropping out.

"Shh-it." Karl hissed under his breath. "I have to stay in," he said, but he had run out of chips. He bought more from the banker.

Chun had been admiring his own string of matching cards. They were lovely. He rose from his seat to toss in his chips. "Five and I raise you five," he said, watching with delight as the men followed him in.

The last card had been dealt. Gil had the strongest hand, a pair of nines. He bet the limit. With an ace and a king showing, Karl reluctantly stayed in. Chun's cards were now a variegated mix but the numbers were right for a possible straight: a good hand for bluffing. He doubled the bet. Yun's power was in his pair of eights. Adding his chips to the pot indicated a third match or a second pair.

Gil now doubled. Karl slowly began to count his chips then stopped. "One of you guys ain't bluffing," he said, gathering up his cards, concealing his pair of aces. Chun and Yun finished counting their chips at the same time and threw their share into the now sizeable pot. With his staying in the game, speculation grew around Chun. The players had been viewing his cards with disdain, unimpressed by the mismatched numbers and hues.

It was time to show their hand. Any one of them could be a winner. They maintained an outward calm but the heat of their eyes and their hard attention gave them away.

Gil turned over a nine, three of a kind. Yun clacked his tongue. "Look at this, will you?" he said, slapping his bottom card over. He displayed two pairs, evidence that he had played it right. All eyes turned on Chun. He casually turned over his card, filling the inside hole of a straight.

"You lucky son-of-a-bitch!" Gil was flabbergasted.

A grin ran across Chun's face. "A lousy four and five of spades. I thought, what the hell can I do with them? Seven of spades next. You could have used that, Yun, remember? Maybe a straight flush, I thought. The trey of hearts took care of that, but who could drop out now? Then you hit me with a six. I couldn't believe it, an inside straight. . ." He shook his head in disbelief. Standing to haul in the chips, Chun began sorting them according to color. He chuckled then began again. "A lousy four and five of spades. I was going to throw them away. . ."

"Olly, Olly oxen free!" The shout came from the street.

"The boys! I forgot about them. I have to bring them in," Chun said, getting up from the table. "Deal me in. I'll be right back."

Chun returned with Harold and John at his heels. He instructed the boys to greet the guests then sent them to bed.

"Say Chun, have you heard about the plans for a building?" Yun asked.

"Can't say I have."

"It's for a meeting hall. Place to meet. Kids can get together and have dances. Office space for the newspaper too. We need it."

Chun arranged his cards; Karl had dealt a new hand. "What happened to Korean independence?" he asked in mock innocence.

"Have to move with the times. We need a new building. Can't stay on Temple Street forever. My company's going to put up five thousand. Everyone's donating something. It'll give your boys a place to go and stay out of trouble. We don't want our kids getting away from us," Yun said.

Chun plucked the discards from his hand. "Give me three," he told Karl.

"Think your company can make a donation? We Koreans don't have a building we can call our own."

"Did you open, Sam?" Chun asked. Samsung nodded.

Yun went on. "Another five thousand . . . I don't mean for you to put up all that, but another five grand and we can start building."

Chun rearranged his cards. Without looking up, he said, "I'm not interested in donating money some guy can use for himself."

Yun laughed. "You don't have to worry about that. We've got control. Can't control money you send overseas. Run into a bad apple in any barrel. But you don't have to worry. The money's going where we say it is."

"I tell you what. If you stop talking about it, I'll start thinking about it," Chun said.

Yun turned to Gil, but before he could open his mouth, Gil said, "Talk to my wife. She's the one who handles the pocketbook."

Yun was caught short by the information. He dropped the subject.

"Mrs. Lyu's a fine woman," Koh said. "My wife talks about her all the time. Says she's heard that Mrs. Lyu knows more about running an organization than anybody."

"Yeah, she can run anything," Gil said.

Chun hid behind a cloud of smoke. Some of it stuck in his throat and he swallowed hard. Ashes dropped from his cigarette onto his lap. He brushed them off.

—6—

"Yobo! Come give me hand. Faye's fallen asleep." Haesu was at the screendoor.

Chun lay down his cards and hurried to help her. He held the screendoor open with his foot, took Faye's limp body from Haesu's back and carried her to her bed. When he returned to the parlor,

Haesu was sitting on the edge of the sofa, bent over as she reached behind her to beat her lower back with her fist.

"She's getting too big for me to carry," she complained.

"Can I do anything for you, *nu nim?*" Samsung asked, already half way out of his seat.

She waved him down. "No thank you." She stretched her back as she stood then walked to the table. Koh rose to his feet.

"Koh Kwang Yong from Reedley," Chun said as he returned to his seat.

"You probably don't remember, but we've met," Koh said. "Temple Street. Many years ago. That turbulent meeting when your group walked out. Your oldest boy was a little tot then." He held his palm open toward the floor to indicate how small Harold was.

"Why, that was almost fifteen years ago," she said, as if nothing that far back should be remembered. Yun and Gil made a feeble attempt to stand, but she waved them down. "Who's winning?" she asked, looking over Chun's shoulder.

"Your husband's the lucky son-of-a-bitch," Gil said.

She flinched at his coarse Korean. "Don't let me interrupt your game," she said.

Chun picked up the cards and began to shuffle them. "You must be tired," he said, feeling cramped with her standing over him. He could almost hear her counting the chips.

"Why don't I make some *nang mien* for us?" she suggested. "It's such a warm night."

"Good idea!" Gil exclaimed, as if it was exactly what he had in mind. "You're famous for your *kimchi.* I hope you have some."

"Of course." She pushed through the swinging door. "Who wouldn't have *kimchi?* It won't take long," she said as the door closed behind her.

"My wife makes the worst *kimchi* in the world," Gil said, shaking his head tragically. "Tasteless, tasteless, tasteless."

Chun leaned forward to push his chips to one side and make room for the bowl of noodles. He had forgotten about Loretta's *kimchi* and left it in the icebox until green and white scum laced the white cabbage. Lucky for him he hadn't eaten any.

"Aristocratic women don't know how to cook," Yun declared. "They had servants to do that for them in Korea."

"Naw," Gil disagreed. "It's an art like everything else. Some women have a talent for it and some don't."

"That better be it," Karl said. "Every Korean woman I know claims to be a *yangban*."

The men laughed. Every Korean knew the ancestry of everyone else. Everyone knew the false claims from the true, knowing that some lied because they thought that thousands of miles of ocean would conceal their low birth. Any attempt at deception only became a target for further ridicule.

"It's stupid. What good is it to be a *yangban* in America?" Samsung wanted to know.

"Better not knock it," Karl said. "If you haven't got that, you haven't got anything."

His words struck a nerve. Chun had decided long ago that there was nothing he could do about the state of Korean or American politics. He had taken each day as it came, satisfied he had fulfilled his duty if Haesu and the children were clothed and fed. If Karl was right, all that would add to nothing.

Chun listened to the rat-a-tat of Haesu's knife on the chopping board. She would agree with Karl, he thought.

"That's why you should have your own business," Yun said. "Don't let anyone push you around."

"At least I have a chance of becoming vice-president," Koh chimed in.

"Why not president?" Gil asked slyly.

His question brought a chuckle from the men. They knew that Koh would be president over Yun's dead body.

Gil began playing with his chips, picking up a stack then dropping them one by one to rebuild the column. "We're kidding ourselves," he said soberly. "We haven't got a Chinaman's chance in legitimate business. The limits have been set and we can't go beyond them."

"Maybe the limits are high enough," Chun said. "Maybe they're as good as we can get anywhere." He knew Haesu would disagree with him. Despite the fact that she was the one who had decided they should return to America, she would disagree with him.

The smell of onions and garlic drifted from the kitchen.

"Sheesh. . ." Karl hissed. "This conversation is beginning to depress me."

"That's the trouble with you," Yun said, "you get depressed. You don't do anything. You just get depressed."

"Do, do, do. You've got a million do's to turn into profit for yourself," Karl snapped.

"He got his picture in the Reedley newspaper as one of the examples of a successful 'oriental' businessman," Koh said in Yun's defense.

"So now we're all supposed to be like him," Karl said, pointing his thumb at Yun while looking at the other men.

"Easy, Karl," Chun warned.

"Initiative," Yun said. "All you need is initiative."

"Fuck initiative!" Karl told him.

The swinging door squeaked as Haesu locked it in place. "This door needs oiling," she said. "I could use some help carrying out the food."

Chun wondered if she had heard Karl. She hated that word as much as he did. It was one of the few subjects they agreed on.

Samsung got to his feet. "I'll help," he said. After he had carried out the last heaping bowl of noodles, he returned to the kitchen to get a chair for Haesu.

"I'm not eating," she said. "Could you please ask Chun to come in here?" She followed Samsung to the door and pulled it closed after him. When Chun walked in, she waited for the door to stop swinging before she whispered, "Quit now! Make up some excuse and quit now!".

Chun drew in air between his teeth. "It's too early. How would it look if I quit without giving them a chance? Stop worrying and go to bed. Sam and I will take care of the dishes." He started for the door.

She grabbed his sleeves. "If you lose, it will be over between us. The house is all we have left and I won't let you take that from me and the children."

Chun's heart went to his throat. He didn't tell her he had already made arrangements to borrow money on the house. He forced a laugh. "You've been seeing too many movies. Now let go of me or my *nang mien* won't be any good." He walked out of the kitchen, confident that no matter what happened to him, she would never allow herself to be a 'divorced woman'.

No one attempted to hold a conversation as the men noisily slurped up the thin white noodles. They kept a continuous supply in their mouths even while plucking *kimchi* from the bowl and meat from the platter with their chopsticks.

His mouth still full, Gil mumbled, "Your wife's *kimchi* is the best." A piece of noodle fell from his chin to his tie and became lost in the flamboyant pattern. Chun knew it was there to stay. Haesu tested the noodles by throwing a length of it against the wall. If it stuck, it was done.

Gil's manners were beginning to draw Chun's derision, standing in the way of his respecting the man.

Belching between the words, Gil suggested they raise the limit. "No more of this amateur stuff."

"Best idea I've heard yet," Chun said.

The cellophane crackled as Samsung tore open the pack. He snapped the bottom against the side of his hand and a cigarette lunged forward. He offered it to Chun.

"Thanks," Chun said. A scratch of his fingernail set the tip of a wooden match aflame. He lit his cigarette then shook out the match. As he leaned forward to pass the cards to Samsung, the smoke went into his eyes. He pulled out his handkerchief to wipe the tears from his cheeks.

"You look like you've been to a funeral," Yun commented.

"Damn smoke stings," Chun said. He wouldn't admit his eyes also burned from lack of sleep. They had been playing Poker for seven hours.

After the limit had been set, the low risk players' supply of chips had steadily depleted. Chun wasn't interested in taking his friends' money. "Anytime anyone wants out, feel free," he said.

Karl tapped his solitary chip on the table. "I've got no choice. I'm down to my last five bucks." He looked at Samsung. "Want to call it quits?"

"I think I'll stick it out and play what I've got. You go on home. I'll find a way," Samsung said.

Karl cashed out and left.

A few hands later, Samsung said, "I can't stay awake. Count me out for awhile." He set his chips aside, made his way to the sofa, and was soon snoring.

The four remaining players moved in toward the table and paid close attention to the game. Sleep tugged at their brains but they were determined to stay alert and play it smart. At the end of each hand, their shoulders drooped and their elbows fell away from the table. No one said anything about quitting.

Chun concentrated with such intensity that blood was drawn to his head. Eyes glassy and red, he looked as if he had been drinking. While contemplating his moves, he would pick up some chips and play with them in his hands. As long as he had plenty to play with, he did not worry. Another hour had passed when he noticed that his supply was getting low. "I need a glass of water," he said, abruptly rising from his chair. "Anyone else want some?" he asked, already making his way to the kitchen.

"I could use some coffee," Yun called after him.

The gas went on with a 'poof'. He couldn't let the game slip away from him, Chun told himself. He could use some coffee too. He turned up the gas. "Be right out," he yelled.

Koh folded his elbows on the table and dropped his head into his arms. Gil moved over to the wing-chair, locked his fingers in front of him and dozed off. Yun waited for his coffee.

The coffee was steaming when Chun put the cup in front of Yun. Yun blew on the brown liquid. As he raised the cup to take a sip, his lips quivered involuntarily.

"I'll get you some cream and sugar," Chun said. He returned with a can of evaporated milk in one hand and a sugar bowl in the other.

Yun poked a matchstick through the skin of milk plugging the holes in the can. Chun decided it wasn't coffee he wanted and went to the mantel for a new deck of cards; a new deck might bring him luck, he thought. He ripped open the transparent wrapper. The sound woke Gil.

"Huh? Oh, Jesus . . . how long have I been asleep?" He looked at his watch and saw that only ten minutes had passed. "Feel like I've been asleep for hours," he said. "I'll have some of that water now." He got up to help himself.

Koh blinked as he raised his head. "Is it time for me to leave?" he muttered.

"Wake up!" Yun told him sharply.

Chun shuffled the cards. They slid against each other like silk, slipping out of the deck and spilling onto the table. Chun gathered them up. "Let's make the game interesting," he suggested. "Let's raise the limit."

Gil was wiping his mouth with a "GL" monogrammed hankerchief. He stuffed it into his hip pocket. "Might as well have a little fun, eh?"

It was Yun's deal. As he handed him the cards, Chun said, "Kids know about fun. My son kicked the can tonight, outran the kid who was 'it' and made himself the most popular boy on the street. He laughed as hard as he ran. I never played that game when I was a boy."

"My son's crazy about football," Yun said.

"Never played that either, not the way it's played here," Chun said.

"You've got to be big to get into that game. We're not built for it." That was Gil's opinion, the biggest man among them.

"My son Gary's tall for his age," Yun said, dealing out the cards.

"Tell him to play basketball like the other Korean boys. Quick and accurate, that's all it takes," Gil said.

"That may be, but he wants to play football."

Gil shrugged. "That's too bad." He tossed in a couple of chips. "I'll open with ten."

"What's the limit?" Koh asked, still trying to wake up.

"No limit, I thought." Gil answered.

Chun's heart skipped a beat. He didn't remember suggesting that but he said. "Okay with me."

Chun wondered where in the room a piano would fit. Haesu would probably move out his roll-top desk. Then where would she put his desk? Maybe now he'll be able to convince her to get rid of some of the furniture. He would throw out the ebony rocker: the children were wearing out the rug rocking it across the room.

"I'll call you and raise you twenty." Gil's voice startled Chun. His mind had been wandering; he must have missed something. Glancing at his cards, Chun said, "Let's see . . . that was ten on Yun's bet, wasn't it? You raised him twenty. . ." He quickly counted off the chips. "Here's ten more."

"It's not your turn!" exclaimed all the players.

Chun felt like a fool. He should have been paying attention; he was not playing a child's game. "No? Oh, sorry. Well, it doesn't matter," he said, leaving his chips in the pot.

Disquietude fell over the players, their concentration unhinged by Chun's careless move. The slack in tension seemed to diminish the game.

Chun pretended to be absorbed in his cards. He saw that Gil's potential pair of Kings was the only hand that could beat his.

Chun's cards looked like a possible straight. What he had was a pair of Jacks. It could still be the winning hand but he decided to bluff and play as if he had a straight. He lit a cigarette, forgetting that his last one still burned in the ashtray. He kept raising the bets until everyone dropped out but Gil.

"This is what is called 'the moment of truth'," Gil said as he toyed with his hidden card.

Koh laughed a silly laugh. "I thought that's what it was when I dropped out."

Gil ignored him.

"Well, let's have it," Chun said.

Gil turned over a King.

Chun slowly blew out the smoke he had drawn deep into his lungs and gathered up his cards. "It's yours. You're too smart for me," he said.

Gil hauled in the chips. "There's one chance in two hundred and fifty for a straight. Did you know that?" he asked cheerfully.

"Figures don't mean anything. It's a fifty-fifty chance. You either make it or you don't," Chun replied.

"Want to call it quits?" Yun asked.

Chun said nothing as he got up and walked to the corner of the dining room. Under the silk shawl, the black steel safe had gone unnoticed. Tossing the shawl aside, Chun began to work the combination lock. The others looked away, not wanting to pry. He swung open the thick door and reached inside. The money stuck to his damp palms. It would take too long to count off the bills, he decided. He grabbed all there was then returned to the table.

"Shouldn't you lock it up?" Koh asked.

"Go ahead," Chun replied, knowing it was empty.

"What are you waiting for?" Yun asked Koh, hurrying him.

Koh scrambled out of his chair and pushed the door to the safe closed. He turned the dial several times before carefully replacing the silk shawl.

"Don't you have some business to attend to?" Yun asked impatiently.

"What? . . . Oh yes, I have to meet someone at nine. Company business. I'll have to give myself a little time to get cleaned up . . ." Koh rambled on.

Chun looked at the clock on the mantel. "We've got three hours," he said.

—7—

The coffee pot lid was jammed again. Chun heard the glass dome hit the sink as Haesu yanked the cover free. She had been up long enough to feed the children and send them on to Sunday school. She was now fixing breakfast for the men.

"Count me out this hand," Chun said. He went to the kitchen to intercept Haesu. He did not want her coming to the table.

"Who's winning?" she asked as she scraped the burnt crumbs from a slice of toast.

"Don't know yet." He picked up the skillet and started out.

"Wait. Put the eggs on separate plates. It doesn't look good served in the pan," she said.

He lifted the lid to look. She was right. The whites of the eggs were curled, the edges turned to brown lace and the yolks were solid. "You get ready for church. I'll take care of this," he said.

Throughout the early hours of the morning, Samsung had intermittantly awakened. When he heard the size of the bets being made, he had gone back to sleep. The smell of breakfast made him sit up. One look at the over-cooked eggs and the ripple of blackened bacon and he lay down again.

Picking at his eggs, Chun kept an ear open for Haesu. When he heard her heels snap against the kitchen linoleum, he stood up. She was slipping on her white gloves when she walked in. Chun took her by the arm and led her back to the kitchen."You go on to church. I'll take care of the dishes," he said.

She pulled away from him. "What's the matter with you?" she wanted to know.

"Go on, go on," he insisted. "I'll clean up." He took her by the arm again and led her to the back door. "A woman has no place in there," he said.

"What?" She looked at him as if he had lost his mind.

He hissed through his teeth. "Do I have to explain everything to you?" He waved her out and shut the door.

While Chun hurriedly collected the dishes and dumped them into the sink, Gil went to the bathroom. He came out with his hair combed, his face washed and smelling of soap. Except for his loosened tie he looked as if he had just arrived.

Breakfast, another cup of coffee, new cards, more cigarettes, nothing changed Chun's losing streak. When he was down tossing a few lonely chips from one hand to the other, Koh said, "Maybe we should end the game. Don't you think so, Mr. Lyu?"

It was the first time he addressed Gil directly. His obsequious manner drew Chun's scorn.

Gil shrugged his shoulders. "It's up to the loser." The condescension in his tone irritated Chun.

"Quit? Why should I quit? Go ahead and deal. I'll be back in a minute." Shutting the door securely behind him, Chun went to the phone in the hall. He dialed two digits of Charlie Bancroft's number then changed his mind and hung up. He couldn't bring himself to ask his friend for help again. He sat on the wooden chair Haesu kept by the phone. She had put it there after Mr. Yim had died. She often told the story about having to reach out with her feet and drag the chair to her when Clara had called with the shocking news. "What if I had fainted?" Haesu would ask.

It was the first time Chun had ever sat in the chair. He was never on the phone long enough to sit. He leaned forward and rested his elbows on his knees, using this moment of solitude to map out a strategy for the remainder of the game. With less than a hundred dollars left, there was no point in cashing in; the money wouldn't even pay for the piano. What could he do with so little money, he wondered. It wasn't enough to support any strategy, he concluded. Convinced he had no choice but to go back and try to win with what he had, he stood up, stretched his back, and returned to the game.

"What's the verdict?" Yun asked. "Time to quit?"

"I'm already late," Koh said.

"Do what you want," Chun said, "but I'm in."

Yun swallowed a laugh. "I have to hand it to you, Chun. You don't quit easily."

"No reason to quit," Chun replied.

As Yun was about to deal out the cards, he announced, "Draw. Jacks open."

They were stuck with the game for a couple of rounds, sweetening the pot with ante. It was Gil's deal again when Chun was cheered by his cards: a pair of sevens and a pair of Jacks. He opened.

Yun threw down his cards as if they were not worthy of consideration. Gil stayed in without bothering to raise the bet. Koh tossed in his share of chips.

"I tell you what," Chun said, "let's bet the pot." He was out of chips but he had confidence in his cards.

"Sure, why not." Gil said, ready to agree to anything.

Koh took back his chips and folded.

"How many do you want?" Gil asked Chun.

Chun set his cards face down on the table. "None."

Gil gave a thin sliding whistle then tossed out three cards. He slowly plucked three more off the top of the deck. His face told nothing. "Okay, let's see those cards," he said to Chun.

Unable to control his smile, in a single movement Chun turned his cards over, spread them out to reveal the two pairs, then reached over to gather in the chips. "It's about time," he said.

"Hold it there!" Gil ordered. He laid down his cards. "I had two Queens." he explained. "The first card I drew was a good-for-nothing seven. Then came a lousy deuce. I thought, shit, I've had it. But coming in last, looking as pretty as a movie star, was the Queen of Diamonds. Tough luck. Chun . . . sorry."

"Chun!" Koh began to sputter. "You . . . you could have had a full house. With that seven you could have had a full house. You should have discarded one and . . ."

Yun interrupted Koh with a look of disgust. "What kind of poker player would draw one card?"

Chun ignored both of them. "Well, Gil, as you say, that's the name of the game. Luck, pure luck."

"That's right," Gil said without argument.

"Count it up and let me know what I owe you." Chun said.

Samsung had been lying quietly listening while Chun was being wiped out. After the men had left, he got up. "Have they gone?" He wanted Chun to think he had been asleep.

"Yes, they're gone."

Ordinarily, Samsung would have asked about the game, but without a word he put on his shoes. He was relieved when Karl arrived to take him home.

"Guess what I've just heard?" Karl entered without waiting to be asked in. "I was having coffee at Hank's Cafe and some of the guys said they heard Gil's been around because he got kicked out of Reno. Got caught cheating!"

Samsung's face lit up. "Do you mean he didn't really win?"

"Right. As soon as I heard, I raced over here." Karl turned to Chun. "We can make him give us back our money."

Chun smiled wanly. "You mean yell 'cheater' like some kid?" He shook his head. "Don't believe everything you hear. Probably some sore loser started the rumor, someone who can't take losing. Gil doesn't cheat. He's smart. He knows how to play the game."

—8—

Sunlight streamed through the window at a slant, lighting everything in its path. No children's voices from the street broke the silence.

Chun was alone. He stared blankly at the table, blind to the crumpled bits of cellophane that sparkled in the morning sun and the fresh cigarette burns on the rose-colored blanket.

Cheat? A gambler's no gambler if he has to cheat. Gil's a big-time gambler, everyone knows that. And he's smart. A man can take losing to a smart player. What fool would admit losing to a cheater? Chun asked himself. That's like being cuckolded, twice with one act.

His lips smacked as he thought, What does it matter? Either way I'm left with nothing.

He would try to empty his mind. He picked up a few crumbs and rolled them between his fingers, pieces of Haesu's fried egg. He toyed with it, stretching it like a rubber band. She never was good with American food. He wanted to laugh but no sound would come from his lips, only silent chugging breaths. Her *nang mien* was the best. Gil thought so, made a pig of himself. Some of it was still stuck to his tie. The thought of it brought a smile to Chun's face.

His smile erupted into laughter, laughter that would not stop, a vomit of laughter that made tears stream down his cheeks. Suddenly, a chill came over him. The air felt as raw as Sunchoun in winter and his teeth began to chatter. He longed to lie with Haesu, to press against her satin underslip and warm his hands on her breasts. His longing ceased when he realized he would have to tell her what he had done.

Chun shuddered and rubbed his arms.

PART THREE

FAYE

F I V E

Papa never said much but when he spoke, my brothers and I listened. I had to listen if I wanted to know what was going on. No one bothered to explain anything to me, the 'baby' of the family.

One night at dinner, Papa said. "There's nothing for me in L.A., Coachella Valley, they say there's work there. I'll be catching a ride with one of the truck drivers at the market."

I never understood why Papa had sold his business to Mr. Yun or why he had given most of the money to Mr. Lyu. I only knew that his doing so had changed everything.

It seemed like any other night when Papa left for the market. Only this time, he carried the leather valise he had carried when he met us in Korea.

At first, home seemed an easier place to live without Papa: no more of his short sharp commands, no need to worry about waking him in the middle of the day, no reason to fear that Momma would nag him until he walked out in anger. I began tagging after my brothers, pestering them until they included me in their games of kick-the-can. I climbed fences and scrambled up trees to prove there was no reason to exclude me. I laughed aloud and yelled. "Olly, Olly, oxen free!" as hard as anyone, filling Papa's absence with noises I was once not allowed to make. I skinned my knees and tore my dresses and Momma could not use Papa as an excuse to stop me.

But I began to miss the other things that had gone with Papa:

185

gone was knowing when he was at work and when he would be home, gone was his assurance that there were no two ways about things, gone was the weekly allowance and the rattle of coins in my metal bank. I had emptied the miniature replica of a bank building when Momma needed the money to pay the milkman, turned the Corinthian columns and the words "First National Security" upside down to shake out the coins.

When the new ways became old, I wanted home to be the way it was before.

"Why Coachella Valley?" I asked Momma.

"Just for awhile," she told me. "He's had bad luck."

Sometimes she blamed Papa. "He shouldn't have gambled," she would say, and sometimes she blamed others. "They cheated him."

Now and then, Papa would send word home through truck drivers. They stopped by the house and said things like, "Chun says to tell you he's okay. He ain't found nothin' good yet, but said to give you this." They would hand over a ten, once in a while a twenty, dollar bill.

When Momma grumbled, "Might as well be twenty cents." The truck drivers stood up for Papa. "Times are hard, Mrs. Chun. Plenty of men looking for work. Your husband ain't the only one," they said.

Twenty dollars seemed like a lot of money to me, but unpaid bills were lying all over the house. Unopened windowed envelopes filled the crystal punchbowl, sailed to the floor from the top of the mantel, fell out from between magazines and newspapers.

The bills never got paid. Momma threw them out when we moved. We had to move. Mr. Bancroft said there was no choice. Papa had borrowed money on the house and never paid it back.

I could not imagine living anywhere else. When I saw Momma packing our things into cardboard boxes, I wished that we could leave everything as it was and carry the house with us the way Papa carried his valise. Momma was packing several boxes at one time. Into one box went the things she planned to sell to the junkman, into another went old clothes for the Goodwill. Into the biggest box of all went the things she was throwing away. She threw all the unpaid bills into that box.

"You can't do that, Mom," Harold told her.

"What good is it to carry them around? We don't have the money to pay them," she said.

I tugged at Harold's sleeve. "Will we go to jail?" I asked.

"No. You don't have to worry. You're still a baby," he said.

"I'm ten," I reminded him. "Almost eleven."

"Great. You're big enough to bring in some more boxes," he said.

I brought in two empty cartons from the back porch and set them on the floor next to Momma. "Why do we have to move? Papa will never find us," I said.

"We have no choice. I've found us a house on 36th Place. Not too far from here."

"How will Papa find us?" I wanted to know.

"I'll tell Mr. Bancroft," she promised.

Mr. Bancroft was just a name to me. I have never seen him, but from the way Momma and Papa talked about him I imagined him to be something like God. I thought that if he wanted to, Mr. Bancroft could see to it that we stayed in our house. I wondered why we were being punished.

Our house on 36th Place was a small white stucco bungalow with a red tile roof. It looked like the playhouses of rich children. There was only one bedroom, so Momma and I slept in the living room. Uncle Samsung helped Harold and John put most of the furniture in the garage. He was upset with Momma for not calling him sooner.

"I don't want to be a bother to anyone," she told him.

"I'm not just anyone, *nu nim*. Next time, you're to call me," he said sternly.

After he left, Momma found a ten dollar bill on the kitchen sink. She looked at the money as if she didn't know what to do with it. "You see, this is why I didn't tell him. Samsung can't afford to give us money." She turned her back to me to pull out a handkerchief from her apron pocket and wipe her eyes.

I went and sat on the front steps. Our house was set far back from the street. According to our colored landlady, the main house once filled the front part of the lot. "A beautiful Spanish mansion," she had said. But it had burned down. She now lived in one half of the double garage, renting out what used to be the guest cottage until she could rebuild her home. She had planted shrubs to cover the gutted foundation, now overgrown and hiding our house from the street.

I wanted to cry. Even if I sat on the steps all day, Papa would not be able to see me.

No truck driver dropped by anymore. Now and then, Momma sold pieces of our furniture for money. One day she made a deal with the junkman: if he could open the safe, she would sell it to him for five dollars.

"Papa's not going to like that," John told her.

"Your Papa's not here. If there is something in it, he would want us to have it," she said.

The junkman brought a friend who put his ear to the safe as he turned the dial, listening the way a doctor listens to his patient's heart. It didn't take him long to open the safe.

"If it's that easy, nothing is safe in there," Momma said.

"Nothing in here anyway, ma'am," the safe-opener said.

"Nothing?" Momma kneeled down and swept her hands across the shelves. "Could there be a secret compartment?" she asked.

"I doubt it, ma'am."

The junkman handed Momma a five dollar bill. Then he and his friend lifted the safe onto a dolly and rolled it down the driveway. I followed them, trying to think of ways to make them bring back the safe. It belonged to Papa. It was the only thing left that belonged to Papa; Momma had already sold his rolltop desk.

The men grunted as they tried to lift the safe onto the wagon. The junkman slipped and his horse neighed. I hoped they would think it wasn't worth the struggle and give it back, but they kept at it until the safe was on the wagon. It was a rickety wagon and looked as if it would collapse under the weight of the steel safe. It didn't. I sat on the curb and watched Papa's safe slowly disappear into the distance and I could no longer hear the clippity-clop of the junkman's horse.

We lived in the house on 36th Place for six months before the landlady got tired of waiting for her rent. "I hate to ask you to leave, Mrs. Chun, but I can't live without the rent money."

Momma nodded. "I understand. You can't help it."

Momma went househunting and found one on Denker Avenue. The Che family was moving out and used only a week of their month's rent. They did not expect Momma to repay them, but she wrote their names and the amount owed them in a small black ledger. Uncle Samsung's name was at the top of the list. I asked her what she was doing and she said, "Someday I'll pay everyone back."

Moving even further away from 37th Place made me unhappy. "Papa will never find us," I complained.

"Of course he will. He'll ask around until he finds us," Momma said. Then she added with a scoff. "How far could we go? We can't move beyond Vermont or Western Avenues or Jefferson and Exposition Boulevards."

She made it sound like we lived on a board in a game of Monopoly.

"I hate moving," I said.

"It's only until Papa comes back," she said.

I wanted to believe her but Papa had been gone almost a year. The day Momma announced, "I'll have to make some money," I knew she was giving up on Papa.

"How are you going to make money?" Harold asked.

Momma sucked air between her teeth. "I don't know. I don't want to be gone all day, away from home, away from you children. And I don't want anyone telling me what to do. I know that for sure."

"If you have a boss, you'll have to do what he tells you," Harold said.

"You don't know what it's like," Momma said. She grabbed the first thing she could get her hands on, which happened to be John's bag of marbles. "If you're a maid or a houseboy, you'll be called by the ringing of a stupid bell." She shook the bag as if it were a bell. "Chun!" she shouted, shaking the bag vigorously. Marbles flew all over the room, hitting the radio, bouncing on the table top and dropping to the floor. It sounded like a round of gunshots in a gangster movie.

John and I burst out laughing. We tried to stop when Momma said, "It was humiliating."

Harold gave us a look of disgust. "It's not funny," he said.

John and I fell to the floor to gather the agate balls. Our eyes met under the table. We quickly covered our mouths to muffle our laughter. After we put all the marbles back in the bag, we stood up. "None of you will ever have to go through that," Momma said solemnly.

I thought of the look on Momma's face when the marbles scattered around the room and my cheeks puffed out to hold in laughter. But John made a funny face and I spat out the air. "I'm sorry, Momma. I couldn't help it."

Momma sighed. "You'll never understand what your Papa and I went through."

Before Momma could find a job, we were forced to move again. I was getting used to it, but hated each move more than the one before. The house on 36th Street, however, was more to my liking. It was wood-framed with three bedrooms and only three blocks from our house on 37th Place. "It will be easy for Papa to find us here," I told Momma. Harold said that each move got easier because there was less stuff to pack.

"Maybe we'll become hoboes," John said.

"Don't be silly, John," Momma answered.

Every night at dinner, Momma read the Want Ads aloud, skipping the Domestic Help column and the ads that required experience. "I know that something will come up that will be just the job for me," she said.

One Saturday morning, I was playing hopscotch with my new neighbor, Bertha, when I heard Momma calling. "Yah! Faye-yah!". I was balanced on one leg ready to hop to the next square.

"Keep on going, Faye. Pretend you didn't hear her," Bertha said.

"I can't do that," I said, bringing down my other foot. I picked up my lagger and started for home.

"Mama's baby!" Bertha shouted after me.

I didn't bother to look back. She was colored and did not understand Korean families. Momma took me wherever she went. She would not leave me with Harold and John anymore; they were hanging around with boys in the neighborhood whom Momma considered 'rough'. I had heard her tell Aunt Clara on the phone, "I don't like this neighborhood, but I can't bear the thought of moving again. Chun should be here. The boys won't listen to me." She had sounded unhappy. I remembered wanting to tell her not to be sad anymore, that Papa would be back and everything would be as it was before. Instead, I had gone to my room and wrote in my diary, "I solemnly swear to mind Momma, to not upset her or make her sad."

"I'm going to look for a job," Momma said. "You're going with me."

I washed my face and changed into a clean dress. Then Momma

and I caught the bus on Western Avenue and rode toward Hollywood. We got off at Melrose Boulevard.

Glass fronted buildings crowded the sidewalk. Company names were painted on the windows, stating their business: Western Auto, Prudential Insurance, Empire Realtors, important names that made Chun's Wholesale Produce sound small and insignificant.

"Where are we going?" I asked.

Momma read from a scrap of newspaper she held in her hand. "5432," she said.

"This is only 5418," I said. "Why didn't we get a transfer?"

"I had no idea where it would be," she explained.

She was always doing that to us, I thought, made us wander around unfamiliar streets because she had 'no idea' where a place was. Once she sent Harold to pay the gas bill before they turned off the service. It was on Seventh Street, that was all she knew and tore off the address from the billing envelope and handed it to him. He walked for miles before he found the number, not asking anyone for directions because he did not want to appear stupid. He still talks about it, as if he's looking for someone to blame.

Momma followed the sidewalk and acted as if she knew where she was going. The lower half of many windows were curtained or painted out. I wasn't tall enough to see over them but Momma was. She peeked into every one.

"What are you looking for?" I asked.

"I'm not sure, but I'll know when I see it." She said it as if she made perfect sense.

It was warm and we were walking on the shadeless side of the street. I went ahead of Momma, eager to get where we were going. A large building, the vanilla color of Spanish missions caught my eye. I read the sign then read it again to be sure. "There's the Paramount Studios!"

"What? Where?" Momma was all excited.

"Down the street." I pointed to a large complex of buildings. "See? It says, 'Paramount Studios'!"

She quickened her pace. "Maybe we'll see some movie stars."

The thought made my heart pound. We walked faster. It was almost as if we were in a race to get there. We were in such a hurry that we nearly missed 5432. Set in and tucked between the Wallenstein Enterprises and the Superior Office Supply, the door was easy to miss. "Paris Fine Embroidered Handkerchiefs" swirled and looped across the glass pane.

"Oh, here it is." Momma sounded disappointed.

I stopped in my tracks. "Nuts," I said.

"Don't say that word," she ordered.

We were still breathing hard as we climbed the wooden stairs. Our shoes thumped on the hollow steps and echoed throughout the empty stairwell. "Enter" a sign on the door instructed. Inside, a counter as high as my chin separated us from those who had business on the other side. Beyond the sea green wooden barrier, squares of raw-edged fabric were stacked on long tables. Women were bent over their sewing, leaning toward the light, drawn to it like moths. At the end of one of the tables a woman was running an iron over the finished pieces. She placed them in a pile that never grew. As soon as the stack began to form, other women took the pressed handkerchiefs, counted them as one counts the pages in a book, then folded them into triangles, fitting them into flat square boxes. I had seen similar boxes in department stores. I've always known how fruit and vegetables made their way to the produce stands, but I've only seen handkerchiefs as they appeared at the linen counters: pristine, delicate, and untouchable. I stood on my toes to get a better view, feeling privileged to observe a process unknown to the clerks at department stores. The women looked at me, the frown created by following their intricate handiwork still on their brows. I fell back on my heels and looked away.

"Yes?" The only man in the place walked toward us. His belly pushed against his white shirt but was cinched in by the belt that held up his brown pants. A large nose took up most of his face and his blue eyes narrowed when he spoke. "What do you want?"

"I saw this in the newspaper," Momma said as she handed him the torn advertisement.

He turned to give the women a look that sent them back to their work. He did not bother to read the ad. "Have you had any experience?" he asked, then added, "Have you done this kind of work before?"

"Yes."

"Where? Where have you done this kind of work?" He spoke haltingly and repeated himself as if he thought Momma would miss the meaning of his words.

"In Korea, all during my childhood."

I sighed. Why did she have to tell him that? He won't know where that is.

"Korea? I mean what company? I mean who was your boss? Korea? Isn't that something like China or Japan?"

Momma hesitated. I had to smile. I knew he would ask. People always ask.

"No, not the same," Momma said.

"Oh, too bad. If you could sew like them people, I know I could use you."

"I sew as good as them," she said, as if there were no two ways about it.

He went over to pick up a couple of handkerchiefs from the stack the women were packaging. "Think you can do this?" He showed the embroidered pieces to Momma.

She gave it a quick inspection. "Oh yes," she said.

Her answer surprised me. I didn't know she could embroider.

"When can you start?" he asked.

"Right away," she replied.

"It's too late to start today. You'll have to come in on Monday."

"Come in? No. I'm not going to work here. I'm going to work at home." She reached for the ad. "See? 'Work in Your Home' it says right here."

"You'll have to come here first to learn. The girls work here then when I see what they can do, I let them take the work home." He was beginning to sound impatient.

"No. I can only work at home. That's easy work for me. You try me. I'll take some home and when I bring them back, you decide." She shook her head emphatically. "I can't come to work here."

The women were staring at us again. I went to sit in a chair, away from their prying eyes. Mothers of most of the girls I knew were polite and agreeable but Momma always seemed to get into arguments. I picked up a magazine and flipped the pages. My face felt hot.

"I can't pay you very much until I see the kind of work you do," the man warned. I looked up in time to see him narrow his eyes.

"How much you pay?" Momma asked.

"It depends. Most of the work runs about two or two and a half dollars."

"Each?"

His eyes popped open. "EACH? Hell no! A dozen. That's twelve handkerchiefs," he said, making Momma appear stupid.

I put down the magazine and got ready to leave.

"Two and a half dollars? That's all?" she asked, making him sound cheap.

"Listen lady, you should be able to do a dozen or more a day." His tone was hard.

Momma bit her lip. "You give me five dozen to take home, I'll bring them back in five days then you decide."

"The most I can pay you is a dollar and a half to begin with. That's for one dozen and only if the work is acceptable. That means if it's good enough in my opinion. That means that I'll decide after I see your work."

"Okay, that's okay."

The way Momma made up her mind took him by surprise. "Now you realize that I'm doing you a favor. I'm trusting you with sixty pieces of linen and four spools of thread." He sounded angry.

"Yes, I know," Momma said calmly.

He stood there for a moment. Then a smile came to his lips. "My name is Mr. Seligman. What's yours?"

"Chun. Mrs. Chun. C-h-u-n." She spelled it out for him. Everyone in the family had to spell it out whenever someone asked our name.

Mr. Seligman pulled out a sheet of paper from behind the counter. "Fill out this form," he said then went to get Momma's package ready.

I walked over and stood by Momma relieved that everything was settled. She began writing slowly, deliberately, the way she always wrote longhand. I have seen her whip through rows of Korean letters and Chinese characters but she always wrote English slowly. "Yah!" she whispered to me. "What does this mean?" she asked in Korean. I read 'residence' and said, "Same as address." She nodded and continued to fill out the form.

"There's a sample in here for you to follow." Mr. Seligman placed the package on the counter then examined the application form. "Hi . . . Hu . . . What is this? How do you pronounce your name?"

"Haesu Chun. Mrs. Haesu Chun."

"Hey Sue. That's easy. I put a sample in here for you to follow. Hey Sue. Come back in five days. That'll be Wednesday."

"Thursday," Momma corrected him then added, "Thank you."

I never knew when to be proud of Momma or when to be

embarrassed. I hated having people stare at us and sometimes Momma seemed to go out of her way to make trouble. But the way Mr. Seligman smiled at her told me she had done something right.

At home, Momma cleared off the mahogany dining table, placed a floor lamp beside her chair, turned on the radio, then sat down to work. We usually went to bed after the Richfield ten o'clock news, but Momma stayed up to sew while I went to sleep. In the morning when I woke up, she was already at the table. I would have thought she had been there all night except that she was wearing her robe. I don't know how many times I heard her muttering under her breath as she pulled out the stitches to do over again, but it was a lot. Her work had to be as good as the sample.

—2—

It was while Momma was working at the dining table that I learned to cook rice. She yelled the instructions to me while I was in the kitchen. "Keep rinsing the rice until the water is clear. Then add water to cover the rice and it reaches the first joint of your finger."

"Which finger?" I shouted back.

"Bring it here and let me see." When I brought the pot to her, she poked her little finger into the water. "Just a bit more," she said as she wiped her hands with her apron.

"When did Halmoni teach you to cook rice?" I asked, proud that my first pot of rice was cooking on the stove.

She laughed. "No one taught me. I taught myself after I came to America. We always had cooks in Korea."

I pulled out a chair and sat down. "Did you ever play hopscotch?"

She unraveled a length of thread from a spool and bit it off. "Of course. But the game I loved most was jumping on boards, something like a seesaw but instead of sitting down, we stood up. If I had a good partner, I could jump higher than anyone." She licked the end of the thread and pushed it through the eye of the needle. "Another thing my girlfriends and I did in the spring was to take a picnic lunch to the mountains and go looking for *kosari*." She tied a knot at the end of the thread.

"*Kosari* grows in the mountains?" I had only seen the dried edible fern after it had been soaked and made into a salad.

She nodded. "While the snow is still on the ground; young shoots that are still curled and tender," she said as she began to sew.

It was while she was telling me about washing her hair in mountain streams that we heard the rice boil over. I scrambled out of my chair and ran to the kitchen.

"Take off the lid and lower the flame!" Momma ordered.

As soon as I took off the lid, the frothy bubbles settled down into the pot. I lowered the flame. Before I could ask, Momma yelled, "Put the lid back on." I sighed with relief. Everything was under control. All I had to do was follow Momma's instructions.

At dinner, Harold and John complained that the rice was too dry. Momma looked at me and said, "It's not bad for the first try, baby." She said 'baby' the way Koreans say, *nae dari,* tenderly and filled with love. She once told me there was no English translation for *nae dari* but that 'my precious child' or 'my darling' was close. I liked Momma's way of saying 'baby' best.

I began to cook rice every night and soon discovered that the first joint of my forefinger measured the right amount of water. The boys no longer complained. While the rice steamed, I visited with Momma. I learned about the things she did when she was a young girl in Korea: about her having to walk through forests where tigers lived, about her love for roast corn in the fall and roast chestnuts in the winter. She filled my imagination with her remembrances until her memories became mine. Stories of her childhood ended when she said, "Until I was sixteen years old, I had nothing to worry about. Then I became engaged to your Papa." I never asked her to go on, afraid she would say something against Papa. I only begged her to repeat the stories she had already told me.

Thursday, when I came home from school, Mamma's chair was empty. A note on the table said, "Bring the baby carriage. Meet me at the bus stop." The message was for me. Harold had to deliver newspapers and John was out selling magazine subscriptions.

The carriage was jammed in the corner of the back porch, filled with empty bottles and bundles of newspaper, ready for the junkman. I piled everything on the floor, knowing that before Saturday I would have to put everything back into the carriage. As soon as we heard the call, "Rags, bottles, papers," and the clop of horseshoes on the asphalt pavement, Momma would tell one of us to wheel the carriage to the curb and sell everything in it.

The straw-colored wicker baby carriage, its white damask lining torn and gray with soil, was part of our household furnishings:

whenever we moved we took it with us. I have seen baby pictures of me lying in the carriage when it was new. Harold suggested we junk it with the bottles and papers, but Momma said, "We can't get anything for it and it does come in handy."

I buttered a piece of bread, sprinkled it with sugar, and started for Western Avenue. Managing the floppy bread in one hand and pushing the carriage with the other, I followed the carriage on its zig-zag course. The wheels were worn and bent out of shape. They no longer rolled straight. At Western Avenue, I stuffed the last bit of bread into my mouth to have both hands free to turn the carriage at the corner.

As soon as I made the turn, the sounds of people working, walking, shopping, and driving cars became louder. Colored people were yelling to friends on the street. Most of the owners of shops lived upstairs or in back of their businesses. Cooking smells hovered over their cash registers. I looked at the gaudy window displays as I pushed the carriage, passing by the handmade signs that said, "Come In."

As I neared the poultry I held my nose, careful to avoid running the carriage into the rabbi who sat on a wooden lug box in the path of the late afternoon sun. He was reading, deaf to the din of squawking hens and the gutteral gobbles of turkeys. It was his job to purify the birds when they were slaughtered, when they would be silenced forever. Harold had told me that the rabbi made the poultry kosher.

Count Basie's music filtered into the street. Some boys were hanging out around the record shop. We shared the neighborhood with Blacks, but when they grouped together, it became their territory. I pretended to look at something on the other side of the street and walked rapidly by them.

"Hey! China girl! Ain't you a little young to be pushing a baby carriage? Come on, give us a look-see at this miracle of nature."

I knew his name. It was Lucerne Luke; he lived on our street. He was dark, muscular, and intimidating. I always knew when he was around, but I would try to avoid him.

He flicked the brim of his cap with a snap of his fingers then grabbed the edge of the carriage. "Hey, slow down there, China girl. What's your hurry? I'm not going to hurt you." He looked into the carriage then jumped back in feigned shock. "What's this? An empty baby buggy? Isn't this a shame? A tra-ge-dy." He grinned at his companions. Without changing their stance, without moving from the spot they had staked out for themselves, they smiled. "This chick needs help," Luke went on. "What d'ya say, man? We can help China girl fill the buggy with a bronze bundle of joy. A baby Buddha." He did not bother to look at me as he sauntered back to his buddies, laughing quietly.

"Man, no baby of yours is going to be bronze," one of Luke's friends said with a chuckle.

Lucerne Luke gave him a look of surprise. "Whatchu mean, man? When I mix up the colors, anything is possible." He emphasized the words 'what' and 'anything'.

They looked away from one another to laugh, a quiet chugging laugh.

I saw my chance and ran. No one was chasing me but I wanted to get as far away from their gibes as I could. I never knew what to say to them; nothing glib or clever came to me. Anything I said to them fell flat, like a 'lead balloon' as John says. I crossed the street to the bus stop. Lucerne Luke had resumed his place among his friends. They continued to watch the scene on Western Avenue, as if waiting for something to happen that would amuse them. They were through with me.

"Whatchu mean, man?" I repeated to myself, trying to sound like Lucerne Luke. I tried several times under my breath, but it didn't sound right. Harold and John knew how to talk jive; they learned because they did not want to get picked on by the boys in the neighborhood. But Momma would not allow them to speak it in the house. Once, when Harold and John bantered in jive talk, Momma said, "Stop that! You sound like Amos and Andy." I had laughed when the boys took it as a cue to shuffle out of the house, swaggering like Lucerne Luke and his friends. Even Momma had laughed.

A bus arrived and pulled up to the curb. The door opened and released boys and girls carrying schoolbooks and men and women clutching the handles of shopping bags. Momma was not among them. As the bus roared by, I slid my gaze down the street. Lucerne Luke caught me looking and waved. I spun around and stared into the window of the drugstore, pretending to be absorbed with the display of razor blades, aspirin bottles, and bandages. I read the labels over and over again until the next bus arrived. The door at the front of the bus hissed open and Momma stepped down. She was carrying a large package.

"Wow! How many dozens of handkerchiefs did you bring?" I asked, giving her a hand.

"Ten. It's heavy," she said. We dropped the package into the carriage. "It took time to count them and then the buses were full. Did you wait long?"

"Kind of. Is Mr. Seligman going to pay you more?" I struggled with the crooked gait of the carriage.

"Two dollars and a half, just like everyone else." She helped me guide the buggy. "I'd better get Harold to oil the wheels," she said.

"You never told me you could embroider," I said.

She smiled. "You're too young, baby. You don't know anything," she teased. She looked beautiful when she smiled.

I slid my hands along the handle bar closer to hers. "I'm almost eleven."

"I know," she said.

We were walking by Lucerne Luke. He tipped his cap and bowed.

"Pay no attention to him," Momma said to me in Korean.

I helped Momma count the handkerchiefs and divide them into six piles.

"A stack for each day," she explained. "It will help me keep track of where I am." She would be counting the days that passed by the number of handkerchiefs she sewed.

The next night, Momma took time from her sewing to cook for the members of her political group. Papa had called them the Five Cave Dwellers, but Momma said their real name was Koreans for Progressive Reforms. They used to meet regularly, but after Papa left and we began moving from house to house, the meetings were often postponed.

When Papa was home, I could not understand why Momma had to meet with the men, but with Papa gone, I liked having them in the house. Uncle Yang was my favorite; he took time to tease me. The others were more serious, but I considered all of them close friends of the family. I knew them so well that I could mimic the mannerisms of each: blink my eyes like Uncle Yang, shout and wave my fist like Uncle Lee, sit all huddled up like Uncle Kim, or gaze at the ceiling and smack my lips like Uncle Min.

My mimicry amused Momma, but she told me, "Don't let them see you do that. They'll think you're disrespectful."

They usually met in the parlor, but Momma was behind in her work so they sat around the table while she sewed.

"Can't you put that down for a minute?" Uncle Lee asked impatiently.

"I'll be up all night if I don't work on them now," Momma told him.

Uncle Lee threw up his hands. "What kind of meeting is this? A secretary is supposed to be writing, not sewing," he complained.

"I'll write it down later," Momma said, pulling the needle through the cloth.

"Do you do that all day?" Uncle Yang asked. "My back would kill me if I sat like that all day."

Momma waved her hand toward a pile of unfinished squares of linen. "I have to finish these by tomorrow."

Uncle Yang reached into his pocket and pulled out a twenty dollar bill. He was blinking like crazy. "It's for the food," he said, putting the money on the table. Momma thanked him but she did not touch the money until everyone had left.

Before the next meeting, she tried to teach me to cook meat and vegetables for the men, but had to throw out what I had cooked.

"I'll just have to tell them they can't meet here anymore," she said.

"Maybe after I practice," I said, knowing I could never cook Korean food like Momma.

"No. There's no reason you should be cooking for them."

When she told the men her decision, they would not hear of it.

"Never mind the food," Uncle Kim said.

"I'll take the minutes," Uncle Min said.

"I'll stop in Chinatown and pick up something to eat," Uncle Yang offered.

"Our organization's a joke," Uncle Lee declared.

"I'm sorry," Momma said. "I just don't have the time."

Everyone became used to seeing her sit at the table sewing. Ladies from her church dropped by and sat at the table to gossip. At first, Momma stopped to make them coffee. But one night she told me, "They're taking up my time with their foolish gossip." When she continued working while the women talked and no longer served coffee, they quit coming to visit. Aunt Clara's phone calls also became less frequent. She told Momma that she was reluctant to take her from her work. She never came to visit. Ever since the operation on her face, Aunt Clara rarely went out of her house.

The K.P.R. held fewer meetings because Momma was too busy working to do anything about Korean independence. Soon, she had only the radio to listen to and Harold, John, and me to talk to; mostly to me because the boys were finding more to do away from home. I became so used to seeing Momma sitting at the table that seeing her anywhere else seemed strange.

I carried reports of what had happened to me while I was away from home to the dining table and waited for Momma to tell me what I should make of it all. I omitted only information that I thought would upset her or were of no consequence. Each day's report differed little from the one before. But Bertha promised changes.

"Why don't you come out to play after dinner?" she asked me one afternoon.

"I have my homework to do," I said.

"That doesn't stop your brothers," she said.

"They have to be in by nine," I told her.

"A lot can happen between seven and nine," she said.

"What do you mean?"

"Come on out and find out for yourself."

That night, I asked Mamma. She said, "Absolutely not! You cannot go out after dark, not in this neighborhood."

"What about the boys?" I asked.

"They're boys and have to learn to take care of themselves."

"It's not even a school night," I whined.

She motioned me to a chair. "Come and listen to the radio. You don't understand now, but someday you'll thank me."

"I'd be just outside. What could happen to me there?" I asked, plopping into a chair.

"If I didn't love you, I wouldn't bother to forbid you to do anything," she said.

"Can't you trust me?"

Momma stuck her needle into the pin cushion to lean forward and turn up the volume on the radio. "Sshh. I want to hear this."

I slid off my chair and crawled under the table. Lying on my stomach, I wondered how she could justify treating me one way and the boys another. I knew it was an argument I could not win. Even Papa and the boys would side with her. They would say I'm too young to understand. I sat up and raised my voice.

"Momma, are you glad you're a woman?"

"Of course. Where are you?" She peeked under the table. "What are you doing down there?" She went back to her work and said, "Although, if I had been a man, I certainly wouldn't be sitting here sewing."

I crawled out from under the table and sat in my chair. I folded my hands on the table and said, "See what I mean?"

At nine o'clock, we heard the back screendoor slam. "We're home!" Harold shouted.

I got out of my chair and ran back to see my brothers. I gasped when I saw John. He was holding a blood-stained shirt over part of his face. Harold put his finger to his lips to silence me. He motioned me back into the dining room.

Momma had put down her sewing and was rubbing her eyes. She folded her arms on the table to form a pillow for her head. "My back aches, Faye. Could you pound your fists over it for me?"

I started beating Momma on her shoulders and worked down to her lower back then worked my way up.

"Where's Harold and John?" she asked, her voice waving in and out as I pounded.

"They went to their room," I said, alternating striking her with the side of my fists and the edge of my opened palms.

"Oh, that feels good," she warbled.

I traveled over her back, sometimes vertically, sometimes horizontally, and sometimes in circles. At first, her back felt as hard as stone, then gradually became softer.

"Momma?"

"Umm?" she murmured.

"When is Papa coming back?" I felt her muscles tighten under my hands, but she did not answer.

—3—

At breakfast the next morning, Harold told Momma that John had gone to find out about a morning paper route and she believed him.

Bertha claimed to know all about it. I passed her on my way to school.

"Bet you'd like to know what happened to your brother," she said. When I didn't say anything, she went on. "But you're Mama's baby and you'd tell."

"I would not," I said, not sure that I wouldn't.

"Bet you're dying to ask me," she said.

"No." I said and skipped away from her. I thought I may be better off not knowing.

Harold did not have to make up an excuse for John's absence at dinner. Momma was too busy to sit with us. "I have to learn how to do this new pattern. Faye, make the rice. There's leftovers and *kimchee* in the icebox," she said.

We ate in the kitchen without Momma. Her eyes were so hard on her work that John could go a whole day without her looking at him.

In the morning, I heard the call of the junkman and the clippity-clop of his horse.

"Hurry, Faye. Take out the carriage," Momma said.

I pushed aside the marquisette curtain to see how much time I had. John was pushing the carriage to the curb, steadying a box that was balanced across the width of the carriage. His blood-stained shirt covered the contents.

"What are you waiting for?" Momma asked.

"John's doing it," I said, watching him through the window. The junkman pulled his horse to a stop and leaped to the ground. He lifted the shirt to look underneath. John was anxious for the man to make up his mind, holding out his hand for the money before the junkman was ready. As soon as he was paid, John wheeled the empty carriage around and ran with it up the driveway.

"What are you looking at?" Momma wanted to know.

"Nothing," I said, closing the curtain.

The back screendoor slammed as the junkman's call and the sound of the horse's hooves moved down the street. John sauntered into the dining room and placed the money on the table in front of Momma. She looked at the bill. "Five dollars! I didn't know we had that much junk," she exclaimed, glancing at John. She moved her eyes back to her work and then looked at John again. "What happened to you? Have you been in a fight?"

"Aw, some kid told me to go back where I came from," he said.

She inspected his face, feeling his nose and the bones on his cheeks. "Nothing seems broken," she said.

"I'm okay," he said.

"Go back where?" I asked. "to Denker Avenue or 36th Street or 37th Place?"

"Very funny," John said.

Momma laughed as she picked up her sewing. "Next time, ask him that."

I didn't have to ask Bertha anything. Right in the middle of my turn at hopscotch she blurted out. "That yellow brother of yours snitched. Lucerne Luke is in Juvenile Hall because your brother snitched." She kicked dirt at me.

"What are you talking about?" I said, kicking dirt back at her.

"He got beat up, didn't he? That's nothing compared to what he's going to get," she said.

I picked up my lagger. "He told my brother to go back where he came from."

"Is that what your brother told you? Ask him again. He's lying."

"Maybe you are," I said and started for home.

As soon as I walked in the door, I knew something was wrong. Harold was sitting at the table and Momma had pushed aside her sewing to listen to him.

"Where's John?" I asked.

"At Uncle Yang's," Harold said quickly.

"What made John do it?" Momma asked. My entrance had not made a dent in her attention.

"He didn't know the stuff was stolen. When the police asked John where he got the things he was selling, he told them. Lucerne Luke gave the things to John to sell and promised him a percentage of everything he made. John thought he could make some money to help us out. He wouldn't have done it if he knew they were stolen. As soon as he found out, he sold everything to the junkman."

"He gave me that money," Momma exclaimed.

"He panicked. He didn't want to get caught with the stuff and he didn't want to get caught giving the money to Luke."

Momma got up from the table and started pacing around the room. "We shouldn't have moved to this neighborhood. I told Aunt Clara that, but we had nowhere to go." She walked to the buffet and fiddled with the crocheted scarf. "What are we going to do?"

She walked back and stood behind her chair. "Why isn't your Papa here?"

"John didn't steal anything. He can't go to jail anyway. He's a minor. He'll be all right, Mom," Harold said. "If I had known what he was up to, I could have stopped him," he said, blaming himself.

"John's not a bad boy. He was only trying to help me," she sighed, blaming herself.

Later, when Momma was busy cooking and couldn't hear, I told Harold, "Bertha said John has more coming to him."

Harold shook his head. "John was stupid," he said, blaming John.

I did not know whom to blame. It seemed like things were happening to us and we could do nothing about it. I wondered what good it was to have Momma home all day. She was stuck to her chair and could not stop what was happening right outside our door.

John could not stay with Uncle Yang forever so Momma wrote a letter to Papa, addressing it to the farm where the last truck driver to bring Momma money said he had seen Papa. She wanted to send John to him, safely away from the neighborhood. A week later, the letter came back unopened. "Not here" was scrawled in pencil over the envelope. John came home.

Momma no longer looked forward to the postman's delivery. She told me to toss the windowed envelopes into the crystal punchbowl. "I'll take care of them later," she said.

"There's one from Juvenile Court," I said, reading the return address.

"Juvenile Court? I guess you had better open it."

I opened the envelope carefully then read the letter to Momma. She listened until I had finished.

"John and me? When did you say?" she asked.

"In three weeks. They want Papa to come too," I said.

"Hmph! Let them try and find him," she said.

Three weeks later on a Wednesday, Momma ordered us to wear our Sunday clothes to go to court. "I don't want anyone to think John came from a poor family," she said.

"Why do I have to go? I didn't do anything," I said. I didn't tell her that I was of afraid of the police.

"We're all going because whatever happens to John happens to his family. That's something for you and Harold to think about too.

I'm going to tell the judge that it wasn't John's fault. He did it for me, for his family. I'm going to tell the judge that if he sends John to jail, he will bring disgrace upon our family. I'm going to tell him that for Koreans, the family comes first," Momma said.

"Are you really going to tell him all that?" I asked.

"Of course!" she said.

I wanted more than ever to stay home. I could see Momma standing before the judge in a room filled with spectators telling him about Korean families and everyone asking, "What's a Korean?".

I was relieved when we got to Juvenile Court and were ushered into the waiting room of the judge's private office. John was called in alone first.

"I hope he doesn't make John say anything he shouldn't," Momma said.

"John can't lie to him," Harold said.

Momma pulled out a handkerchief she had been working on and began to sew. After she had hemmed the edge of one side and was beginning on the second, we were called into the judge's office.

I expected the judge to be big and have white hair, but there wasn't a strand of white in his brown hair. He was thin like Papa and had large blue eyes. He sat behind a huge desk. John was standing in front of him.

"Please sit down, Mrs. Chun. I've been going over the case with John. He tells me that you're going through hard times, that his father has left home," the judge said.

Momma frowned at John and said in Korean. "Why did you tell him that?" She turned to the judge. "Mr. Chun had bad luck. We'll be all right. John worried about me. He's a good boy. We'll pay back everything."

The judge smiled at her. "There's nothing to pay back. It's not quite that simple. John's broken the law. I've gone over the report carefully and believe that John did not know that he had been handling stolen goods. He is a minor and this is his first offense. I can't prevent it from going onto his record, but I am going to put him in your charge. You will have to see to to that he stays out of trouble."

"What do you mean?" Momma asked.

Harold quickly translated everything into Korean for her then added, "Just say, 'thank you'."

Momma's eyes grew enormous as she gave Harold a look. She bit her lip then said, "Thank you" to the judge.

"When Lucerne Luke is out on probation, I'll order him to stay away from your brother." The judge now directed his words to Harold. "He may plan a reprisal of some sort. John must be very careful."

Harold nodded then told Momma. "I'll explain later."

I knew from the look Momma had given him that Harold was in trouble. She waited until we got home to speak to him. "Don't ever forget that I am your mother. Under no circumstances are you to tell me what to say," she told him.

Everything was falling into place again, I thought.

That night, I dreamt about Lucerne Luke. His eyes were bulging out of their sockets. He had huge wings and was hovering over-head as I ran to find a hiding place. I kept looking up at him to see how close he was until I stumbled into a deep hole. I woke up in the morning with a stiff neck.

I screamed with pain as Momma tried turning my head in different directions.

"You need to put the sun's heat on it," she said. She grabbed a pillow and dragged me out to the front yard. She studied the sun's position then pointed to a spot on the ground. "Lie down," she ordered. I howled while she turned me about to place my neck under the direct sunlight. "Now hold it there until you sweat," she said.

"Everyone's going to see me," I complained. "Why can't I just take an aspirin?"

"Nature's the best medicine," she said and went back into the house.

All I could think of was how embarrassing it was to lie where every passerby could see me. Whenever I heard footsteps on the sidewalk, I closed my eyes, pretending not to notice the intruder. As I began to feel the benefit of the heat, I relaxed. When Bertha woke me up, my neck was sticky with perspiration.

"What's the matter with you, girl?" she asked, standing over me.

"Nothing," I said, feeling no pain or stiffness as I turned to look at her. "Nothing's the matter," I said, sitting up. "John's not in trouble and Lucerne Luke can't touch him."

She laughed. "Girl, don't you know anything? Luke ain't no fool.

He's not going to personally handle your brother." She shook her head. "You people don't understand anything."

I stood up. "Oh yeah? Look at this." I turned my head from side to side. I looked up at the sky then down to the ground. I looked Bertha in the eyes. "We people understand magic." I said and walked into the house.

—4—

I did not mind losing Bertha as a friend. I was confident the judge could keep Lucerne Luke from John, but Bertha would try to fill me with doubts. As long as Luke was in custody I considered John safe and found me a new friend.

I met Jane on my way to school. We started right in talking to one another. When she saw me at recess, she said, "Let's meet after school and walk home together." When we discovered that we were going to be in the same gym class, we jumped and squealed with delight.

"Which team are you going to sign up for?" I asked.

"Let's sign up for volleyball," she suggested.

We stood in line together. At my insistence, she stood in front of me. She was shorter and more petite than I. Just like Momma would want me to be, I thought.

"Is your hair naturally curly?" I asked. "It's so pretty."

"Sort of. I don't need a perm, but I have to set it if I want it this curly." She pulled a shiny black curl straight then let it spring back.

"Mine's like wire. A perm makes it all kinky. I hate it," I said.

She ran her hand over my straight bobbed hair. "It's black and silky like my mother's," she said.

We had moved up to the sign-up table. Jane gave the teacher her full name and my heart sank into my shoes. Her last name was Nagano, a Japanese name. Every March First and just about every day in between, Koreans reminded each other to hate the Japanese. She signed up for volleyball and waited for me.

"Next!" the teacher snapped.

I gulped. "Faye Chun."

"Speak up. I can't hear you," the teacher bellowed.

I cleared my throat. "C-h-u-n," I spelled it for her. "Faye with an 'e'."

"F-e-y?" she asked.

I wanted to die. "No. F-a-y-e." I said.

"Which team?" she asked impatiently.

I had been struggling with that same question as soon as I learned Jane's full name, wondering if I should end the friendship now.

"Volleyball," Jane told the teacher. "We want to be on the same team."

"Volleyball's filled up." The teacher looked over the sign-up sheets. "There's space in baseball and basketball."

It was being decided for me, I thought with relief. "Basketball," I said.

Jane tugged at my arm. "How about baseball? I'm too short for basketball." She turned to the teacher. "Can the two of us sign up for baseball?"

The teacher sighed as she erased Jane's name from the volleyball column and wrote our names on the sheet marked 'baseball'.

Jane linked her arm in mine. "Let's share lockers," she said.

"Okay," I said, convinced there could be no harm in sharing lockers.

After school, we parted at the corner of Normandie Avenue and 37th Street, promising each other to meet in the morning. I skipped all the way home. I ran into the house and told Momma, "I have a new friend. Her name is Jane."

"That's nice. Bring her home sometime," Momma said.

"She lives kind of far from here, way on the other side of Normandie."

"Some Saturday, then," Momma suggested.

"It would be too hard for her to find us," I said and went to my room to change my clothes.

Whenever I came home late from school, Momma knew it was because I had stayed at the corner of Normandie and 37th to play with Jane. To keep her from worrying, I told Momma, "Jane's a straight A student. She's very popular, the president of the Scholarship Society."

"I'm glad she's a nice girl. Why don't you invite her over?"

"She spends most of her time studying," I said.

Jane had invited me to her house several times, but I had made excuses without ever telling her about March First. She knew that

on Thursdays I had to meet Momma at the bus stop with the baby
carriage, but she was not convinced by my excuses on other days.

"My mother wants you to come for dinner. When can you come?"
Jane asked.

"My mother wants you to come to our house too, but she's busy
with her work so I have to cook. That's why I can't come to your
house on any night," I said. For good measure I added, "My
mother would give me permission if I asked her, but I won't
because it's too hard for her to do her work and cook too." I made
myself sound noble while lying to her.

It was harder for me to lie to Momma. I told her everything Jane
and I did without ever telling her Jane's last name. Then one
Thursday morning, Momma told me something that changed everything.

The early morning light was shining on Momma's hands. "Mr.
Seligman likes my work. He thinks I am good enough to teach
other women," Momma said.

"That's good," I said, gathering my books to leave for school.

"Better bring John's wagon to the bus stop. The carriage is too
broken down. I'm going to bring work for some of the ladies in the
neighborhood."

"You'll have to carry more handkerchiefs on the bus. Why don't
they go to Seligman's themselves?" I said, making my way to the
door.

"The ladies asked me to do it. They don't speak English very well.
They need the work and it will mean a commission for me."

"What ladies?" I looked at the clock on the mantel. I would have
to hurry if I did not want to miss Jane.

"Oh you know. Mrs. Kano, Mrs. Watanabe, and Mrs. Hiroshi.
You're going to be late if you don't leave now," she said.

I stopped in my tracks. Those were Japanese names. I took my
hands off the doorknob and walked to the table. "You're bringing
work for *them*?"

"It's strictly business. Run along or your friend will leave without
you," she said, waving me out.

I opened my mouth to speak, but decided it could wait and ran
out the door.

I had missed Jane in the morning, but we met after school as
usual. She was never late on Thursdays, knowing that I had to meet

Momma at the bus stop. "Race you," she said, challenging me. "Skipping," she added.

We laughed harder than we skipped and collapsed at the corner. Panting, our hair clinging to our damp faces, our cheeks red with heat, we stayed sprawled on the cement sidewalk. "My sisters are putting a skit together. Ask your mother if you can come for dinner tomorrow night," Jane said. "It will be fun."

I sat up and looked straight at her. "You know what? I think I'll just do that."

Her eyes grew wide. "Swell!" she said.

At home, I brushed off John's wagon and pulled it to meet Momma. I could hardly wait for her to get off the bus. We packed the bundles into the wagon and started for home.

"You've brought a lot of work for the Japanese ladies. When are they coming to the house?" I asked.

"This evening."

"Momma, Jane Nagano asked me over for dinner tomorrow. It's Friday so I don't have to do my homework. Can I go?" I spewed it out when all along I had planned to work up to it gradually.

"Nagano? So that's why you've never brought her home," she said.

I felt the perspiration form under my arms. "I guess I forgot to tell you . . ."

"Don't lie to me, Faye." Momma stepped out of the way as the wagon swerved.

"I didn't mean to lie. I was afraid you wouldn't let me keep Jane as a friend." I started to walk faster.

She quickened her pace to keep up with me. "You know what the Japanese have done to our people."

"Not Jane. She's the nicest girl I've ever met."

"You know the rule. No Japanese friends."

I walked even faster, raising my voice to cover the distance between us. "What about Mrs. Kano, Mrs. Watanabe, and Mrs. Hiroshi?"

"I've told you. It's strictly business. That's not the same as you and Jane." She stopped to shout at me. "Faye! You wait for me!"

Tears began to fill my eyes and blurred my vision. "Jane's my friend."

"What? I can't hear you! Stop where you are," she ordered.

When she caught up with me, I blurted out, "I haven't got

anyone. You're always at that stupid table." I couldn't stop myself. "The boys are always out together. Papa's gone and I don't have anyone." I threw down the handle of the wagon and ran into the house.

I was under the cover of my bed when I heard Momma drop the bundles of unsewn handkerchiefs on the table. I hid my head under the pillow when she came into my room.

"I'm sorry you're so miserable," she said. "Everything would be different if your Papa were here taking care of us." She sat on the edge of the bed. "We'd be rich if we were in Korea. None of us would have to work. But we came back to America because the Japanese were so cruel and there was no freedom."

"Jane could never be cruel," I said. "You're the one who's being cruel, keeping me from being her friend."

"You should be spanked for saying that," she said, bringing down her hand on my seat. "I guess you'll just have to find out for yourself. I'm going to give you permission to go to Jane's house to play. But you cannot have dinner with them. Is that clear?" She stood up and left the room.

I couldn't help myself. I laughed into my pillow.

I tried to sleep, shutting my eyes tightly to invite sleep to come, unable to keep from popping them open to see if the night was over. Jane and I had giggled at every word when I told her I could come to her house. I smiled in the dark remembering. When tired of waiting for sleep, I began to worry. Momma was usually right. I thought of torture chambers and Koreans shouting "Mansei!". My head began to ache. I ran the conversation with Jane through my mind again and tried to forget that she was Japanese. Sleep finally came when I decided what dress I would wear to Jane's house.

"Do you like *arare*?" Jane asked.

"I love it." I often craved the sugar and soy sauce coating on the Japanese rice cracker.

"We always have some with our tea," she said.

"I love it," I said again and smiled.

The outside of her house looked like mine: three steps led to a cement porch and an asphalt shingled roof pitched over the one-story wood-framed house. But her porch was bigger. Hers was large enough to hold a swing and a half-dozen potted ferns. Jane held the screendoor open and I stepped into what, until that moment, had been forbidden territory. The sharp smell of camphorwood pushed at my nostrils. The rooms were arranged like those in my house and the furniture were similar to ours, but nothing seemed like home. Not a scratch on the tables or a speck of dust anywhere. Hanging perfectly straight on the wall were two pictures: one of Mount Fujiyama and the other of the Crown Prince of Japan. Snapshots of Jane's family were turned just-so on the mantelpiece.

"Your house is nice," I whispered.

Jane smiled and led me to a man dressed in a gray suit. He was sitting in a large green easy chair reading a newspaper. Jane bowed. "Father, this is Faye Chun." The newspaper came down and he nodded. Momma would have said he was dignified-looking. I could not imagine him prying anyone's fingernails with bamboo sticks, but I was relieved when he returned to reading his paper.

"Excuse us, father. I'll take Faye into the kitchen to meet mother." She bowed to the newspaper then led me out of the room.

"Is your father going out?" I asked in a whisper.

"No. Why?

"He's wearing a suit."

"He always wears a suit," Jane said as she pushed on the kitchen door. "Why are you whispering?"

I shrugged my shoulders. "I don't know."

Mrs. Nagano was a few inches shorter than Momma and looked as soft as a pillow. She smiled warmly and raised her hand to approximate my height. "Tall girl," she said. I was shorter than she but a half a head taller than Jane. "American food," Mrs. Nagano declared, nodding her head in agreement with herself. "I made Japanese dinner. Too bad you can't stay. You have tea with Jane. I bring to the dining room."

Jane's sisters were also in the kitchen: older sisters I had heard about. Margaret, the eldest, had pushed aside the salt and pepper shakers and the bottle of soy sauce to make room for her books at the kitchen table. She was the studious one, the sister Jane wanted to be like. Dale, the middle sister was helping Mrs. Nagano prepare the meal. They stopped what they were doing to say "hi".

I knew that Jane had an older brother. "He's in Japan attending school," she said. She put her lips to my ear. "He's really there to meet a girl. My parents want him to marry a girl from Japan. They think the girls in L.A. are too Americanized." Jane looked at me in surprise when I told her that no one could make my brothers live in Korea just to find a girl. "Doesn't your mother care about family tradition?" she asked.

"Oh sure. We're *yangbans*," I said.

"What's that?"

I paused, wondering where to begin. "Never mind, it's too hard to explain."

Jane took me by the arm. "Come on. I'll show you our family shrine."

At the back of the house, in a glassed-in porch overlooking the garden, potted plants had been carefully arranged around a high narrow table. Two lacquered urns stood on the table. "My grandparents' ashes," Jane said softly.

"I'll stay here," I said, backing into the hallway.

Jane bowed to the urns before joining me. "You're not afraid, are you?"

"No," I lied. The thought of having anyone's ashes in the house sent a shiver through me.

"Tea, tea, tea," Mrs. Nagano sang as she pushed through the swinging door. As the aroma of toasted *arare* mixed with the fragrance of camphorwood, I recognized the scent I had associated with Jane. Out on the streets in the sunshine, when we played and perspired, Jane emitted a mystifying and elusive trace of a smell that I was not able to identify. In her house, the odor was strong and pervasive. I suddenly felt like an intruder, barging in, making discoveries that were none of my business.

Mrs. Nagano waited while Mr. Nagano folded his newspaper. He took the cup from her hands. "Aah, the tea smells good," he said as he ran his nose over the cup. "There's nothing like green tea from Japan. Don't you agree, Faye?"

"Uh, well, uh," I stammered. "My mother usually makes coffee."

"Jane tells me your parents are from Korea," he said, as if they should know about Japanese green tea.

"I think the tea we drink is Chinese," I said.

As he nodded, he brought his cup to his lips and blew gently. "Do you speak Korean?" he asked before taking a sip.

"Yes. We speak it at home. My mother's English isn't very good." To keep him from thinking Momma was stupid, I quickly added, "But she speaks Japanese and can read Chinese."

He raised his eyebrows. "Is that so?" He put down his cup. "Where did she learn?"

"In Korea. She had to."

He was quiet for a moment then said, "I see. Did she teach you Japanese?"

I shook my head. That was the last thing in the world she would do. Momma always sounded angry when she spoke Japanese, as if she were punishing each word as it came out of her mouth.

My mouth was dry but I hesitated to bring the teacup to my lips, afraid I would hit my teeth and spill the tea. I helped myself to more *arare*.

Jane took my arm and shook it gently. "I wish you could stay for dinner. My sisters prepared a skit for tonight. We take turns on Friday nights entertaining each other. It's their turn and they said it's going to be funny. Please stay."

"Jane," Mr. Nagano interrupted. "Do not insist. Faye's mother has her reasons and we must respect them. Perhaps your sisters can give their skit now. Call them in and ask your mother to join us."

It was settled. All Papa had to do was say something and it was settled too. Only he would have said all that in half the number of words. On second thought, Papa would not have said any of it. We never entertained one another at home.

The ladies came from the kitchen and took their places. Mrs. Nagano turned a dining chair toward the parlor, brushed off imaginary crumbs, then sat on the edge of the seat. Jane took my hand and we sat on the floor in front of the performers. I began to feel warm with excitement. My skin tingled as I waited in anticipation.

Margaret moved in close behind Dale until no one could see her. As Dale put her hands behind her back, Margaret brought her hands around and tucked them into the pockets of Dale's apron.

How clever, I thought. Margaret's hands were to appear as if they belonged to Dale.

"Ladies and gentlemen. My first number will be 'Home Sweet Home'," Dale announced with Margaret's hands clasped in front of her. Margaret raised her hand to Dale's lips while Dale cleared her throat. As Dale burst into song, Margaret's arms floated in the air like Jeanette McDonald's in *Naughty Marietta*.

I thought it was wonderful and wanted to roll on the floor with delight. "Bad manners," Momma would have said, so I noticed the way Jane laughed and followed her example with a delicate lilting laugh. When Dale ended with ". . . there's no-o place like home," my sides ached from having restrained my laugher. I applauded loudly.

For their second act, the performers exchanged places. Margaret began her monologue. "A child said, 'What is grass?' fetching it to me with full hands . . ." Dale's graceful hand movements accompanied the poem. I became entranced. Momma would recite poetry to me, but always in Korean. ". . . Or I guess it is the handkerchief of the Lord," Margaret was saying. The words gave significance to Momma's work, I thought. She ended with, "And now it seems to me the beautiful uncut hair of graves".

"Oh, Margaret. That was nice," I said. "Did you write it?"

She laughed. "I wish I had. It's from *The Grass*, by Walt Whitman."

Mrs. Nagano said something to Mr. Nagano. I recognized the word *"Chosen-jin"* and knew it was about me. I felt ill at ease. Was it about my ignorance of Walt Whitman? I wondered, or about the way I laughed, or the way I don't drink Japanese green tea? Was it about my being Korean? We had our opinions about the Japanese; perhaps they had formed some about us. Did Jane have to beg her parents for permission to invite me to her house?

Mr. Nagano smiled at Dale and Margaret with approval. "You have improved a great deal. You have developed duplicity into a fine art. It is difficult to tell if you are two acting as one or one acting as two."

The word 'duplicity' opened a crack in my memory. I had tried desperately to forget a secret, tried so hard that I could never forget. I remembered Captain Yamamoto of the Taiyo Maru.

I stood up. "I have to go now," I said.

Everyone looked surprised.

"I have to help my mother," I explained.

Mrs. Nagano nodded. "Wait. I'll wrap some *arare* for you." She started for the kitchen.

"No. No, please. No, thank you," I said.

"No?" She turned back. "Next time, you stay for dinner," she said.

"I'll walk you to the corner," Jane offered.

"Never mind. You stay here. I'll see you on Monday," I said, making my way toward the door.

Not until I was out on the street headed for home did a sense of relief come over me.

The sun was down. I walked rapidly. Someone could be hiding behind the thick stumps of the palm trees, someone like Lucerne Luke. What did Mrs. Nagano say? It was driving me crazy not to know.

In the open space of a vacant lot, I stopped to break off a few clusters of baby-pink roses. The Cecile Brunner bloomed over a neglected heap of dead branches. As I turned away, the hem of my dress hooked itself on a thorn. Several threads broke as I pulled free. Nuts, I muttered to myself. I looked to see if there was anyone around. "Damn!" I said aloud.

I hurried homeward as the twilight breeze stirred the scent of narcissus and wild roses. " 'a scented gift . . .' something . . . something 'dropped' ". I wished I could remember the poem. My birthday was coming soon. I could teach John the skit. Papa would sit in the wing chair. Momma would turn her chair toward the parlor, and Harold could sit where he wanted. Momma could make coffee and Papa would not have to wear a suit. It would be a birthday party and everyone would be polite to one another.

I turned the corner to our street and broke into a trot. *The Grass*, by Walt Whitman. I'll look it up at the library.

—5—

Momma sniffed the roses before tucking them in the pocket of her apron. "They're sweet," she said. "Set the table quickly. You're late." She went to the stove to dish out the rice.

"I hurried home as fast as I could," I answered. I thought the first thing she would do was ask me about Jane's house. I grabbed a handful of chopsticks and rushed around the table, setting a pair at each place.

Momma did not say another word until the bowl of rice was making its round at the table. "I received a letter from Gilbert Lyu today," she said.

"What's he want?" Harold asked, dumping a paddleful of rice on his plate.

"Papa's been in a hospital in Reno. He's very sick." Her voice cracked as she said it.

"Reno? But that's in Nevada," John said.

We thought Papa was still in California. Nevada seemed so far away to me.

"Papa's been working at the Golden Nougat Hotel," she said.

"Golden what?" John laughed. He looked at Harold and me and we giggled. We knew what she meant. "Nugget, Momma," he corrected her. "You can't eat it."

"After you eat the nougat, you can fill your teeth with the nugget," I said.

We laughed, but Momma did not.

Harold reached for the platter of meat and vegetables. He slid a portion onto his mound of rice. "What's Papa doing there? Why hasn't he sent home any money? What's the matter with him?"

"He's been working as a . . . what do you call them? You know," she bit her lip, "they carry suitcases."

"A bellhop?" Two grains of rice popped out of John's mouth as he said it.

"I guess so," she said with a sigh.

"Papa? A bellboy? Carrying other people's suitcases?" Harold found it hard to believe.

"Never mind that now," Momma said sharply. "He's been in the hospital several weeks. Mr. Lyu says Papa doesn't seem to be getting better. Harold, you'll have to go see him."

Harold gulped down his mouthful of food. "Me? How am I going to get to Reno? Where in Reno?"

"I have ten dollars for you. Maybe you can get a ride at the market."

"How the heck am I going to do that? All the way to Nevada?" He picked at his food then laid down his chopsticks.

"Try . . . please." Momma sounded desperate.

"What will I do when I get there?"

"Someone from the family has to be with him. You're the eldest. I can't leave you children or I would go." The roses fell to the floor as she pulled a handkerchief from her pocket to blow her nose. "Whatever happens, we cannot let Papa be alone now." Her voice was small, like a child's.

Harold sat back in his seat and heaved a sigh. He was frowning but said, "Okay, I'll try."

Love was in Momma's eyes as she handed him his chopsticks and said, "Eat some more. We have to bring Papa home . . . one way or another."

I slid off my chair onto the floor and gathered up the flowers.

A few days after Harold left, I received a birthday card. Momma had recognized Mr. Lyu's handwriting and opened it by mistake.

"It's from Papa," she said. "I thought it was for me."

Two crisp dollar bills fell from inside the card. It was the first time Papa had ever sent me anything. I gave the money to Momma. All of us gave what money we had to her.

"Thank you, baby," she said.

Jane remembered my birthday. She gave me a present wrapped in white tissue tied with a red ribbon. "Open it on your birthday," she said. She knew that I couldn't stay to play. "Not until we hear from Harold. My mom's really worried," I had explained. I took the present home and put it in my drawer.

Momma worried so much that she was beginning to have dreams. She would tell John and me about them at breakfast. "Papa keeps coming to me in my dreams wearing a white gown," she said.

"Sheesh! You and your dreams, Mom." John pushed aside his cereal. "Dreams don't mean a thing. You're just talking 'old country' heebie-jeebies. Papa's not going to die no matter what you dream."

"I can't help what I dream. And they always mean something," she insisted.

I didn't know enough not to believe in Momma's dreams, but John refused to listen to her and walked out of the house when she began talking about them.

"We were in this beautiful garden. He was walking toward me but the closer he got to me, the further I would find myself from him. He looked peaceful," she told me.

"Can't be our garden," I said, thinking of the weeds and patches of dirt.

"No, not here. It looked like the garden of the first apartment your Papa and I lived in. Dahlias were blooming everywhere." She put down her sewing. "That may be a good sign. When Mr. Yim died, all the blossoms had fallen off."

"In real-life or in a dream?" I wanted it to be a good sign.

"In my dream," she said as she started sewing again.

"That's good," I said with relief.

My birthday fell on a Saturday. I took Jane's gift from the drawer and took it to the table to unwrap it. I was more excited about opening that one gift than any I could remember.

"What's that?" Momma said.

"My birthday present from Jane. I can't guess what it is. It rattles when I shake it. I hope it isn't breakable." I untied the ribbon and pulled off the sheets of tissue and exposed a colorful tin box with Japanese writing on it. A picture of the contents made my mouth water. "*Arare!*" I exclaimed.

"That's very nice of your friend," Momma said.

"Her whole family is nice," I said. We had never discussed my visit to Jane's house. "I was wondering, do the Japanese hate Koreans?"

"Why should they? We've never done anything to them," she said. "Why don't you save those until after dinner. I'll send John out for some ice cream and we'll have a party."

"Ice cream and *arare*?" I screwed up my face as I imagined the taste of the two combined. "Let's skip the ice cream until Harold and Papa come home," I said.

Momma sent John out for spareribs instead. She cooked them my favorite way, and for dessert we had Chinese tea and *arare*. Everything tasted delicious. But the tea kept me up and in the middle of the night, I heard Momma moving about. "Are you sick?" I called from my bed.

"I'm all right. I had a nightmare, that's all."

Harold was slouched on the sofa with his face scrunched into his chest when I came home from Sunday school. I was happy to see him but said nothing because no one said anything to me.

"Surely somebody was going to Reno," Momma said. She sounded angry.

"I've told you. The roads over the summit were closed. I got a ride to Stockton and waited for a ride to Reno. I was running out of money. What if I couldn't get to Reno and couldn't get back?"

"If only the two dollars had come earlier," she said.

"Two dollars! What good is two dollars? We just didn't have it, Mom." He sat up to pull the pillow out from behind him. He wrapped his arms tightly around it and held it close. "We just didn't have it. It isn't my fault . . . Jesus. . . ." he choked then began to cry.

I had never seen him cry.

"If only we were in Korea," Momma's voice was husky. She cleared her throat. "We would be rich."

She was thinking about the land again. Whenever she needed money, she thought of it. But she never wanted money badly enough to sell her land. "Someday you children will inherit it all. It belongs to our family. If I were to sell it, the money would soon be gone and we would have nothing," she would say. The name of the town where the land was located made us laugh. John and I would waddle around like ducks as we chanted. "Qwaksan, Qwaksan, Qwaksan."

Harold reached into his pocket for a handkerchief. He wiped the tears from his eyes and blew his nose. "Write to *Halmoni*. Tell her to sell the land," he said.

Momma shook her head. "I can't do that. *Halmoni* won't understand."

Papa's dying may have only been in Momma's dreams, but I was beginning to feel it had already happened. A few days later, when I came home from school, and found Momma on the sofa crying, it wasn't necessary for her to tell me, "Papa died". I crawled onto the sofa to lie next to her and cry, but no tears would come. "Papa died" were just words. Nothing had changed. He had been gone for months. I wanted him back, but I had gotten used to his being away.

There must be something wrong with me, I thought.

"Don't cry, Momma," I said and went to my room. I kicked off my shoes to lie on my bed. Jane would be home now, bowing to her father before sitting down to a snack of tea and *arare*. I pictured him sitting in his chair reading, wearing his suit, and the tears began to come.

I thought Momma was going to lie on the couch forever, but that evening she was busy making one telephone call after another.

"What are you doing, Momma?" I asked, happy to see her up.

"I'm calling people your Papa and I have helped and give them a chance to help us back." She stayed on the phone until she had borrowed enough money to have Papa's body brought to L.A.; bring him home for a proper funeral. She wrote down each person's name and the amount she had borrowed. The list in her small black ledger covered a page and a half.

"Can you imagine?" she asked us all, "it costs more to have Papa's body sent than it does to buy a ticket for a regular passenger?"

"Maybe Gilbert Lyu could set Papa up in one of the passenger seats," John said without thinking.

I couldn't help it. I pictured it and thought it was funny.

"John!" Momma scolded, slapping him hard on his back.

"Ow, Mom. I was just kidding. I didn't mean anything," he said.

None of us could imagine Papa dead. Death was just a word. Even the certificate confirming his death meant little to us. It had arrived before Papa. Harold was reading it when he suddenly said, "Damn!"

"Don't say that word," Momma told him.

"For 'color or race' they wrote 'Chinese'," he said.

Momma muttered under her breath. "Put it away," she said, waving it aside. She was no longer interested in what the certificate had to say.

The lid kept falling as Momma tugged and pulled the thick wool cape from the trunk. When she finally got it out, she threw the black cape over my shoulders. I sagged under its weight. "Why do I have to wear this? It looks awful," I complained.

"Just this once. You have to wear something black. We're lucky it fits."

"I look like I belong to the Salvation Army," I grumbled.

"John wore it in Korea. Remember how cold it was?" Momma put on her new black hat, then carefully drew the black veil over her face. The hat matched her black dress. "It's expensive," she had said when she first tried on the dress, "but it will have to do me for at least a year." She told me then there were rules for widows that she would have to follow. Black was to be her color now that Papa was dead.

The men at Pearson's Mortuary wore white gloves. They guided Momma everywhere as if she could not see, as if she were blinded by the chiffon veil. Perfect strangers told us what to do and when to do it. They whispered their instructions as if they were afraid of waking someone. No one at our house spoke with hushed voices.

The service was like a Sunday sermon, but Papa's name was mentioned along with Jesus and God. I had never seen Papa in church. Mrs. Gilbert Lyu sang "Rock of Ages." As usual, her voice shook on the long notes. Harold and John tried to hide their smiles. They could not see Momma's look of warning behind her veil so she leaned over and tapped Harold on the shoulder to sober him up. When the service was over, white-gloved men led us to the open coffin where Papa lay.

I caught my breath. I wasn't prepared to see him so still. Such silent sleep. He always snored. He used to make us laugh, he snored so loudly. Please snore, Papa. He had on a new suit. Maybe it was a special occasion, but he would have preferred his white shirt and gray corduroy pants. John nudged me on; we were being directed to a waiting limousine.

None of us had ever been in a Cadillac. The interior was padded with soft velvet that muffled our voices. Papa was in the Cadillac ahead of ours. He's never been in one before either. The driver started the engine and we followed Papa's limousine, making our way through L.A., slowly wending our way across town to the Evergreen Cemetery. Traffic stopped to let us pass, allowing us to get to the cemetery without interruption.

"How many cars are there?" Momma asked.

The boys looked back and counted about twenty.

"That's quite a lot. Your Papa's having a nice funeral," she said as she raised her head and held the veil above her face.

That was better, I thought. I hated the veil.

"Didn't you think he looked nice?" she asked no one in particular.

Harold looked shocked. "God, Momma! What are you talking about?"

I had heard several people say to Momma, "Mr. Chun looks so nice." It must be something one says at funerals. "I thought he looked strange," I said.

"That's the way he's supposed to look," John said.

Momma ignored us and went on. "You'll get to see the plot I chose. There were two available at the price we could afford. One had water seeping into it so I chose the other one. It's on a slight hill and dry. I thought Papa would like that better." Her voice broke and she began to cry. She pulled the veil over her face.

I didn't know what to say. She talked about Papa as if he were still alive. I felt hot and slipped out of the wool cape. I was beginning to hate funerals.

When we arrived at the cemetery, Aunt Clara was standing at the curb waiting for us. She had a veil over her face. She always wore a veil whether or not there was a funeral. I remember she was pretty

before she ruined her face. "She fell in love with the wrong man,"
Momma had said. Aunt Clara hugged each of us as we came out of
the limousine and helped me with the cape.

"Must it take an occasion like this to bring you out?" Momma
scolded her as if she were a child. "I want you to come to the house
afterwards," she added firmly.

Aunt Clara nodded as she took Momma's arm and they walked to
Papa's grave together.

The coffin was closed but I knew Papa was in there; friends had
carried him from the chapel to the hearse and from the hearse to
the grave. They placed the coffin on a metal grate and white-gloved
hands hooked the gray box to a steel crane. Black grease stained
the gloves of the hand turning the crank that slowly lowered Papa
into the ground.

He won't be able to get out. Stop! I wanted to say.

Dummy. It's already dead, John had said. We were on our way to
Korea. Papa was going to join us there. Remember? But that was
only a turtle.

The words froze in my mouth and exploded into a scream. As
more followed, a man from the Pearson's Mortuary grabbed me
and led me back to the Cadillac.

I pulled away. "Let go of me! He's my Papa. You didn't even
know him."

He grabbed me again. "You're messing up his funeral, kid," he
said with his teeth tightly closed.

He shoved me into the limousine and slammed the door. I sat on
the floor where I could not see out and no one could see me.

Please turn back the clock. Change the ending. Shut out time.
Not long ago time, but lately time and most of all, now. Momma forgot
to tell me about American funerals. Someone should have told me.
I beat my fist on the velvet seat. "Damn, damn, damn," I said. I
knew no one could turn the clock back.

As soon as we got home I threw off the cape. Momma took off
her hat and went to the kitchen to prepare the food. Guests would
be coming to the house and she wanted to be sure there was plenty
to eat. When some of her lady friends arrived, they shooed her out
of the kitchen and took over.

"Chun looked so nice, so peaceful, just like he was sleeping. They
do such a good job of make-up these days, you can hardly tell
he's . . ." Aunt Clara's voice trailed off.

Momma was clearing the dining table. "Sometimes they look better than when they were alive." She looked for a place to set her sewing basket.

"Haesu! What a thing to say!" Aunt Clara exclaimed.

Momma stopped when she realized what she had said. "I didn't mean that the way it sounded. I only meant that . . . Well, Clara, you know that he wasn't the handsomest of men." She shook her head sadly. "Poor Chun. Such bad luck. I'm glad he's had a nice funeral though." She clucked her tongue. "Too young. Only forty two."

I waited for her to go on, to say, "the good always die young" the way she usually does, but she stuffed the sewing basket inside the buffet and slammed the door shut without saying anything.

"I hardly recognized him in that suit," Aunt Clara said.

"Cost eighteen dollars. I don't know where any of his things are. All Gilbert Lyu sent was this empty bag." She reached down alongside the buffet and lifted up Papa's leather valise.

Out on the street at curbside, steel doors were slammed shut, sounding like popcorn exploding in a pot that was warming up. Guests were arriving. Momma would be making excuses for my behavior at the funeral. "I'm going to my room, Momma." I said.

Aunt Clara beckoned to me. "Poor Faye, too young to understand all of this." As she leaned over to take my hands, the veil fell away from her face. I saw her gray complexion. She had meant to have it whitened, but having her skin peeled had left it looking dead. Above her high cheekbones, her eyes bulged as if she were frightened. The operation was to make them larger. Momma had told me that Aunt Clara could not fully close her eyes anymore, not even when she slept. I kissed her cheek through the veil and vowed I would never fall in love with the wrong man.

I reached for the valise. "I'll put this way," I said and carried it to my room.

Perfect strangers had put us through the funeral and blamed me for ruining the ceremony. Papa would not have allowed them to get away with that. I put the valise at the foot of my bed.

I wished we could do it all over again. Only this time, a different ending.

It was dark when I awoke; no sound of voices, only the sound of Momma's scissors as she scraped it on the table. She was sewing.

The rasping sound of sleep came from the boys' room and I lay there listening to them breathe.

What happens to Papa now? At Sunday school, the minister said that good people go to Heaven forever. Heaven's out there somewhere. I swept my hand across the darkness through an edgeless void. Forever. Papa's going to have to explain forever that he is not Chinese. No end to forever. No edge to space and no end to time. I sat up and reached out again. Nothing. My heart began to race and I had a sinking feeling in the pit of my stomach. What happens to Papa now? I broke into a cold sweat. What will happen to me? God, if you're out there say something so I won't be scared anymore. Nothing.

I jumped out of bed and flung the door open.

"Oh! Faye! You frightened me," Momma said.

"Momma! What happens to Papa now?"

"What? Oh, you must have had a nightmare. He's gone to Heaven. Have yourself something to eat then go back to bed."

"Where is Heaven, Momma?" I demanded to know.

She flipped her hand in the air. "Somewhere up there, I guess."

"How long is forever, Momma?"

"Faye," she ran her hand over the stack of raw-edged, unembroidered cloths. "I have to finish these. Now go eat." She went back to her sewing.

I wanted to rip the handkerchief from her hand, but I rubbed my arms instead. I was getting cold standing in my barefeet; my teeth began to chatter. "I don't believe there is a Heaven," I said, unable to control the shake in my voice.

She gave a deep sigh. "I'm too busy to talk about it now."

I went back to bed, leaving the door wide open. I hoped sleep would take the fear out of me. I squeezed my eyes shut, forming another void. Tears seared the arid emptiness. I was still awake when Momma went to bed. I was still awake when her breathing became deep and measured. I was still awake when night turned gray and I could see the blurred image of Papa's valise. I fell asleep as day began to break.

SIX

"Did you get that, Faye?" Miss Song rasped. "You write that it was moved by Lily Yun and seconded by Gracie Park that in July we are to have a day hike at Elysian Park, including a tour through the Hires Rootbeer plant."

"I got most of that," I said, scribbling quickly in the black notebook where we kept the minutes of the meeting. Miss Song had told us that rootbeer flowed from the taps at the Hires bottling plant and Lily had said that sounded like the goose that laid the golden egg. I thought all that should have gone into the minutes, but Miss Song said I should only record decisions our club made.

"Pay attention. We're going to take a vote now," Miss Song said. The club was her idea. After she was graduated from U.C.L.A. with a degree in Sociology, Eleanor Song became a social worker and called all teenage Korean girls together to form an organization. We named ourselves after the national flower of Korea, The Mugunghwa Club.

I thought Miss Song should have been a P.E. teacher. She was stocky and stood with her feet apart like a coach of a football team. Her voice was deep and raspy. Once, Gracie called her "Mr. Song" by mistake. Some of us cringed with embarrassment while others laughed.

"Miss Song, Miss Song," Nancy Lee called, waving her hand in the air. "When are we going to give the Tin Can Hop?"

"Just a minute. There's a motion on the floor. The president is

227

supposed to call for a vote. That's you, Alice."

Under Miss Song's prompting, Alice called for a vote and the motion was passed.

"Record the results in the minutes, Faye."

"Yes, Miss Song."

She waited while I wrote everything down. "Now we'll discuss the Tin Can Hop," she said. The Hop was her idea; one had been given at her highschool. Admission to the dance would be cans of food that were to be distributed to needy families on Thanksgiving.

I raised my hand. "Miss Song, what do you mean by 'needy'?"

"Poor people," she said and looked for another question.

"Where are we going to find them?" Lily Yun asked. Her father had bought Papa's business and owned a packing house in Reedley.

"Don't worry, we'll find them," Miss Song assured her.

I hoped she did not mean us. Momma wouldn't stand for that. Papa's funeral was four years ago and she still owed people money for it. But according to her, we weren't poor; we just did not have enough money.

The motion to have the dance in early November was passed.

When we heard the sound of scuffling feet and the scraping of chairs on the other side of the partition. I hastily wrote, ". . . made a motion to adjourn the meeting" and filled in Gracie's name as her hand went up.

Several hands from both sides of the moveable wall pushed the partition aside, opening up the hall of the United Korean Association. The boys had formed a club of their own, calling themselves "Cavaliers". Like we, they met on Friday nights.

The girls in charge of the refreshments fluttered around the kitchen uncapping bottles of Par-T-Pak sodas and ripping open bags of potato chips. The girls in charge of music plugged in the turntable and put on a Glenn Miller record. The boys sat around.

I had on a new dress and looked for ways to show it off without drawing attention to my feet. My saddle shoes were covered with layers of polish and looked as if they were made of chalk. The ghostly whiteness exaggerated their size, reducing my ankles to spindles. When I helped push the chairs and tables against the wall, I moved quickly, giving no one a chance to get a good look at my shoes.

"Who is he?" Gracie's voice drifted to my ears. "He looks like Dennis Morgan."

Dennis Morgan was one of my favorite actors. I turned to look. Boys from out of town often came to the N.A.K. building on Friday nights. Word had gotten around that it was a place where young Koreans met to socialize. The out-of-towners were usually from the San Joaquin Valley. Muscular and tan from working in the fields, they could be distinguished from the city boys of the Cavalier club. This one was no exception, only he was handsomer than most.

"Somebody ask him to dance. You do it, Alice," Gracie suggested. Alice was the girl the Cavaliers voted they most wanted to be marooned with on a deserted island.

"Why should I? It's not my idea," Alice protested.

Someone changed the record and turned up the volume.

When I hear that serenade in blue.
I'm somewhere in another world alone with you . . .

While the girls were still arguing, *he* walked toward me. I was sitting on the edge of a table and drew my two limestone blocks of saddle shoes into the shadows under the table.

"Hi!" His face broke into a broad grin. His white teeth glistened against his bronze skin.

"Hi," I answered back.

"Wanna dance?"

"Okay." In one move, I stepped onto the floor and put my hand on his shoulder. His eyes never fell to my feet. I thanked God it was a slow piece; I could not jitterbug. Only savages dance like that, Momma said.

"My name's Willie Koo. I'm from Reedley," he said.

"Oh, really?"

"No, Reedley. Willie's my name." His eyes twinkled as he laughed at his own play on words. He started right in talking about himself. I listened until I forgot about my shoes. He lived with his uncle and worked at the Yun's packing house until he was old enough to drive his uncle's truck. He wanted to get out of 'hicktown,' he said, and see the world. This was his first trip to L.A.

"Don't your parents ever come to L.A.?" I asked.

"I haven't any," he answered. "They're both dead."

I forgot to move my feet and he stepped on my shoes. "Oops, sorry," he said, breaking away to see if he had damaged anything. I

quickly drew him close to resume the two step. "My father's dead
too," I said. As soon as I said it, I regretted it. It was a terrible thing
to have in common. But Willie was the only young person I had met
who did not have a father.

"No kidding? I don't remember my mom. She died when I was
born." He looked around the room. "This is really great. You guys
always get together like this?"

"Every Friday night. Don't you belong to a club?"

"Ain't that many Koreans in Reedley. How old are you, anyway?"

His question took me by surprise. "Me? Fifteen, uh, going on
sixteen."

"You don't happen to have a sister, do you?"

"What? Why?"

"I'm eighteen. Just graduated. Ready to see the world. And here
I am. L.A. is really something."

"Uh huh." I said. No one seemed to think me old enough for
anything.

Serenade, serenade in blue . . .

Willie did a fancy turn and dipped. As I fell toward him, the
hard contours of his leg pressed through my dress. I had never felt
a boy against me before. The blood rushed to my cheeks.

"What's your name?" he asked.

I told him.

"Fay? Like in Fay Wray?"

"With an 'e,' " I said, "F-a-y-e."

"No kidding? Well, I'll be seeing you, Faye with an 'e'."

Willie began showing up regularly on Friday nights. As an out-
of-towner, he could not join the Cavaliers but they allowed him to
draw from the pool of girls for dates. All of us knew how it worked:
the boys decided among themselves who would ask whom to be his
date. By gentlemen's agreement, no one stole another's claim. The
arrangement may have been to the boys' liking, but a girl had little
choice. If she refused an invitation, she was doomed to stay at
home.

Willie began asking me to be his date. I had no way of knowing if
it was because he wanted me or because no one else did. Anyway, I
fell into being his girl.

Being Willie's girl meant that I would be included when the boys took their girls bowling, or to movies, or to Simon's Drive-in for a hamburger. I wanted to be the kind of girl boys liked to be with so, while watching movies, I studied the way Hollywood stars walked and talked. I thumbed through magazines to see how starlets fixed their hair and dressed. I learned to do my own hair, but clothes required money.

"Look at these shoes, Momma." I had delayed polishing them for the occasion. "They make me look like Frankenstein's monster. I need extra money to buy clothes. I can work, get a part-time job or help you sew."

"Never. If necessary, I'll stay up all night working to give you what you want. But you will never work for money," she said.

"Why not me? What's so special about me?" I said, hoping I would find the words that would change her mind.

"Not just you. Because of your family. Women of the *yangban* class do not work for money."

"You do."

"Because I have no choice. But here in my house where no one can see me."

"In America, it's all right to work for money, for girls to work like boys. It's nothing to be ashamed of," I insisted.

She put down her sewing to wave her finger at me. "You are not like other American girls. If you try to be like them, you will be nothing special." She picked up her sewing. "You don't need new clothes to be a lady."

"Who wants to be a lady?" As soon as I said it, I knew I was in for it. She was going to remind me about our family position in Korea, about the Japanese depriving us of our rightful due. "Oh, never mind," I said and walked to the back porch. She was right about one thing: I wasn't like other American girls. No one at school spoke to me or behaved towards me as if I were like any American girl. Most of them were nice enough. I even considered Ruth Johnson one of my best friends until she told me, "You know, Faye, I don't think of you as being Korean anymore," as if there was something wrong with being Korean. We never double dated. She went to school dances but I was never asked. If it wasn't for Miss Song, I wouldn't be anyone's girl.

I found an old paring knife and scraped off the layers of white polish from my shoes then applied a new coat of milky paint. They still looked ragged. I could not help wondering what good it was to be a *yangban* if I couldn't dress like one.

I used the last drop of shoe-white then went to the carriage to drop the bottle in the box for the junkman. I looked up in time to see John climb over the fence. He dropped to the ground then disappeared behind the garage.

Soon afterwards, the doorbell rang. "Answer the door, Faye," Momma shouted.

The policeman was sweating and breathing hard. When he saw me he said, "Well, at least I've got the right place. Do you have a brother about this tall?" He held his hand at the level of his forehead. "Wearing a light blue shirt and tan pants?"

I shrugged my shoulders. "I have two brothers," I said.

"One of them run in here a few minutes ago?" he asked.

"No."

"What is it?" Momma asked me in Korean.

"It's a policeman. He's looking for a boy," I said.

Momma came to the door. "What boy?"

The policeman showed Momma John's height and described the clothes he was wearing.

"What he do?" she asked.

"Tried to steal a bicycle. Was it your son?"

"I don't know. He's not here," she said.

"Ma'am, I saw him run into this yard. I know he belongs to you."

Momma looked at me. *"Opah pwasse ni?"*

I shook my head to indicate I had not seen my brother.

The policeman took a card from his wallet and handed it to Mamma. "I'm Officer Richards. Better have a word with your boy. Tell him it's best for him to cooperate with us. The store owner said he had seen your boy hanging around when some other things had disappeared."

"Maybe he looks like someone else," Momma said. "We don't steal. We pay back what we owe. I call you . . ." she looked at the card. "Officer Richards."

After he left, Momma told me, "Go find John."

I walked through the house and out the back door. By turning sideways I was able to squeeze through the space between the fence and the garage. Step by step, I edged toward the back of the garage. I stopped when I heard John's voice.

"We've got to get rid of the stuff, man," John said.

"It's you they seen. You're the one in trouble, man," a voice replied. I did not recognize the voice.

"That's why I can't keep it here. Take it. Get rid of it," John ordered.

"I know I can count on Luke to take them," the voice said.

"Man, just don't tell him where you got them," John said.

"Gotcha."

I heard shoes kick against the fence as someone climbed over it and ran away.

Someone jumped on some loose boards in the garage then I heard the door scrape open.

"John?" I called.

His face appeared around the corner of the garage. "What are you doing there?"

"I came to tell you a policeman came looking for you. Momma knows." I sidled out to him.

"Shit! I thought I had lost him."

"What are you up to anyway?" I asked.

"What's it to you?"

"If you get into trouble we'll all be in for it. What did you try to steal for anyway?"

He sat on the ground and picked up a handful of dirt. "Know of any other way to get a bike?"

"Work for it. Save your money," I said.

John laughed as he threw the dirt in the air. "I'd be too old to ride a bike by then. Figure it out, Faye. We won't ever have anything we want."

"Don't say that, John. Harold will find a job. He'll be able to work full time," I reminded him.

"Think all he has to do is worry about buying things for us? Why do you think he went to Fresno to look for a job?"

"I thought it was because he couldn't find anything in L.A."

"Jesus, Faye, You don't know anything. He went away to get away."

"You're lying."

"Okay, I'm lying. Have it your way."

"Better go talk to Mom. The policeman left her his card."

"What did Mom tell him?"

"You know, that she'll pay for anything you took," I said.

"Shit!" He stood up. "Go on in and tell Mom I'll be home later."

"Don't get into anymore trouble," I said.

"Who are you to tell me what to do? Go on in and tell Mom what I said," he ordered then turned and walked toward Western Avenue.

I hated keeping secrets from Momma, but I wasn't anxious to give her bad news.

"John will be home later. He says you shouldn't worry."

"We'll see," she said.

I went to the kitchen to wash the rice. The water splashed over the sink onto my shoes, sending a spray of white on the floor.

I held the door open for Willie. He was carrying a lug of cucumbers. "The first of the season, Mrs. Chun. You'll be the first lady in L.A. to make *oi kimchee*," he said. On top of the cucumbers lay a bunch of yellow daisies. "Those are for you," he said to me.

While he took the lug to the back porch, I found a vase and put the flowers in water. I didn't notice Willie creeping up on me. He turned me around and planted his mouth on my lips. "Stop that!" I said, pushing him away. He giggled silently and grabbed me around the waist.

"Yah! Faye-yah!" Momma called.

Willie let go of me like a shot. I laughed at him quietly and walked out of the kitchen. "What do you want, Momma?"

"I'm worried about John. Would you and Willie see if you can find him?"

"Sure, Mrs. Chun," Willie said. He had followed me out carrying the daisies. When he set them down, the yellow blossoms seemed to light up the whole table.

"They're very pretty," Momma said.

"I'm taking Faye bowling. We're meeting some kids at the alley. Maybe John will be there," he said.

"Tell him I want to see him right away," Momma said.

I grabbed a sweater and was about to go out the door when Momma said, "Be home by ten o'clock."

"Ten? Our tournament won't be over by then," I complained.

"Ten-thirty then."

"Alice Choy doesn't have to be in until eleven," I said. Momma always used Alice as an example for me to follow.

"Ten-thirty is late enough," she said with finality.

As we walked toward Willie's truck, I complained, "My Mom's so strict."

"I don't blame her. If you were mine, I'd watch over you like a hawk," he said, squeezing my hand.

"But she overdoes it. Feels she has to make up for Papa, I guess."

"At least you have a Mom to make up for your not having a father."

I pressed against his arm. "I shouldn't be complaining, should I?"

"It's okay, baby. Cry on my shoulders anytime. I can take it," he said boastfully.

As we drove by *Curries'* Ice Cream Parlor, I looked in to see if John was there. Whenever we had extra change in our hands, we would walk the mile to *Curries'* to have an ice cream cone. He wasn't there.

"They make the best ice cream," I told Willie.

"That's a long way to go for ice cream," he said.

"The library's right across the street. I go there a couple of times a month," I said. "I first went to look up a poem by Walt Whitman and it got to be a habit." I thought about Jane. I hadn't seen her for several years. When she joined the Japanese Culture Club and I joined the Mugunghwa, we drifted apart. But I've never forgotten her or her sisters' skit. " 'A child said, What is grass?, fetching it to me with full hands . . .'," I recited to Willie.

"You're in trouble, kid. Didn't you read the sign, 'Keep off the grass'?" Willie replied, mimicking my cadence.

I laughed. "It's really a swell poem. I don't understand all of it. It ends with, 'And to die is different from what anyone supposed, and luckier'."

"Luckier?"

"That's what it says. I understand dying being different from what anyone supposed. Learned it the hard way. I was a mess at my father's funeral, made a fool of myself. Momma had to tell everyone, 'It's her first funeral. She doesn't know how to behave.' I wanted to die."

"I wouldn't know how to act either. I've never been to a funeral."

"Not even your father's?"

Willie hesitated, as if he were arguing with himself. "He hasn't had one," he said, finally. "I say he's dead because he never considered me alive. No one's ever owned up to being my father, but I've got a feeling I know who it is and he ain't dead."

"What are you talking about?"

He hesitated again. "Aw, forget it."

Whatever it was had made him sad. "You'd get a kick out of the book on etiquette I've read about funerals," I said cheerfully.

"There's a book on it?"

"I looked it up. It tells you what to wear, what to do, and how to think. It said that 'death has lost much of its terror'. It said that, 'death is accepted with simple fortitude by sensible people'."

Willie gave a laugh. " 'Sensible people'," he said, as if no such thing existed.

"How do you like this one . . . 'etiquette requires complete control by the bereaved woman'?"

"You mean, crying at a funeral is a no-no? Who wrote that book anyway?"

"Can you imagine a Korean woman in 'complete control'?" I asked sardonically.

"That's like asking a Korean to hate *kimchee*," he said, chuckling. "What does 'bereaved' mean?"

"That means losing someone who died," I answered with confidence. I had looked up the word.

"You sound like you memorized the book," Willie said.

I wondered if he was teasing me. I had read the pages over and over again, trying to comprehend the reasons behind the rules. Nothing Momma had taught me helped me to understand.

"I'd feel so strange trying to think and act like that. That's why I read it so many times. It said, 'Leave the family in mourning alone with their grief'. Everyone came to the house. They helped Momma cook then sat around to eat and keep her company."

"Sounds like the best part of the funeral," Willie teased.

"I've read the book but I still think I wouldn't know how to behave at a funeral," I said with a sigh.

"Why worry about it? No Korean will be reading the book," Willie reassured me. "How'd we get on this subject, anyway?"

"Whitman's poem." I settled back into my seat. " 'All goes onward and outward, nothing collapses'."

As Willie opened the door, the rumble of bowling balls rolling down hardwood floors and the sharp crack as they hit the tenpins made me want to have a try at it. No other place in the world sounded like a bowling alley.

Alice waved when she saw us. "We've already reserved the lanes," she shouted.

I cupped my hands around my mouth. "Have you seen John?"

She nodded and pointed toward the pool room.

"Will you get him, Willie? He won't listen to me. Tell him he should go home right now," I said.

I sidled down the row behind Alice to talk to her. She was wearing a plaid skirt and a cardigan sweater that picked up the red in the plaid. Silver barrettes held her permanent-waved hair neatly in place. She had on rented bowling shoes, a brand new pair without a single crack in the blue number '5' painted on the back of the heels. She looked terrific.

"Whoever loses has to treat the winner. Noodles at Hangchow Restaurant," she said.

"Who's coming?" I asked.

"C. K. is picking up Lily. Jimmy brought me. He's in there with John," she said, nodding her head toward the pool room.

"I see they finally got some decent shoes," I said, pointing my chin at her feet.

"The last pair of 5's."

"I wear 7's but I'd better get mine before they're gone." I left her to go to the registration desk.

Willie had a serious look on his face as he walked toward me. "Is something wrong?" I asked.

"I was going to ask you the same thing? John said he's going home as soon as he finishes the game. He wanted to know when I was going back to Reedley."

"Why?"

"That's what I was wondering."

"But he is going home?"

"Oh yeah. He said to tell you he's going home."

I was relieved. Momma wouldn't be worried about him much longer.

"JAMES LEE!" a voice boomed over the loudspeaker. Jimmy came out of the pool room to claim the lanes assigned to us. John followed him out. He looked at me then turned and went out the door.

"Did you get your shoes?" Willie asked.

I held up a battered pair of ecru shoes. "Seven is a popular size.

The man said they're all beat up like this."

The sight of them made Willie laugh. "You ought to buy yourself a pair," he said.

I sighed. "My Mom would say, 'you don't need your own bowling shoes to be a good bowler'."

Willie put his arms around my waist. "I'll get you a pair for Christmas."

By the time C. K. and Lily arrived, we had bowled a game. Willie didn't mind their being late. He did not like Lily. "She's a stuck-up little snot," he once told me. He had worse things to say about her father. "That S. O. B. is so full of himself. When he comes to the packing house, he expects everyone to kiss his you-know-what because he's given them a job. He expects gratitude for slave labor," he had said. I remember being perplexed. "Mr. Yun? He bought my father's business. He's responsible for collecting the money to build the N.A.K. building. He's a bigshot in the community. What's he done to you?" Willie had muttered to himself then told me, "I hate his guts."

Lily opened her navy blue canvas bag and took out a pair of bowling shoes. "I can't stand the thought of wearing shoes someone else has worn," she said with a shudder.

"Good idea. Think how they must feel," Willie said.

Lily ignored him. "The fit has to be exactly right or your feet begin to hurt." She bent down to untie her saddle shoes. "Aren't these a nuisance to polish? How do you keep yours so white, Faye?" I had tucked my shoes under the seat.

Before I could open my mouth, Willie said, "She read a book on it."

"Well I'm sure you didn't," she said to him.

I put a restraining hand on Willie but couldn't shut him up. "No, but Faye told me about it. It takes a special kind of spit." He hacked to bring his sputum up. "Got plenty for you," he gurgled.

"Jesus, Willie. You haven't got any class," C. K. said in disgust.

I punched Willie in the ribs. "That's repulsive," I said.

"Willie's a country hick," Lily said. "He doesn't know any better."

Alice rolled back her eyes. "Cut it out, both of you." She took a kleenex from her purse and handed it to Willie. "Get rid of it," she said.

I looked at Lily, expecting her to say something. But she wore her expression of disapproval without saying another word. Prim in a pale blue sweater that set off her brown checked skirt, she seemed sure of herself. I had noticed earlier that the brown of her saddle shoes matched the brown of her skirt. I'd be sure of myself too, I thought, if my shoes matched my dress.

We had bowled two hours when Willie announced, "Last game if we want to eat. Faye has to be in by ten-thirty."

I could have hit him over the head with a bowling ball. "Don't let me break up the game," I said.

Jimmy began adding up the score. "Well, I know for sure that Alice and I want to eat. We left you guys in the dust. You're low man, Willie. You and C. K. will have to treat."

"That's nothing new. I'm the original low man," Willie said.

Everyone laughed but me. I saw nothing amusing in what he had said.

The streets that led to the Hangchow Restaurant went through the heart of old Los Angeles. Our voices wobbled as the wheels of the truck bounced over streetcar tracks and fell into gutted asphalt.

I grabbed the ledge of the window as we bounced over a pothole. "You shouldn't say bad things about yourself," I said.

"Why not? I beat the other guys to the punch," Willie said.

"Or give them ideas."

He took a moment to think about what I had said then chuckled, "Do you take everything so seriously?"

Do I? I wondered. Everyone else had laughed. "Not everything," I said.

He put his hand on my thigh and gave it a squeeze. "Stick with me, baby. We'll have plenty of laughs."

I pushed his hand away. "That's not funny," I said.

The others were waiting when we arrived. The six of us entered the restaurant and crowded into a booth. It was difficult to see anything. The dim light barely reflected off the brown shellacked walls. We brushed off the seats of the bentwood chairs before sitting down. "Don't they ever clean this joint?" Willie grumbled.

"Whose idea was it to come here?" Lily asked.

Willie and Jimmy looked at each other in mock amazement. "We always come here," Jimmy said.

"Doesn't everybody?" Willie added.

Everyone but Lily laughed.

From the booth next to ours, the hollow sound of Chinese words sprinkled with pidgin English climbed over the top of the partition. The other cubicles were silent. The restaurant was practically empty. There would be no excuse for slow service. While we waited for attention, an old Chinese man sat behind the cash register reading his newspaper.

Willie pushed aside the dingy curtain and shouted, "Hey! Garçon!"

The man looked up. Willie held up his arm and pointed to his watch.

Scowling, the man snapped, "Next time, come early."

Willie leaned toward the center of the table and in a lowered voice said, "Next time, we won't come at all."

Everyone laughed but Lily and me.

"You have to know how to handle these guys," Willie said, after our meal was served. "Put a little pressure on and you get service. Old Yankee know-how." He gave me a wink.

C. K. pushed back on his chair to look out. "He's still reading his newspaper."

"One thing you have to say for him," I said. "He has a lot of character." I smiled and waited for the laugh.

"What?" Willie asked. He didn't get it.

"Never mind," I said. "What time is it?"

He looked at his watch. "Holy Smokes! We have to beat it." He pulled out his wallet and laid down a ten dollar bill. "This ought to do it."

"That's too much!" C. K. protested.

"Forget it," Willie said. He once told me there was nothing worse than being a cheapskate.

We ran to his truck and scrambled in. Willie turned the key to the ignition and slammed his foot on the starter. The engine whined but refused to turn over. "Damn it!" Willie said. He pulled on the choke and kept at the starter until the engine finally took fire. He grappled with the steering wheel to maneuver out of the tight parking space. "Trading in this pile of junk for a new semi. I'll be able to make a lot more money."

"That's great," I said.

At every Boulevard Stop, the engine threatened to die. We were half way home when it finally gave up. "Shit!" Willie hissed. "We'll have to push it to the curb."

I got out to help him. When the truck was snug against the curb and in gear, we walked to the corner and stood in the dark to wait for the J car.

"We're late, Faye. What am I going to tell your Mom?" Willie asked.

"She's probably asleep. Besides, she's my Mom. You won't have to tell her anything."

He smiled so broadly that I saw his teeth glimmer in the dark. "Thanks, baby." He put his arm around me. "I wish you didn't have to go home at all." He pulled me close and snuggled his face in my hair. He ran his lips over my ears. It tickled and I pulled away. "Don't!" I said, laughing.

"Don't!" he mimicked. He took my hand and pulled me to him. I was no match for the strength of a country boy. My hands became hot from struggling with him. I felt moist all over. He pulled my hips against him to feel the hardness between his legs. He released me only to pull me against him again, repeatedly in a rhythmic movement he seemed unable to control.

Clang! Clang! I broke free and ran out to the street to wave down the approaching streetcar. I didn't wait for it to come to a complete halt before clamoring aboard. I slid into the front seat where I would be in full view of the conductor. The streetcar started up again as Willie dropped the coins in the box. He fell next to me and smiled. I looked out the window.

"You liked it," he insisted. "Go on, admit it."

"Stop it!" I said to him in Korean. I stared out the window, confused by the contradiction of excitement and revulsion, unable to sort them out by the time we reached our stop. I tugged the cord to ring the bell. Willie stood up and stepped aside to let me pass, his lips curled in a smug smile. His smile was getting on my nerves.

We ran the three blocks to my house. The light in the dining room was on. "I've gotta hurry back. I'm going to see if Jimmy can give me a hand with the truck. See you next week," Willie whispered hoarsely. He started to run down the steps when the front door flew open.

"Willie! Come in here!" Momma called to him. "Why are you late?" she demanded to know.

"No, Momma . . . don't. Let him go. Don't ask him. Ask me," I pleaded.

Willie hushed me up and led me into the house. "It's my fault."

He spoke to her in Korean so that she would understand, haltingly as he searched for the words. He told her about the slow service at the restaurant, about the dead engine, about the infrequent running of streetcars at night. *"Mi yan ham ni da,"* he said, ending his explanation by saying he was sorry.

"It's very important to keep promises. I said ten-thirty and you said all right. I don't know if something happened to you. Parents worry about their children," she said.

Willie nodded to show he understood. I waited for someone to say something to me.

"Next time, if we're going to be late, I'll call you," he promised.

"That's good. But try not to be late. Faye has to keep a good reputation."

After Willie left, Momma began closing up the house.

"Why didn't you talk to me?" I asked.

"He has to know what I expect. He doesn't have any parents to tell him. Now go to bed," she said as she switched off the light.

She left me standing in the dark as if I wasn't there at all, cutting me off from the light, leaving me to grope my way to my room. Willie had helped himself to my body and Momma put my reputation in his hands. I wished I was rid of them both; I could take care of my own reputation.

—2—

"Call John to breakfast," Momma said.

I went to the boys' bedroom. "He's not here," I called out.

"Where is he? He came home last night. He saw you and Willie, and came home, talked to me, then went to bed."

"He probably went out early," I said.

"No. I got up at five to finish sewing. I would have heard him." There was panic in her voice.

I looked around John's room for a clue. In the closet, alongside of Harold's clothes, hung empty hangers. I rushed to my room to look in my closet. In the far corner where I kept Papa's valise, dust outlined the perimeter where the leather case had stood. I walked to the kitchen.

"He's run away," I said.

Momma went to his room to see for herself. "Where could he go?

Maybe he went to Uncle Yang's. Scared because of the policman. I'll call him."

"He won't be there."

"How do you know?" she said, making her way to the phone.

"He took Papa's valise."

She dropped into the chair by the phone. "What are we going to do? We can't ask the police for help." She threw her hands into the air. "We can't do anything. We'll just have to sit and wait."

Rrrrng! Momma jumped out of the chair, fumbling the receiver as she took it off the hook. "Hello, hello. Who is it? Who? About John? You know about him? Oh, that." She listened for a long while then said, "I let you talk to my daughter." She handed me the phone. "I can't understand him."

It was Officer Richards. "I told your mother that I can't do anything to your brother if there are no charges against him. In other words, tell her to go see the bicycle shop owner. Give him a good sob story. He'll drop the charges and your brother won't have to be taken into custody. Understand?"

"I think so," I said. He gave me the name and address of the shop before hanging up.

I explained what he said to Momma but left out the part about telling a 'good sob story'. All she had to do was tell the truth. I gave her the address.

"It must be the one we walk by all the time," I said. I must have walked by the shop hundreds of times pulling the wagon to meet Momma at the bus stop.

"There? So close to home" she said softly.

Momma changed her clothes and announced she was leaving to speak to the bicycle shop owner.

"Don't you want me to go with you?" I asked.

"No. You stay home. Maybe John will call."

I didn't expect to hear anything from John, but I did as she asked. If John had wanted us to know where he was going, he would have left a note. He knew that we could not go to the police for help.

She was only gone an hour. "Is everything all right?" I asked.

She nodded. "Forty dollars. The man said he was sure John stole more than that but would take forty dollars and not send John to jail."

"Forty dollars? Does he have any proof?"

"I didn't ask him. I have to pay him. The police know that John tried to steal a bicycle."

"He has to have proof. Besides, John didn't steal a bicycle. The man's blackmailing you!"

"Even if he is, I have to pay him," she said, with resignation. She was giving in without a fight. I couldn't stand it. "Momma, you don't have to pay him anything." She didn't believe me; the wrinkles on her forehead stayed. "Momma, it's stupid not to let me work. A summer job . . "

She waved her hand at me. "Don't bother me with that now."

"Then sell the land," I said. "What's the point of hanging on to it?"

A fire lit in her eyes when she looked at me. "I hope that someday you will know why I keep the land. Until you do, don't talk to me about it."

I wished I knew now. I was tired of trying to make sense of it. But it wasn't time. Momma's anger was coming down on me and I found myself welcoming it. "Okay, Mom. I'm sorry I upset you," I said. "I think I'll go to the library." I couldn't think of anyplace else to go.

Momma always did what she believed to be fair and honest. But nothing was getting any better. I would think that if she were making the right decisions, trouble would unknot itself and her luck would improve. Forty dollars. She was already at her sewing night and day just to make ends meet. She can't squeeze more hours out of a day. Qwaksan. Qwaksan. Why won't she sell the land?

It was too warm to walk on shadeless Jefferson Boulevard. I stayed on the quiet streets where sprinklers cooled the air and trees shaded the sidewalks.

What I couldn't do with forty dollars. Any old dress or sweater would no longer do. When I first noticed the swelling under my nipples, I had run to Momma, frightened and wondering how fast and how large my breasts would grow. She just laughed and said, "In Nature's time." I showed her the embarrassing bumps of my nipples when I wore matted sweaters. "No one notices," she had said. John noticed. He whistled whenever he could tell my nipples were hard, even when he was with a group of Cavaliers. Some big brother! Why won't she let me work?

At Vermont Avenue, a colored girl rushed out of a grocery store and bumped into me. "Watch where you're going, girl!" she said, throwing me an angry look. Her expression changed suddenly and she screamed, "Faye!"

"Bertha? I thought you had moved to Texas." I put my books in one arm while she shifted her bag of groceries and we hugged.

"It's lousy in Texas." She noticed my books. "Going to summer school?"

"No, to the library."

"I've got to get off my feet. Where can we sit?" She looked around.

I noticed then that she was pregnant. "When did you get married?" I asked.

Her mouth dropped open. "Girl, you haven't change nohow. I'm not married." She took my hand and led me to the bench at the streetcar stop. "Whew! it's hot." She tucked the bag of groceries under the bench out of the sun.

"What's wrong with Texas?" I asked as she pulled me down to sit next to her.

"Take everything that's wrong with L.A. and double it. Hotter than blazes, can't not only live where you want, can't sit where you want. Have to look like a nigger, dress like a nigger, and act like a nigger. I wasn't ready for that. I came back, lived in east L.A. for awhile, then found a place on 35th. A block from here," she said, nodding her head in the direction of her place. "You still living in the same house?"

"Yea. We haven't had a chance to move," I said.

"Your Mom still doing that work?" She sewed a running stitch through the air.

I nodded. "How can you have a baby and not be married?"

She laughed. "God, Faye, don't you know anything yet? It was a mistake. I fooled around at the wrong time. Bet you can't guess who I did it with."

I shook my head. She always managed to make me feel as if I had blindfolds over my eyes. But I wasn't going to let on that I did not know what she meant by 'it'.

"Remember Lucerne Luke?"

"Him?" I took her hand. "You haven't seen John around, have you?"

"No. Why?"

"I just wondered." I wasn't sure whether or not I should be relieved.

"Have you got a boyfriend?" Bertha asked.

"Sort of," I replied.

"Well, watch out or you'll be left holding the bag."

"Oh."

"What I'm saying, girl, is keep track of your cycle. Don't end up like me."

"Are you getting married?"

"Just because a guy likes to do it with you don't mean he wants to marry you."

"A baby without a father?" That seemed like the saddest thing in the world to me.

"I'll probably put it up for adoption or something. It's not easy to find a guy looking for a ready-made family."

"How about your mother? Won't she take care of it?"

"My folks stayed in Texas. They said, 'It's our home, baby.' Some home! A place where white folks think they're 'good people' if they're civil to us. I wanted none of it."

"Do you have a job?"

"I'm paying my own way." She noticed something by her feet, "Oh, damn! I forgot about the ice cream." The bottom of the paper bag was dripping when she pulled it up. "I've gotta get this home. I'll come by and see you, Faye." She kissed me on the cheek then stood up to leave. "You need someone to talk to you."

I enjoyed seeing Bertha. We didn't argue the way we did in the past. It had meant nothing to me when she told me that she was moving to Texas. Jane was my friend then. That was several years ago. Bertha was back and I was glad to see her.

I made it to the library an hour before closing time. I deposited my books and asked Miss Lane, the librarian, where I could find information on pregnancy.

She looked at me for a moment. "Is it for a science report?" she asked.

"Yes," I lied.

I read in an hour everything I could about male sperms, female eggs, gestation, and copulation. I learned that 'sex' was a legitimate word and what Bertha referred to as 'it' and Momma called 'that thing' was sexual intercourse.

Miss Lane was puzzled when I returned the reference books to their shelves. "You can check those out, you know," she said.

"I don't need to, thank you," I said. They contained information Momma would not allow in the house. I checked out a book by Willa Cather and one by Mark Twain and left the library.

Harold was home when I arrived. "Hi! How's Fresno?" I asked.

A lift of his chin meant it was acceptable.

"You sound cheerful," Momma said to me.

"I do?" I said. "Any news about John?"

"I thought maybe you had heard something," Harold said.

"Me? Who would tell me anything?"

Harold turned to Momma. "Don't worry. He'll pop up. Where could he go?"

Momma sighed. "I just wish I knew."

We found out two days later. Willie wrote, "John's with me. He told me your Mom gave him permission—confessed later he had lied. I'm writing so you won't worry. I'll tell you about it on Saturday."

Momma was furious. "Why didn't John write the letter himself? I don't like his being with Willie. There's no mother or father in that house," she said.

"Willie's all right," I told her.

"He's a nice boy but he has no family background."

"He's my boyfriend."

"Boyfriend, but that's all."

She slammed the door on other possibilities. I wasn't sure how I felt about Willie. Lily's scorn had raised doubts, but I wasn't ready to be pushed into a conclusion. "He's one of the nicest boys I know," I said.

—3—

I've got it!" Willie announced. I thought he meant the lug box of peaches he was carrying. "I've got my new truck! Come on, Mrs. Chun, let's all go for a ride."

Momma motioned him to a chair. "Tell me about John."

"Didn't you get his letter?" Willie asked as he took the peaches to the kitchen. He came out and sat down. "He said he was writing you a letter."

"No letter," she said sharply.

"Don't blame Willie," I said.

She paused. "I don't blame you, Willie. I'm mad at John."

"He's all right. He's looking around for work," Willie said.

"He's not coming home?" Momma asked.

"I think he's afraid to come back. Said some kids would be after him. He's not a bad boy, Mrs. Chun."

"I know that, but he should talk to me," she said.

"Maybe he's afraid to," I said.

She gave me a look. "Why? Have I ever beat him?" she demanded to know.

Willie jumped in. "Maybe he's ashamed of what he did. Maybe it would be better for him to get out of L.A. for awhile."

Momma stopped sewing to think about what he had said. "And out of this neighborhood," she said. "He always liked the country. He liked it in Korea. He wanted to stay there, but I was afraid . . . The Japanese were so cruel."

"He can't get into any trouble in Reedley," Willie said. "He can get a job in a packing house or work on a farm. He's planning to move into the Hur's boarding house."

"Hur Yul Gok? I know him. A good family. Tell John I want him to live there," Momma said. She got up from her chair. "Let's go see your new truck."

We went out to the curb to see it. It was magnificent. A dazzling white cab was coupled to a platform that seemed a mile long. Momma was impressed. She looked it over and said, "You lucky boy."

"I was going to get a black one but dark colors show the dust so I . . ."

Momma interrupted him. "No, no. White is better. White goes with metal. Righteousness. White tiger," she said.

"White? Not yellow tiger?" Willie asked.

"No, yellow dragon but white tiger," she insisted.

Willie nodded. "I get it. Old-country thinking. Well, how about a ride in the white tiger?"

"You children go ahead. Some other time for me. Holidays are coming, lots of work. I'm making neckties. Nobody buys handmade handkerchiefs anymore," she said.

"You didn't tell me you were making neckties," I said.

"Just started. It's faster than embroidering," she said as she turned to go into the house. "Ten-thirty," she reminded us.

Willie gave me a hand as I hoisted myself into the cab. His face glowed as he climbed in next to me. At the turn of the key, the engine roared and shattered the stillness.

"Listen to that, Faye. That would scare the you-know-what out of King Kong," Willie said with pride. "Let's go see if anyone's at the bowling alley. Let them have a gander at the 'White Tiger'."

At every stop, he revved the engine. I felt dwarfed by the powerful sound, engulfed by the steel monster, as it carried me above all the other cars. When we pulled into the parking lot, the attendant waved us away. "You can't bring that rig in here. It takes the space of six cars," he said.

"So we'll bowl six games," Willie said.

"There's a tournament on tonight," the attendant said, waving us out of the lot again.

"No one we know will be here. We might as well leave," I said.

Willie looked down at the attendant. "So long, sucker." He revved the engine and shot past the startled man, laughing at him to make him feel the fool; it was either him or Willie.

"It must not be easy finding a parking space," I said.

"Yeah, she's a little big for the city. She's meant for the wi-de open road." He twanged the words like a cowboy.

"Must be hard to maneuver," I said.

"It just looks that way. It's a cinch. Want to try it?"

"Oh no. I couldn't drive this thing."

"Sure you could. You'll see how easy it is."

"I mean it, Willie. I can't drive this rig."

"Trust me. I'll be right next to you. You know how to drive, don't you?"

I nodded. "Uncle Yang lets me drive his Model A. But I don't have a license."

"You don't need one. No one's going to catch you." He turned onto 35th Street, put the gear in neutral, and pulled up the emergency brake.

"I'm not kidding, Willie. I won't drive this thing."

"Oh yes you will." He leaned over and turned my face toward his. "Don't be a scaredy-cat." He got out of the cab. As he walked across the front of the truck, the headlights beamed on the fine angles of his tawny face. He looked even handsomer than Dennis Morgan.

"Slide over," he said as he opened the door on my side. He lifted himself into the cab. "I want you to see what a kick it is. Look, there's not another car on the street. Release the brakes, put in the clutch, shift to first, and let her go."

I could see that he wasn't going to let me out of it. I took a deep breath and did as he instructed. The truck shot forward and I slammed on the brakes. He lunged forward then laughed. "Easy, easy. Take it easy."

"Willie. I don't think this is a good idea. I'm scared."

"Scared? I told you not to be a scaredy-cat. That does it. You can't quit now. Just let out the clutch slowly."

I tried it again. The engine convulsed momentarily before settling down to a deep hum. We were soon scudding down 35th Street. Rrrm, rrrm, I revved the engine at the first stop. As I started picking up speed, my movements became automatic and I shifted smoothly from gear to gear.

"Look at me, Willie! I'm driving a semi!"

"I told you you could do it. Just keep it steady now." He slipped an arm around my shoulder, leaving his other hand free should I need his help.

"Can I try the horn?" I yelled.

"That's what it's for," he shouted back.

I pressed the black disc and a joyous bellow filled the air. Willie leaned over and pressed it again. I was in control, guiding the direction of the semi. "I didn't know this could be such fun!" I told Willie.

"Didn't I tell you?" he said, bursting with pleasure.

The end of 35th Street was coming up on us fast. "Hey! What shall I do when I have to turn?"

"You turn, baby."

"Left or right?"

"Make up your mind, but do it fast," he said, sitting up straight.

I heard him but my hands and feet stayed fixed. I couldn't sort the messages in my brain to make any part of my body move.

"Slow it down, Faye. Slow it down!" Willie grabbed the steering wheel with his free hand. He kicked my foot off the accelerator. "Put your foot on the brakes. Press gradually but get it down there." He pulled the steering wheel toward him, turning the semi around the corner. The trailer bounced onto the sidewalk before rolling back on the street, narrowly missing the left rear fender of a parked car.

I pushed the brake as far as it would go and the truck came to a stop. My heart was racing. "Willie, I could have wrecked your truck."

Willie collapsed in his seat then chugged into a roaring laughter. "You had me going for a minute." He took my hand. "You couldn't have hurt anything on the semi. Of course, you might have smashed up that car."

"I must have been out of my mind," I said.

"You were having a good time." He leaned over and kissed the nape of my neck. "You ought to get a truck of your own, Faye. It makes you happy." He tucked my hair behind my ear. Assuming an Italian accent, he said, "But girls donta need a good trucka, they justa need a good . . ."

"Willie!"

"Lucka."

I flashed him a look of skepticism.

"Honest, that's what I was going to say," he insisted. He looked at his watch. "We still have time."

"You'd better drive," I said. I felt unsteady. The thought that Momma might have had to pay for Willie's semi had flashed through my mind.

Willie parked a half a block from my house in the shadows of a sycamore tree. He turned off the headlights. He drew me to him and ran his hand over my breasts; my pathetic inadequate breasts. "You looked beautiful, Faye. All hot and excited. You did a good job, too. Drove like a real pro."

I laughed. "Oh sure."

"I've never seen you like that," he said. He slipped his hand to my thigh and I thought of how he felt when we dipped at the end of a dance.

"I've never driven a semi before," I said.

"Fun, isn't it?" he murmured as he ran his lips over my face then kissed me. I kissed him back.

"I don't know what made me freeze up like that. I could have killed us," I said.

"Don't make your lips so hard," he said.

"What?"

"Relax. Open up a little," he said.

"Like this?" I left my lips unpursed and separated them slightly. We tried it. "Yeah, that's nice," he whispered.

"I'm surprised no one called the police. I was speeding and . . ."

He pressed his lips hard against mine, forcing my lips against my teeth until they hurt. He ran his hands over my body. I put my hand on his to restrain him then let go. Suddenly, he plunged his tongue into my mouth.

I sputtered and yanked away. "Don't do that!"

"Hey, take it easy. Haven't you done that before?"

"You should have warned me. You should have asked me."

"Asked you?" He gave a laugh. "It's not like going all the way," he said. "Come on, Faye, admit it. You liked it."

I opened the door and jumped to the curb. "You should have asked me," I said again and ran home.

Momma came into the bathroom while I was gargling. "What's the matter?"

I spat out the water. "Am I late?"

"No. Where's Willie?"

"He's gone."

"Are you sick?"

"I thought I was going to throw up."

I went to my room and shut the door behind me. I began to undress in the dark. Shame crawled over me like a slimy net as I thought of what Willie had done to me. I had led him on, wanting him to do things to me. I lay awake half the night wondering what had come over me. I fell asleep wondering what would have happened if I had let Willie go on.

I woke up feeling no better than when I went to sleep. I couldn't understand it. I had never felt more joy than when I was driving Willie's semi. And I had wanted to kiss him and be touched. But I was left feeling rotten. I wished I understood—perhaps if I talked to someone. I got out of bed and called Alice on the phone.

"It isn't fun with Willie anymore," I told her.

"Did you get into a fight?" Alice asked.

"Not exactly. Maybe we should have. I can't explain it."

"You're just going through a stage. I get that way sometimes. You'll get over it."

"That's just it. What am I supposed to get over? From what to what? I seem to be waiting for something to happen without knowing what I'm waiting for."

"Honestly, Faye, I don't know what's wrong with you. You and Willie look swell together. You're made for each other."

"Like Clark Gable and Carole Lombard? Like William Powell and Jean Harlow?"

"Are you being sarcastic?"

"I don't mean to be. But don't you think Clark Gable makes Carole Lombard feel happy . . . good . . . something? Are we to feel different because we're not them? I mean, how do you feel about Jimmy?"

"He's okay. Not bad-looking, good personality, pretty smart."

"That's it?"

"What else is there? He's not Clark Gable but do I look like Carole Lombard? You think too much, Faye. Don't think about it so much."

"Maybe you're right. But I think Willie and I should be getting somewhere."

I heard her sigh. "All I can say is, you'd better be sure before you let Willie go. It seems simple to me. Either you want to be his girl or you don't."

As soon as we hung up, I began to formulate the words in my head. I rejected an outright opinion: Willie, your manners are crude. That would be thoughtless. Willie, I get bored easily; it's not your fault. This was no improvement. I thought of an outright lie: Willie, I have a brain tumor and have only six months to live—it's not fair to you; find someone else. That worked for Bette Davis in a movie, but I would have to go on and die. I decided on a straightforward approach: Willie, I don't know why but I don't want to go steady anymore. It's not because of who you are or what you do; it's just not working out.

He was going to be hurt no matter what I said. I only hoped that I would remain as cool as Lily. I did not want to end up like Bertha.

Willie walked in Friday night carrying a crate of Chinese cabbage. He paused at Momma's chair to show her what he had brought.

"A good batch," she declared. "The white looks tender and the leaves are a ripe yellow. Very nice, Willie, thank you. But so much.

We can't eat everything you bring."

"That's okay, Mrs. Chun. Give some away or throw out what you can't use," he said. "Ten-thirty," he promised as we left the house.

After we had settled into the cab of the semi, he asked, "Do you want to drive."

I shook my head.

"I'm not going to kiss you like that unless you want me to," he said.

"That isn't it," I said.

"Are you still mad at me?"

"It's not you. It's me."

"You're tired of me," he said.

"I get so confused," I said. "Maybe I have a brain tumor or something."

"Brain tumor? That's original," he said with a laugh.

"I like you a lot, Willie, but we're locked into each other. You should be free to take out other girls."

"Don't worry about me."

I took a moment to make sure that I wanted to say it. "I should be free to go out with other boys," I said finally.

His lips puffed up as he blew out air. When he had let out all he had, he said, "I get it."

"I'm sorry. . . ." I began, but Willie held up his hand to stop me.

"Don't say it." He sat frozen in silence for a moment then opened the door and jumped to the ground. He came around to my side, offering me his hand as he opened the door. I took, it and dropped to the ground and walked toward the house. He whistled at me and I turned around.

He was standing on the running board looking at me over the roof of the cab. "I'll call you sometime," he said, a broad grin on his face, "after I've killed myself." Still smiling, he slipped into the driver's seat.

Rrrm, rrrm, rrrm. The semi shot away from the curb. I stood there watching as it headed down the street, the blast of the engine fading away. A few moments later I heard the distant bellow of the horn. It brought a smile to my face.

—4—

My weekends were now free. On Thursdays, while Momma was at Seligman's Custom Ties, I turned on the radio and practiced jitterbugging. The Tin Can Hop would be taking place in a few weeks. I would be there without Willie and everyone will know that I'm not his girl anymore.

John came home for the Hop and to spend Thanksgiving with us. He was tan like the boys from San Joaquin Valley and had the muscles to prove he was working hard.

"You look swell, John," I said.

"So healthy-looking," Momma said.

"Beats loading trucks at the market, I'll bet," Harold said.

John beamed. "I like it. Maybe you ought to move to the country, Mom."

"What would I do?"she asked.

John shrugged his shoulders. "Work in the fields or the packing house, I guess."

Momma shook her head. "I can't do that kind of work. Do you have any friends?"

John paused. Blushing slightly, he said, "I have a girlfriend. Beth. She's Mr. and Mrs. Hur's daughter. She's a nice girl."

"Good," Momma said.

"You should have been here last Saturday," Harold told him. "Your buddy, Jimmy, got pie-eyed. Some of the guys took off his clothes and hung them on a telephone pole. When he went climbing after them, they turned the headlights on him."

John and I laughed.

"What's that?" Momma asked.

"What's what, Mom?" Harold asked.

"Pie-eyed," she said.

"Drunk," Harold explained.

She looked at John. "I'm glad you went to Reedley," she said.

Admission to the Hop was a can of food or twenty-five cents. John and I raided the cupboard.

"Some of this stuff has been in here for years," John said, inspecting the contents of the cupboard.

"Momma keeps them in case, for some reason, she can't cook. She never opens a can of anything," I said.

John decided on a can of Franco-American spaghetti and I chose a can of creamed corn.

"We'd better ask Mom if it's okay," I said.

"She'll never miss them," he said.

"We'd better ask anyway," I said.

Momma waved us aside without even looking at us. "Take whatever you want," she said. "You look after Faye, John. Bring her home by ten-thirty."

"Mo-om," I whined. "I'm not a baby. I can take care of myself."

John grinned. "Do what big brother says."

Harold came out of his room. Although he had on his work clothes, he looked dressed-up. His tan shirt and blue denim pants were clean and ironed.

"Are you coming to the dance?" I asked.

"After work, if I'm not too late," Harold replied.

"There's more cans of stuff," John said.

Harold gave a laugh. "I'm not going to carry a can around with me. That's for kids." He took a quarter out of his pocket. "I'm getting in with this." He flipped the coin in the air and caught it the way James Cagney would. He turned to Momma. "I'll see that they get home in time."

I looked at John. "Do what big brother says," I told him.

John and I walked to the U.K.A. building. As always, he stayed several paces ahead of me. He hardly said a word to me but I felt close to him. If I wanted to, I could bring up almost any subject of our past and he would know what I was talking about. And we were bound by nature; nothing could ever change that.

We were a block away from the hall when we heard the music.

"Harry James," he said.

"Artie Shaw," I said.

"Wanna bet?"

"You'll lose. It's "What is This Thing Called Love?". I've been practicing jitterbugging to it."

"You? Better not try it unless you're good."

"What do you mean?"

"Some have it and some don't," he said.

"Have what?"

"Rhythm, the body, the whole thing. Don't go on the floor thinking you're a Ginger Rogers and end up looking like Zazu Pitts."

"I don't know how I look," I said.

"Forget it then."

I did not tell him, but I intended to give it a try.

Alice was at the door collecting the cans. "We're doing great," she shouted above the music. "We have enough to fill at least ten boxes."

"Then what are you going to do with them?" John wanted to know.

"Distribute them to needy people for Thanksgiving," Alice said.

"Like the Salvation Army?" he asked.

"Only to Korean families." She reached around him for the cans of food held out by people standing behind us.

I pushed John on. "We're holding up the line."

"What needy families is she talking about?" he asked me.

"I don't know," I said. "Only Eleanor Song and the people who get them are supposed to know."

"She'll have a tough time finding a Korean family who'll think of themselves as 'needy'."

I nodded. The same thought had occurred to me when the Mugunghwas first voted on the project.

Willie's admission to the Hop were two crates of apples. He gave a nod of his head to John then slid his glance by me. He hung around for awhile then left without dancing.

"Why didn't he stay?" I asked John.

"I guess you broke his heart," he said.

"He doesn't want anyone to think I gave him the brush-off," I said.

"But you did, didn't you?"

"It's not the end of the world. Kids break up all the time," I said. I would have respected Willie if he had stayed and asked me to dance. It would have meant we were still friends.

C.K. stood next to me for a long time before he nudged me with his elbow. He pointed to the floor and spun his fingers around in circles. "Sure," I said and took his hand to walk onto the dance floor. It was a fast piece by Woody Herman. C.K. pushed me away then pulled me back. He spun me around and I began to move my feet in frenzied patterns. Whenever he drew me toward him, we did our fast steps together. I felt all feet at first, but as the beat of the band persisted, I could not help but move in time with the music. When it was over, I was sweating and breathing hard.

"Neat, Faye. You're a great dancer," C.K. said, wiping his brow with the back of his shirt sleeve.

The next piece started right up. It was slow. Without asking me, C.K. slipped his arm around my waist and began dancing. "I didn't know you were that good. How about going to the Christmas dance with me?" he said.

"Sure." I knew Momma would approve: C.K. was from a good family. His father was a well-known Korean patriot.

Three days later, Eleanor Song arrived at the house carrying a carton of food. Alice had told me that with the quarters collected at the dance, turkey, milk, bread, and eggs were added to the canned goods. Miss Song entered the house smiling and set the carton on the dining table in front of Momma.

"Happy Thanksgiving from the Mugunghwa Club," she said.

Momma bit off the thread she had been sewing with and said, "Thank you. What is the box for?"

"Food for Thanksgiving. Faye must have told you about the Tin Can Hop," Miss Song said.

"A dance," Momma said.

"Yes, to collect food for Korean families for Thanksgiving," Miss Song said, still smiling.

"All Korean families?" Momma asked.

When Miss Song's smile changed to a sympathetic expression, I said, "Excuse me. I was cleaning up my room. I'd better go back to what I was doing." I left them to go to my room.

Miss Song should have told me we were on her list. I could have saved her the trip.

I heard Momma ask for a definition of 'needy'. I heard her tell Miss Song that she never asked for charity. Did Miss Song have any idea how humiliating it was to be given charity when it was not asked for? Momma wanted to know.

There was no way I could shut the door to my room without their noticing. John tip-toed into my room from the bathroom. He held his finger to his lips, then fell on my bed and rolled with soundless laughter.

I heard Momma rummage through the carton. "For a Korean family?" she said. Her voice was hard. She began reading the label of a can aloud, slowly because it was written in English. "Fran . . . co American Spa . . . ghe . . . tti."

John pulled the pillow over his face to silence his laughter. I covered my mouth.

Momma continued. "I don't mean to sound ungrateful. I know

you meant well. But I cannot accept this food. You'll have to take it back."

Miss Song sputtered, "I . . . we . . . the girls . . . We didn't expect . . . that is, I don't know what to say, Mrs. Chun."

"Eleanor, imagine yourself in my position. How would you feel? I work hard to take care of my children. I don't ask for anyone's help."

I peeked out the door in time to see Momma handing the box to Miss Song.

John and I waited until Miss Song had left before going to the parlor. I settled onto the couch to read while he went to the kitchen.

Momma sewed in silence, pulling hard when her thread snagged.

John was making a racket, opening cabinet doors and slamming them shut. "Hey, Mom," he yelled, "Where's the Franco-American spaghetti?"

"What?" she asked, then realized what he had said. *"Aek i nom,"* she scolded in Korean. Suddenly, she laughed. "Was that ours?"

John came out of the kitchen. "Gosh, Mom, you act as if we're rich."

"We'd be rich in Korea," the three of us said in unison and laughed.

On Thanksgiving we had roast pork. No one in the family was crazy about turkey.

When John went back to the San Joaquin valley, Harold went with him. The Song Brothers' packing house needed truck drivers.

"If the pay is what Uncle Samsung says it is, I can send you fifty bucks a month," Harold had said.

"Never mind the money. I want you home," Momma had said. But when Harold told her that he hated loading trucks, she let him go.

The house seemed empty without them. Weekends came at a crawl.

On Sundays, I walked to church alone, happy that I would soon be with my friends. One Sunday I left the house earlier than usual, arriving at church before anyone. I sat on the cement steps and waited. I stood up when I saw Alice come running toward me, waving her hand.

"Faye! Have you heard?"

"Heard what?"

"The Japs bombed Pearl Harbor!"

"What? Where's Pearl Harbor?" It must be somewhere in the Far East, I thought.

"Hawaii. It means war for the United States. Everyone's talking about it. Where have you been?"

"Right here," I said, remembering I left the house before Momma had turned on the radio. "What do you mean, war?"

"Just what I said, war. A sneak attack. Typical of the *wae nom*, isn't it?"

The week's Bible lesson fell on deaf ears as everyone tried to comprehend what being at war meant. Afterwards, we stood outside the church and talked about Pearl Harbor, saying things like, "Those stupid Japs," "Punks dropping bombs on the U.S. " "The Americans will sink the 'rising sun' so fast it'll be over before we know it."

We didn't notice the car slowing down along the curb where we stood. "Hey!" a man yelled from the car. We turned to see what he wanted. The brown-haired, blue-eyed man made sure his three companions were paying attention before he growled at us. "You stinkin' Japs. Go back where you came from!"

Alice and I looked at each other. "We're not Japanese," we told him.

Reverend Lim had been standing at the top of the stairs waiting to greet his parishioners. "Go away or I'll call the police," he warned the man.

The man's spit landed at our feet. "Go back where you came from!" As the driver began to speed away, the man yelled, "You fuckin' yellow monkeys!"

Reverend Lim ran down the stairs to join us. "I think you children had better get off the streets. Go straight home and stay in your house. People are in a state of shock. Go home where it is safe."

Alice decided to stay at church and wait for her parents. I hurried down the streets I had walked earlier: past the wood-framed houses with their aprons of green grass, past the picket fences that enclosed naked dormant plants, past garage-high poinsettias bursting with fiery blossoms. I ran until I heard Momma's radio from the street. As soon as I walked in the door, she shouted, "The *wae nom* bombed Pearl Harbor!"

I walked over and turned down the volume of the radio. In the same loud voice she said, "The fools. They can't beat the United States. They'll get what they deserve. At last, Korea will have her independence."

The radio announcer spoke of sneak attacks, ships sinking, fires, deaths, war. He said nothing about Korean independence.

"Momma. War means we could all be killed."

"Oh no, don't you worry. They'll never touch us here. The Americans will smash them right away. The Japanese will be defeated. Now be quiet. I want to hear this," she said, turning up the volume.

It wasn't long before the phone began to ring. Koreans were getting in touch with their countrymen. They talked excitedly as they cursed the Japanese, cheered for the United States, and planned their country's independence. The telephone became inadequate and meetings were called. Momma pushed aside her work to attend. She told me about them later.

"We're going to get together. United Koreans to help the United States. Men are going to volunteer for the national guard. People with money will buy bonds. And we're going to wear badges saying we're Koreans."

"Badges?"

"You don't have to worry. You're an American citizen. But we might be mistaken for Japanese."

"That's nothing new," I said.

"The war is new. We don't want people to think we're our enemy."

Momma looked puzzled when I laughed. "There's an old saying about being one's own enemy," I explained.

"So?"

"Never mind. I don't know why it struck me as being funny. It has nothing to do with this," I said.

The Christmas dance was cancelled because of the war. No one would think of dancing when innocent people were dying. As news of bombings in Europe and invasions in the South Pacific flooded the radio and newsreels. I began to care about people I had never met, some living in places I never knew existed. Patriotism became the paramount virtue in the United States. It required hating the Japanese; I had had a lot of practice. Being at war with Japan meant mainstream Americans and I were on the same side.

Momma's group began to meet again. The smell of Momma's cooking and the sound of excitable voices filled the house once more. The war had given Koreans hope for regaining their country and reasons to organize.

"There's talk about sending the Japanese who live on the west coast to camps," Uncle Min said.

"What camps?" Momma asked.

"Somewhere away from the west coast. The government thinks the *wae nom* are spying for Japan," he said.

"Of course they are!" Uncle Lee declared. "A Japanese is always loyal to his emperor. It's in his blood."

"Does that make him patriotic?" I asked. I could not tell if Uncle Lee was praising them or damning them.

Uncle Yang laughed. "Before December seven, it made him a 'good' Japanese. After December seven, it made him a 'bad' American."

"Aeh!" Uncle Kim snapped. "*Sang noms* before and after any date," he said, calling them eternal bastards.

Uncle Yang took out a memo pad from his pocket and read from his notes. "A picket line at San Pedro to boycott Japanese goods. We need signs and lots of people. I'll be taking a carful. How about you, Faye?"

"What do I have to do?"

"Just walk around carrying a sign that says, 'Boycott Japan'."

"That sounds easy. Why not?" I said.

It was easy. A photographer from the Los Angeles Times was at the pier. He took a picture of me carrying a sign and printed it in the newspaper. Momma clipped it out and sent it to Harold, proud as if I were Joan of Arc.

Anything I did against the enemy made me a heroine. I was glad it wasn't Koreans who bombed Pearl Harbor.

I had gone to my room to read when the men arrived for the next meeting. The subject of 'camps' came up immediately.

"There's talk of sending Koreans to camp with the Japanese," Uncle Min said.

"WHAT?" Uncle Lee barked.

I put down my book to listen.

"As far as the United States government is concerned, we are part of Japan," Uncle Min said.

"They can't do that. We can't let them do that," Uncle Yang said. I knew his eyes were blinking rapidly.

"Ignorance! Plain ignorance!" Uncle Lee spewed. "What do they think we've been screaming about all these years? Why do they think we've been demanding recognition as a separate nation?"

"It won't happen," Uncle Kim's voice was calm. "K. S. Ahn is in Washington talking to congressmen," he said.

"Yes, but will they listen?" Uncle Lee said.

"They'd better. No one's going to catch me going to camp with any Japanese," Uncle Kim said.

"Catch no Korean," Uncle Min said.

"I'm staying right here," Momma said. "No one can make me go anywhere."

"We'd better get everyone to send letters to congressmen and money to Ahn," Uncle Yang said. He paused. Probably writing notes, I thought. "We'll have to distribute the names and addresses of influential congressmen and senators to all Koreans in California," he continued.

"Senators. Good idea. Ahn needs all the support he can get," Uncle Kim said.

"Where's Rhee on this? He's known in Washington. What's he doing?" Uncle Min asked.

"Who cares?" Uncle Lee said. "Ahn's our man."

I was impressed. Letters to congressmen and senators in Washington, D.C. Momma's group had a voice and the United States government was going to hear it.

Later, when the Koreans were informed they were excluded from the 'relocation' program, K. S. Ahn became a hero.

Momma sighed deeply when she heard the news. "Justice, at last. No one will mistake us for Japanese. We will be moving about freely in California."

Bertha was the first to make me realize what it meant. I was surprised to see her at our door.

"I came to say goodbye and to let you know I think the whole thing stinks," she said.

"Where are you going?" I asked, holding the door open for her.

"I'm not going anywhere. You're the one. It's so dumb. Hauling everyone off to a camp because they can't tell who's spying."

Momma called from the table. *"Nu gu wat ne?"*

"It's Bertha," I answered. Bertha beckoned me out and we sat on the porch steps. "Not us. The Japanese," I explained.

"That's not you?"

"No, we're not the same." As soon as I noticed it, I blurted out, "You've had your baby!"

She ran her hand over her stomach. "Do you mean you don't have to go?"

I nodded. "When did you have it?"

She hugged me. "I'm glad. I know you ain't done nothing."

"Was it a boy or girl?" I asked.

"I don't know." She cupped her hands around my ear and whispered. "I had an abortion."

"A what?"

"You know, popped it out of the oven before it was ready." She wrinkled her brows. "I had to. I couldn't take care of it by myself."

"Oh, Bertha. Gee, I'm sorry."

"It's okay. I'll get over it. Want to know something funny? Luke wants to marry me."

"Because you got rid of the baby?"

She laughed. "You're really something. He doesn't know about the baby. It's the war. He'll be making money as a soldier; more if he gets married. 'What the shit,' he said, 'let Uncle Sam buy us some good times'."

"Are you going to?"

She shrugged her shoulders. "At least someone would be taking care of me."

"Do you love him?"

She grabbed my arm and rocked me back and forth. "Girl, do you take me for a fool? He may go away and never come back."

I laughed as I pulled away from her. "He'll come back."

"Yeah, then what?"

"Love and happiness. Ta-rah." I spread out my arms to the vocal fanfare.

"Sure. And ice cream and candy." She put her elbows on the step above us and leaned back. "I don't know what I'm going to do. Maybe I can get a job in a war plant. They can't be fussy, they'll be needing people like me."

"A job? Will they need people like me?"

"If they'll take me, they'll take you."

"Yah! Faye-yah!" Momma called.

Bertha stood up to leave. I took her hand. "Let me know about the job. I'm serious," I said. "My mom can't refuse to let me work if it means I'm helping to win the war."

"I'll let you know," she promised as she backed toward the sidewalk. "I'm sure glad you don't have to go to no concentration camp. Ain't that some confession of stupidity? They can't find the spies so they lock everyone up."

"Yeah," I said.

—5—

My arms were beginning to ache from carrying the books. I was probably taking home more than I could read: it never seemed like too many at the library.

I turned onto Normandie Avenue, a street where stores mingled easily with homes, where Momma shopped for seaweed and miso sauce, where Jane and I used to play hopscotch.

An eerie bleakness had fallen over the street, empty of shoppers and people chatting, no one bowing to anyone. Shops were boarded up and the shades of homes drawn. Starred satin flags hung in some windows, silently signifying there was an American soldier in the Japanese family.

Had they cleared out already, I wondered. Hardly any time had passed since the date was announced. Then I remembered. My books were due on the day they were to leave. Only half the day was over and the streets were deserted, sucked clean of a whole community. The cement curb bordered a cemetery of homes.

I had a sudden urge to see our house on 37th Place, to walk the street where I had lived when our family was whole.

Yukio Watashi's voice cut through the air as he told his father to hurry. Mr. Watashi was scurrying about watering the ferns that grew in the bulbous wooden Kikkoman shoyu tubs. Other members of his family were throwing their belongings onto a truck; not their truck from the nursery but one that was almost as big as Willie's semi, the kind that took me on hayrides to Santa Monica beach huddled with my friends, singing, joking, laughing.

No one on this truck was laughing. People stood jammed together. Some held onto the wooden stakes that fenced them in. Women had tied bandanas around their head and men wore their hats low. I could not tell the Kanos from the Hiroshis.

Yukio's father put away the watering can then climbed onto the truck. The man who had given him a hand closed the tailgate. The truck started slowly, the engine straining under the weight of its cargo.

"Faye!" a voice from the crowd of passengers shouted. "Here!" A hand fluttered in the air. I searched for a face and found it. It was Jane. She was smiling. "I'll see you after the war," she yelled.

A book slipped out of my arms as I tried to wave back. I stooped to pick it up. As I looked for Jane again, the truck disappeared around the corner.

I felt sick.

"Lord, child, don't look so sad. There'll be another one coming along soon. They's not going to forget you," a colored man said as he walked by.

I couldn't think of anything to say. I nodded and walked on to 1337.

A colored woman was watering Momma's dahlias. It was too early in the year for any blossoms, but the plants had multiplied, lining the driveway from the backyard to the front.

"The dahlias must be beautiful when they're in bloom," I said.

The woman smiled at me. "Knocks your eyes out. They just keep coming. I keep dividing them and they just keep coming. Pretty soon I won't have room for anything else," she said, laughing as she returned to her watering.

Mr. Watashi's plants will die, I thought. Dust will gather in Jane's house and the *arare* will go stale. What did that have to do with winning the war, I wondered.

As soon as I got home, I told Momma about deserted Normandie Avenue and the people jammed in the truck. "It was terrible, Momma."

She sighed. "Yes, but they've done worse than that to us," she said solemnly.

"Not Jane. Not Mr. Watashi."

"No, but innocent Korean victims too." She thought a moment then added, "Maybe it isn't as bad as you think. They'll be together and safe."

"Baloney."

She picked up her sewing. "Well, there's nothing we can do about it. Just be thankful we didn't have to go with them."

I had no reply to that. "Do you know what I think?" I said finally. "Some things are just plain bad with nothing good about them at all."

The war didn't end right away like Momma said it would. Harold wanted to work his way up at Song Brothers but when the war showed no signs of ending soon, he quit his job and came home.

"I'm going to join up, Mom. Sooner or later they'll be after me. I'm going to apply for officers' training," he said.

Momma's eyes popped open. "How wonderful!" she had picked up the expression from listening to soap operas.

Harold went to the Air Force recruiting office and made all the arrangements. "I'll be a 'ninety-day wonder'," he told us.

While Harold prepared for the entrance examination, I went around with Uncle Yang to sell war bonds. "I've picked the most beautiful girls," he would say as Alice, Lily, and I climbed into his Model A. We had parents who insisted we represent our people. We put on our Korean dresses and were driven to rallies. The master-of-ceremonies would thank us for singing our 'native' songs and dancing our 'native' dances then called us "good Americans". At Pershing Square, Edward G. Robinson smiled at me.

Alice was the first to drop out when she found a summer job.

"It's at the old Walt Disney studios at Silver Lake," she said. "They're making some kind of instrument for navigators in the Air Force. It's a secret."

"How can it be a secret?" I asked. She seemed to know a lot about it.

"Each person works on a single part. Only the top guys put it together and know how it works. My job is easy. There are still openings, Faye. You should apply."

I thought of asking Momma for permission then decided to apply for the job first.

"It's a secret weapon for the Air Force," I told Momma after I had been hired. "I'll be a drill-press operator. A dollar an hour to start. Alice works there." I held my breath. I had gone over the scene in my head a hundred times, imagining what she would say, rehearsing my reply.

She said nothing for awhile, as if she had to think about her response. Finally, she waved her hand in the air. "Go ahead. But only because it's wartime. I didn't raise you to be a . . . a. . . ."

"Drill-press operator. After school starts, I'll be working on weekends," I added, wondering if I had pushed my luck.

She kept on sewing as if she had not heard me.

Uncle Yang put up a bigger protest. "You girls showed them Korea. That's more important than being a . . . a . . ."

"Drill-press operator. I'm sorry, Uncle Yang, but I've already taken the job."

"What am I going to do? Koreans should be represented," he said.

"Call Eleanor Song. She'll find some girls. Prettier ones than Alice and me."

He could not deny it so he laughed.

The day arrived when Harold was to take the examination. I gave him the victory sign when I left for work. When I walked in the door that evening, he was home.

"How did you do?" I asked.

"Okay, I think. It didn't seem too hard."

I crossed my fingers in the air. "Come on, God, be on our side."

Momma laughed. "Don't act silly," she said.

As each day passed, we grew more and more anxious. Finally, Momma told Harold, "Call them, call them. Ask them why they're taking so long."

"I can't do that," Harold said. "You're talking about the United States of America."

"Then I'll call," she said, pushing aside her sewing.

"Never mind. I'll do it," he protested, beating her to the phone.

He was on the line a long time. Then we heard him say. "Hallelujah."

Harold smiled as he told us about it. "The guy wasn't supposed to tell me. I told him I was losing sleep. He said the letter must be tied up in the mail. They went out last week. I said, 'Jesus, what if mine got lost?' 'I see your point,' he said. He left me hanging there while he checked. When he came back, he said, 'You know a slip of the lip can sink a ship?' 'My lips are sealed,' I told him. He said, 'You can sleep now, kid. You're among the top ten percent.'"

"Wow!" I exclaimed.

"Top ten percent?" Momma sat back in her chair and laughed.

"We celebrate." She reached into the pocket of her apron and pulled out a five dollar bill. "Port wine. It's sweet." She handed the money to Harold and waved him out the door.

He was back right away with a bottle of wine and a bag of potato chips. Momma told him to keep the change. We drank out of the crystal punch cups, refilling them until the wine was gone. Momma had to put her sewing aside. She would laugh over nothing and her stitches went out of line. I felt as if I were on fire. My cheeks had turned a flaming red. I saluted before I said anything to Harold. After awhile, I could not say anything without giggling.

"Hey, wait a minute. I've just remembered something," Harold said. He went to his room and came back with the Edwards Military Academy cap perched on his head. He began marching around the room.

Momma laughed so hard I thought she was going to fall out of her chair. "*Aigoo, aigoo,*" she gasped, holding her sides.

"Take it easy, Mom." Harold said, pulling the cap from his head.

She finally caught her breath. "I forgot all about that hat. It's so small for you. It's just a toy." Her eyes began to glisten. "You'll have a real one now."

I had collapsed with laughter, sapped of energy. "I'm sleepy. I think I'll go to bed."

"I think I'll go out for awhile," Harold said.

"It's so late," I noted.

"Never mind," Momma told me.

After Harold left, I asked her, "Why did you let him go out? It's late."

"He's not a boy anymore," she answered.

I lay in bed thinking about our celebration, about Harold, Momma, and me laughing it up. It wasn't something I would say aloud, but war had its advantages.

I was about to leave for work when the letter arrived from the Air Force. I waited to share Harold's big moment. He opened the envelope neatly with a knife. "I'm going to have this framed," he said, grinning. As he read the letter, the grin faded from his face. "It says I didn't get in," he said with gulp.

"Maybe they've sent you the wrong letter," I offered.

"It has my name on it."

"You go to them. Tell them they made a mistake. Go right now,"

Momma ordered.

"Cheez, Mom, take it easy," he said.

"It has to be a mistake. The man wouldn't have lied to you," I insisted.

Harold chewed on his lower lip. "I wonder what happened."

"Go find out. Take care of it right now," Momma demanded.

"Jesus, Mom, quit pushing!" Harold snapped. He tucked the letter into his pocket. "Shit," he said under his breath and walked out of the house.

I had no desire to go to work. I kicked off my shoes and called in sick.

The senior officer told Harold, "Competition was very keen. You were close, but we had to draw the line somewhere."

The junior officer took Harold aside. "I didn't lie to you. It has nothing to do with your score. Orientals are not allowed in officers' training. I didn't know. It's nothing personal."

"Why did you let me take the exam?" Harold asked.

The junior officer shrugged. "It's your constitutional right."

Harold's voice quavered when he told us about it later. I had never seen him look so forlorn.

"Did you tell him off?" I asked.

He scoffed. "What good would that do?"

I expected Momma to explode. I wish she had. She just kept on sewing without saying a word, stopping now and then to sigh deeply. She went to bed that night and did not get up the next day. She had no cough or temperature, but I stayed home to look after her. Every time I asked, "What's wrong, Momma?", she waved me away and turned her back to me. I cooked meat and vegetables the way she had taught me, but she pushed the dish aside and ate only rice gruel and *kimchee*. Harold wasn't eating much either. On the third day, he said, "It's killing her."

"My cooking?" I thought that would at least bring a smile.

"Naw," he growled, "figure it out." He got up from the table. "I've gotta do something," he said and left the house.

Early in the morning of the fourth day, Momma got out of bed and told me I had better go to work.

"I don't know if I want to work anymore. Even if it is wartime," I said.

"We have no choice. United States has to win the war or there's no hope for Koreans." She tied the belt to her robe tighter.

"You've lost weight," I told her.

"The Americans are better people than our enemy," she said, ignoring my comment. She poured herself a cup of coffee. "No country is perfect."

When Harold told her that he had joined the Signal Corps, she said, "Good," then cried.

John wrote to say that after Beth's graduation he was going to join the Navy.

"Don't bother to tell him what happened," Harold said.

Willie dropped us a line from Chicago. He had joined the Navy to "get out of hicktown and see the world".

I went back to work and continued to drill holes in precisely the same place on identical pieces of dull black metal.

S E V E N

I t was late in the year to be planting dahlias. When I brought them
home yesterday, Momma said they should go into the ground as
soon as possible. The tubers were on special at the nursery, twenty-
five cents a dozen, on sale because the tags identifying their variety
and color had fallen off.

"We'll have to wait until late summer to see what we have,"
Momma had said. Then she had chuckled. "It will be like having a
baby."

I stood at the back screendoor sipping on a cup of hot chocolate,
watching her turn the soil. "Do you want me to help?" I asked.

She shook her head. "No, this is my job."

She had time to garden now; money was coming in from Harold,
John, and me. She had been emancipated from the dining table,
free to set aside her sewing without fear of unpaid bills.

"Can I bring you some coffee?" I offered.

"Later. I want to get these into the ground."

Da da-da da da, two bits.

"Someone's at the the door," I told her. "I'll see who it is." I set my
cup in the sink as I walked through the kitchen.

I opened the door to Willie who stood with his arms spread open.
"Surprise!" he said. In his sailor suit, he made me think of Raggedy
Andy.

"What are you doing in L.A.?" I held the door open for him.

272

"The U.S. Navy said, 'Take a few days off, sailor. You deserve it'. So here I am." His teeth glistened as he grinned. It was catching; I smiled at him.

"Momma's in the backyard," I said, leading the way. "She'll be happy to see you." Pushing on the back screendoor, I called to Momma. "Guess who's here."

She looked up, cupping her hands over her eyes, shielding them from the slant of the morning sun. "Willie! My, you look handsome. But you've lost weight."

He took off his cap. "Navy food, Mrs. Chun. I can't eat the stuff."

"Stay for lunch. I'll fix *nang mien* for you," she said.

Willie's eyes grew wide. "Really? My kingdom for a bowl of *nang mien*."

Momma laughed as she dropped her hand from her brow to push the trowel into the dirt. "You can have it for nothing. How do you like Chicago?"

"Can't compare to L.A. I'm stationed in San Diego now," he coughed.

"There are Koreans in Chicago," she said.

"Not like L.A. I went to a restaurant owned by Koreans and to church. The two places I was told to go if I wanted to see Koreans."

"Good. Then you had a chance to eat Korean food," she said.

"At church, but not at the restaurant. They served roast beef, boiled vegetables—the kind of stuff I can get in the mess. I guess no one goes to a restaurant to eat Korean food," he said.

Momma nodded. "You have to grow up with *kimchee*."

"Is Chicago pretty?" I asked.

"Pretty? Parts of it, I guess. It's cold. They don't call it the 'windy city' for nothing."

"What's it like? Is it clean?" I asked.

"No. Dirty brick buildings. The snow falls white but melts to a brown slush."

"A whole city of dirty brick buildings?" I tried to imagine it.

"Not where the rich live."

"Places like Beverly Hills?" I wanted to know.

He shrugged. "Mansions are mansions wherever they are." He walked over to stand by Momma. "What is that you're planting, Mrs. Chun?"

"We don't know. We'll find out in a few months." She swept her hands in front of her. "This will be covered with flowers. Maybe yellow, maybe orange, maybe red. . . ."

"Maybe lavender, maybe white," I added.

"Why maybe?" Willie asked.

"No labels," Momma said. "Faye took a chance."

"I got them cheap. The tags had fallen off," I explained. "Momma loves dahlias."

She nodded. "Generous flowers. Like peonies in Korea. Take so little, give so much. And always more each year."

There was a small explosion in my memory. "I forgot to tell you! You know the dahlias you planted at 1337? They've multiplied. They're growing along the driveway and in the front yard."

"When did you see them?" she asked.

"It was when I saw Jane and all of them on the truck. My God, it must have been two years ago."

"Two years?" Willie laughed, setting off a series of coughs. "What a memory, Faye," he gasped.

"I must have been trying to forget that day. Would you like some coffee?"

"Sounds good," he said, catching his breath.

"Are you ready, Momma?"

"No, not yet. You go ahead."

While Momma gardened, Willie and I sat on the steps sipping from our cups.

"I was hoping some of the old gang would be around but everyone's off to war," he said.

"Jimmy's been overseas for months. Alice said he should be home soon. John must be somewhere in the Pacific. His A.P.O. is San Francisco. Harold's is Seattle. We think he's in Alaska. He sent home some dehydrated soy sauce left behind by the Japanese. It's pretty good."

"Dehydrated soy sauce?" Willie shook his head. "What'll they think of next?"

"The last I heard, C.K. was at Fort Ord," I said.

"I know where he is," Willie said. "He's in officers' training. One of those 'ninety-day wonders'."

"They don't take orientals," I said.

"They do now. They'll take anything now."

"Are you sure?" I lowered my voice so Momma wouldn't hear. "Harold was in the top ten percent but they didn't take him because he's Korean."

"What? Jesus," Willie said with disgust.

"Keep it down. I don't want Momma to hear."

"That's lousy," he rasped. "His timing was off."

"Not his, the Air Force. He's staff sergeant in the Signal Corps."

"Hey, Mrs. Chun," he called. "Faye tells me Harold's a staff sergeant. You've got a smart boy there."

Momma nodded as she sidled over to plant another tuber. "From private to staff sergeant. I'm proud of him. I'm proud of John too."

"The only one left is Faye. Maybe she should join the WAVES," he said. He grinned at me then turned his head to cough.

"You must have a cold," I said.

He nodded, his shoulders bouncing from the spasms.

"Faye has to stay home until she gets married," Momma said.

"Who says so?" I asked.

"I do. In Korea, children do what their parents say. Parents do everything for their children and the children respect them for it." She buried the last tuber in the ground. "I thought I taught you that."

"I'll never get out of L.A.," I whined.

"Uncle Sam will look after her. Pay for her travel, too. Women who join the service don't have to go into combat. They're usually given a desk job," Willie told Momma.

"No, not Faye." She stood up and slapped the dirt from her hands. "Nice girls stay home."

I groaned. "So do cats and dogs."

"Never mind," she said, stretching her back. She turned on the faucet, adjusted the nozzle to a fine spray, then began watering the newly planted tubers.

"Your mom sure is stubborn," Willie said. I rolled my eyes up. "If it hadn't been for the war, I would have been stuck in Reedley for the rest of my life."

"Sometimes I wish I could pack up and leave. But I wouldn't know where to go. I ask myself, how would I live? I tell myself that no matter where I go, I'll end up with a job reserved for 'inexperienced oriental female.' Not many places call for a drill-press operator."

"Join the service. Let them take care of you," he said.

"Then Momma would be alone and I'd be away from my friends."

"Your mom will get used to it. Don't be a scaredy-cat. Don't you want to serve your country?"

"My country? Strange isn't it? I've never been able to say, 'my country'. I've always said, 'the United States' or 'the government'."

He put his cup down beside him. "I have trouble saying it, too."

Momma dowsed the rest of the garden before turning off the faucet. "It's time for me to start the *nang mien,*" she said and went into the house.

Willie's brow grew moist as the sun beamed directly above us. He pulled out a handkerchief from the pocket of his overshirt. "There's no place to put anything in these monkey suits," he complained as he wiped his face. He shook out the hankerchief then spread it on the step to dry. "I've been thinking of going AWOL."

"What? You can't do that. They'll put you in jail!"

"They'll have to catch me first."

"That's crazy, Willie," I said. "It's your cold. As soon as you get over your cold, you'll change your mind."

"Do you know what they've got me doing? They've got me ordering produce," he scoffed. "I ask them to show me the world and they've got me ordering produce."

"Didn't they give you a choice?"

He gave a laugh. "Honestly, Faye, you're something. Ever heard of 'snafu'? You know, situation normal all fucked up? Don't look at me like that. I didn't make it up. The way it works is, you sign up for ship's mechanic if you want produce. It goes along with all kinds of stupidity. Figure this one out. If a guy can say 'Chollie', why can't he say 'Willie'?"

"If you feel that way about it, why did you suggest I join up?" I asked.

"That's different. The service is easier on women."

I laughed at him. "You're really something, Willie. You tell me to go into the sevice while you're thinking about ways to get out."

A gust of wind blew his handkerchief off the step. He grabbed at it but missed and chased it around the yard before catching it. He fell to the ground, laughing and coughing at the same time. He was like a child yet had the rough cut of an old man. I couldn't understand the sadness that came over me, a sensation without a label, like crying when happy, or smiling when sad.

"Willie, you know what you should have done?" I said.

"What?"

"You should have signed up for produce."

Willie belched behind his hand then wiped his face on his sleeve. "The pepper's getting to me," he said. He was the only one sweating.

"Eat more, Willie. You're too thin. I'm going to boil ginseng for you. Your cough sounds bad," Momma said.

"No thanks. I can't eat another bite. And never mind the ginseng. I can't take that stuff. It's too bitter," he said.

Momma took his bowl from him and went into the kitchen. "Just a little more. I'll boil the ginseng later so it won't spoil the flavor of the *nang mien*."

Willie looked at me. "How do you stop a woman like that?"

"You don't. Don't eat anymore unless you want to. She'll boil the ginseng whether you want it or not. She thinks even the vapors help."

Willie started on the second bowl with enthusiasm, but after two bites, he began to pick at the food with his chopsticks. "It's really great, Mrs. Chun, but I'm too full to eat anymore."

"Don't force him, Mom." I stood up to clear the table. "Go sit on the couch, Willie. I'll open the front door. The breeze will cool you off."

After I washed the dishes, Momma put the ginseng on the stove to simmer before she sat at the dining table to sew.

"Is it okay if I play some records?" I asked.

"Nice ones. None of that crazy music," she answered.

Willie requested 'Moonlight Serenade'. "You'll like that, Mrs. Chun."

I put my finger to my lips to warn him to keep silent and showed him the label: Count Basie's 'One O'clock Jump'. As soon as I put it on, Momma shouted, "Yah! *Tuki shil ta!*" declaring she didn't want to hear it.

Willie and I laughed. He went to her. "May I have this dance?"

She waved him away. "That's not dancing music."

I took the needle off the record. "Jitterbugging is for savages," I said before she had a chance to say it.

"Foxtrot looks nice," she said. "Clara tried to teach me but I'm no good."

"Maybe you didn't have the right partner," Willie said. "Maybe you should dance with someone like me." He pointed his thumbs at himself.

"He was a captain," Momma said. "Captain of the Taiyo Maru."

Willie whistled. "A captain? That's out of my class."

"He said, it's not in our blood," Momma said.

"What does blood have to do with it? Me and Faye can cut a rug as good as anyone. Would you like us to show you?" he asked.

"No," she said. "You'll just raise dust."

"One thing I learned in the Navy is that anything the white boys can do, I can do. I'm even smarter than a lot of them," he said with confidence.

"He didn't mean smarter or dumber," she said. "American music doesn't make me feel like dancing. Korean music makes me feel like dancing. It's in my blood. That's what he means."

"Korean music doesn't make me feel anything," Willie said.

Momma clacked her tongue. "That's too bad."

She smiled when I said, "I feel like dancing when I hear Korean music, only I don't know how." Her smile faded when I said, "American music makes me feel like dancing, too. The more I do it, the better I get."

I promised Momma we wouldn't raise dust and Willie and I danced to 'Moonlight Serenade'. His hands were damp and he stepped on my feet a couple of times. He confessed that he was tired. "The next time I come, we'll go out dancing," he promised.

—2—

Over a month passed before I heard from Willie. "Still in San Diego," he wrote. "I've decided to give the medics a chance. They're looking me over. Keep up the morale of a serviceman and drop me a line."

Momma frowned. "I hope he's all right," she said.

Then one day, Willie's letter came from San Fernando Valley.

"He has T.B.?" Momma whispered the word.

"Yes. Jimmy's back from Italy. He's driving Alice and me out to see Willie."

"No. You mustn't go. It's a bad sickness."

"They wouldn't allow visitors if it were dangerous."

"No. You can't go."

"It's too late, Momma. I've already told them I was going. They'll be here soon. I have to get ready," I said and went to my room to get dressed.

Alice and I had decided that it was our patriotic duty to be as glamorous as possible for the 'boys' in the hospital. I rummaged through the crumpled boxes in the closet until I found the one I was looking for and blew off the dust. I took off the lid and pulled out the white ankle-strap shoes. They were still like new. With my first paycheck, Alice and I had gone shopping. She had encouraged me to buy the shoes. "Makes you look sexy," she had said. Momma had never seen them; I had never had the nerve to wear the shoes.

Wobbling in the three-inch heels, I went to the mirror. I brushed my hair until the curls fell loosely to my shoulders, then pinned a cluster of artificial blue forget-me-nots behind my ear. I rubbed ruby red lipstick over my lips then stepped back to see if my slip was showing. My heart began to pound as I braced myself to face Momma.

She had unraveled a length of thread and was biting it off when she cast her eyes over me. "Where did you get those shoes?" The thread hung on her lip.

"I bought them when Alice and I went shopping. Ankle-strap shoes are the latest thing." I hobbled to the window to look for Jimmy's car.

"Nice girls are careful how they look or they might give the wrong impression. I tell you for your own good, your shoes look cheap," she said.

I held onto the arm of the couch to work my way to its seat. "Alice said they looked good on me," I said as I sat down.

Momma licked the end of the thread and slipped it through the eye of the needle. "You ask me or Alice?"

I gave myself time to work up my nerve. I swallowed, then said, "I asked me."

She bit her lip and yanked at a knot in the thread, breaking it. "Look what you've made me do." She pulled a new length of thread from the spool. "I've spent my life at this table, sat here until my back screamed with pain, stayed at this table so I would be here to raise you right. But you pay no attention. Do you think I gave my life to this kind of work so that you could end up a bad girl?"

I sank into my seat. I knew that she was getting ready to go through everything she had to endure since Papa died. She had suffered enough when he was alive, but that was nothing compared to what his dying had done to her. I had heard it all when Harold's friends brought him home drunk the night of his high school graduation and again when John ran away. "Please don't go through all that, Momma. These shoes don't make me a bad girl. Do you want me to look like some goon no boys will look at?"

She threw down her sewing. Her words came rushing out in Korean. "Are you so empty-headed that you don't know what I'm talking about? Good girls do not advertise themselves to men!"

The blood rose to my cheeks. "They're just a pair of shoes! Why do you throw in all that other junk?" I held back my tears.

"Somebody has to tell you. I tell you for your own good."

"Do you know what Willie said? He said I should get out of here and see the world. He said he would have been stuck like me if he hadn't joined the Navy."

"You listen to Willie or you listen to me?" she demanded to know.

I didn't want to listen to either one of them. "I'm listening to everyone. That's my problem." Through the marquisette curtains, I saw Jimmy's car pull up to the curb. "They're here. I have to go. We're going out to eat later. I'll be home before midnight," I said.

She picked up her sewing. "Why tell me?" she said.

I didn't answer. She wasn't really asking.

Jimmy whistled as I walked to the car. "Now I know what I was fighting for," he said.

Alice punched him. "That's what you said to me!"

"There's a war on," he said. "I have to share myself with everyone."

Alice scooted over as I climbed in next to her. "It's good to see you, Jimmy," I said.

Alice gave me a nudge. "I told you those shoes do something for you."

"My mom thinks so too. We had an argument over them."

"Mother knows best," Jimmy quipped. "You look like a million bucks."

"Million bucks," Alice mimicked him. "Since you've been back you're full of those dumb sayings."

"That's the way people talk. No lie. I know. I've seen the world," he said, pulling away from the curb.

"Is that what you learn when you see the world?" She looked at me. "I think I'll stay home."

I laughed. "That's a thought."

"Oh you babes in the woods. You have to get out there to appreciate what you have here," he said.

"Thanks, Jimmy," Alice said.

He grinned. "You can pay me later, baby."

She punched him again. "Don't be icky."

"You two make a lovely couple," I said.

They laughed.

San Fernando valley was an hour or more away from the center of Los Angeles. As we left the city, the air grew hotter. My arm began to stick to Alice's.

"I don't know how anyone can live in San Fernando. It feels over ninety already," I said.

"It will be, when we get there, maybe even a hundred," Jimmy said.

"If I ever leave L.A., it won't be to move to San Fernando Valley," I said.

"This is nothing. You don't know what hot is until you've been overseas and in a tank on a day like this." He held his hand outside the window against the wind. "At least the air is moving."

"You must have drunk gallons of water," Alice said.

"You can't drink the water. Not from the tap. It isn't safe."

"What do you do when you're thirsty?" I asked.

"Drink treated water or bottled stuff. Still get the runs. Half the places don't have flush toilets. If they do, half of them don't work," he said.

"But their civilization's older than America," I said, thinking he exaggerated.

"That's probably why," he said. "Nothing beats the good old U.S.A. If anyone doesn't think so, he ought to go back where he came from."

"That could be everyone but the Indians," I said.

"I'm saying, if a person doesn't like it here, he ought to leave." He was dead serious.

"This is supposed to be a free country. You can say what you like . . . or don't like," I said.

Alice cut us off with a slice of her hands. "No more talk. It's too hot to think."

Alice always accused me of making too much of everything. "Why all the talk?" she would say. "Just make up your mind and do it." I once suggested that she read Plato. "Ugh! Dull's-ville," she had retorted. "I had to read some of his stuff in Civics."

"Men are out there giving their lives for people here at home. They don't deserve traitors," Jimmy said.

"Who's a traitor?" I demanded to know.

"Cut it out, you two," Alice snapped.

"Okay, okay," Jimmy said. "Sorry, Faye. Let's kiss and make up." He puckered up his lips.

That brought another punch from Alice. "You don't have to go from one extreme to the other."

"Later, Jimmy," I said.

We laughed.

The hot wind of the Valley began to carry the scent of orange blossoms. The fragrance followed us to the entrance of the sanitarium. Inside, disinfectants obliterated all smells. We hushed our voices as a nurse led us to Willie's room. She held the door open for us.

As we filed in, Willie lifted himself onto his elbows. The effort brought beads of perspiration to his brows. His skin pulled at his bones. His body had shrunk even more than when I last saw him. I was stunned.

"Hey, man, whatcha doin'? Come on, get out of that bed. Let's go dinin' and dancin'." Jimmy's joviality seemed forced.

"I'm with you, man, I'm with you." Willie fell back on his pillow coughing.

The nurse motioned us to chairs that had been placed away from Willie's bed, then left. I took the artificial flowers from my hair and walked over to place them on the bedstand. "Here, these are for you."

"You look real nice, Faye. A sight for sore eyes." Willie covered his cough with his hand. I backed toward the chair and sat down, tucking my feet under the seat, hiding my white ankle-strap shoes. In the bleak hospital room, the shoes seemed garish. Willie went on. "I know I promised to take you dancing, but you know how the Navy is. Orders are orders." He smiled, his beautiful white teeth dulled by his sallow skin. "How's your mom? Have the dahlias bloomed yet?"

"They're just beginning to open up. The next time you come to the house, they'll put on a real show," I said.

"What are dahlias?" Jimmy asked.

"Flowers, dummy," Alice said.

Jimmy looked at Willie. "How do you like that? She called me dummy. I've been fighting the war for her and she calls me 'dummy'."

Willie laughed. Everytime he laughed, he ended up coughing. "How was it over there?" he rasped.

Jimmy shrugged his shoulders. "Some good, some bad. Except for the food and lousy water, it wasn't bad. Except for the Fascists, the scenery was good. But I'm glad to be back in the good old U.S.A."

Willie nodded. "You're back. You've seen the world and you've made it back." He closed his eyes for a moment. When he opened them, a teardrop fell to his pillow.

"Are we making you tired?" I asked.

He shook his head. "I like your being here. The days have become too damn long for me."

"We'll come whenever I'm in town," Jimmy promised. "I'll drive the girls over."

"Great!" Willie exclaimed. Sweat popped out on his forehead.

We waited for him to cough. The conversation stalled; no one was sure whose turn it was to speak. I thought hard for something to say. Talking about events Willie had missed seemed cruel and I found myself wanting to avoid talking about the future.

"How's the food?" I asked.

"I can't eat the stuff," Willie said.

"Would they allow us to bring something?" I asked.

He shook his head. "Everything has to be sterilized."

Alice gasped. "Is it okay for us to be here?"

"Sure," Willie said. "You can't give me anything."

She didn't seem to know what to say to that.

Willie laughed. "I'm just kidding. Don't worry, you won't catch anything. I'll cough at the wall."

"I didn't mean . . . ," she began.

"Forget it," he said, struggling to finish what he had to say before he coughed.

I looked at Alice to see if we should leave.

Willie slipped lower under the covers. "It was swell of you guys to come."

Alice signaled Jimmy.

"We'll be seeing you, Willie. Should we check with the hospital before we come?" Jimmy asked. "In case they're giving you a bath or something," he quickly added.

Willie nodded then turned toward the wall and pulled the covers over his shoulders. "Hang on to those shoes, Faye. We'll be going dancing."

I didn't feel like laughing, but I did.

—3—

The white dahlias lay on the sink. Momma had covered the stems with a damp cloth to keep them from wilting. I opened the Shopping News to wrap the flowers. A photograph of a colored soldier caught my eye. Private First Class Lucerne Luke, the caption said. He had been cited for bravery posthumously. There was a second photograph of his wife accepting the medal. I looked closely at the face under the wide-brimmed hat. It was Bertha. She looked beautiful. She had been married to a war hero. Bertha was the only girl I knew who took hold of life and made things happen. "Girl, don't you know anything?" she always said to me. Remembering made me smile. I tore out the page with the pictures and set it aside, then wrapped the dahlias in the newspaper.

Momma had been disappointed when so many of the blossoms turned out to be white.

"I like them," I had said. "They remind me of weddings."

"In my dream, before your Papa died, he was in white, but the flowers in the garden were all different colors," she had said.

I turned on the radio to listen while I waited for Jimmy and Alice. A voice, loud and excited, said, "Glenn Miller is missing in action. The plane he was in disappeared this morning." The announcer promised to interrupt the program if there were any new developments. He then put on a recording of 'Moonlight Serenade'. I turned the dial. Every station was paying tribute to the celebrity war hero, playing music that stirred memories of Willie. I turned off the radio and sat listening to Momma scrape the bamboo rake across the backyard until Jimmy's car pulled up to the curb.

"I'M GOING, MOMMA," I yelled, picking up the dahlias.

The radio was on in Jimmy's car. The program was interrupted repeatedly with unchanging report of the bandleader's disappearance.

"Isn't it terrible?" Alice said.

I nodded. "Maybe he'll be found, though," I said.

At every newsstand, bold headlines shouted the news of Glenn Miller's disappearance as if he were already dead. Willie had died of tuberculosis and Momma whispered the word.

"How do you like the wreath?" Jimmy asked, pointing his thumb at the back seat. "C.K. sent some money. Alice and I chipped in for the rest."

A life preserver of white carnations encircled an anchor of dark blue cornflowers. Red roses filled the spaces in between. A white satin ribbon stretched across the wreath with "Seaman 1st Class-Willie Koo" printed in gold.

"That's really nice," I said.

"I called Willie's uncle to see if there was anything we could do. He said Mr. Yun is handling everything," Jimmy said.

"Yun? Lily's father?" I said. "Why him?"

"I didn't ask," Jimmy said. "The uncle's not an easy man to talk to."

"Oh," I said. Odd, I thought, and disappointing. I wanted Willie to have a nice funeral: he hated K.Y. Yun.

"He told me to go directly to the cemetery. No chapel." Jimmy said.

"Isn't that strange?" Alice said.

"Yes," I said. But I knew the Korean community would not be turning out for Willie's funeral; he was an illegitimate child. His uncle or Mr. Yun had probably thought of that.

When we reached the gates of the cemetery, I unwrapped the dahlias and removed the cloth from the stems.

"They're beautiful," Alice said.

"We planted them when Willie came to the house. I mean, my mom was planting them when. . . ." Tears suddenly welled in my eyes and fell onto the petals. I swallowed hard to keep my voice steady. "We were having fun. Planting blind. Waiting for the surprise." My voice broke. The book said that etiquette required complete control by the bereaved woman. Willie had asked about the word, 'bereaved'.

Alice put her arms around me. "I didn't know you felt that way about him."

"I didn't. That's not it. Oh, God," I sobbed. I didn't know what it was. I wiped the tears away but more kept coming. The book said that death had lost much of its terror and was accepted with 'simple fortitude by sensible people'. The author never knew Willie and me. We had laughed at the required behavior. "Liar," I said.

Jimmy got out of the car. "You chicks come when you're ready." He took the wreath and left.

"Liar? Who?" Alice asked.

"Not you," I said, gaining control of myself. "Not anyone in particular." I pulled out a handkerchief from my pocket and blew my nose. "I'm okay now," I said and opened the door to climb out.

Reverend Lim and two of Willie's Navy buddies were standing at the graveside with Jimmy. Willie's uncle stood alone at a distance as did two white-gloved men from Pearson's Mortuary. K.Y Yun was nowhere in sight.

Jimmy had placed the wreath at the head of the coffin, a richly carved coffin with ornate golden handles, a coffin befitting the son of a wealthy man, a man like K.Y. Yun.

I prayed with Reverend Lim that Willie be received in Heaven for eternity. He had made it out of hicktown forever, I thought. I laid the dahlias at Willie's feet then broke the rules of etiquette to sit in Jimmy's car while the men from Pearson's Mortuary lowered Willie into the ground.

E I G H T

A downpour and no galoshes. I was caught in front of the Fair Deal Grocery Store. The rain drummed on the taut canvas awning overhead, poured in sheets over the edge, and splashed at my feet. I backed up between the red Delicious apples and the rust-green Winter Nelis pears. Damn! The burrs of a wooden lug box caught my stockings. A thread snapped and ran as I pulled away. I had queued up for the stockings, stood in line with people who grumbled about wartime shortages to buy stockings that sagged and did nothing for my legs. There was no longer a need to stand in the line for anything. Peacetime goods were coming back; the war was over.

The downpour suddenly turned into a drizzle. I tossed a dime on the counter, grabbed a newspaper, held it over my head, then made a run for it. The rain had collected at the curb and formed a rushing stream. It was impossible to cross the street without stepping into the torrent. Galoshes would have been of little use.

Uncle Yang's Model A stood at the curb shining under the deluge. They must be at it again, I thought. With the war over, Momma and her friends met to plan the business of running Korea. They damned the 38th parallel that divided their country, argued the merits of communism and democracy, discussed the policies of Truman and Stalin, and judged the brilliance and stupidity of Korean leaders. And they talked of going home.

The branches of the Christmas tree screened the living room

from the street. Some branches had more ornaments than others, throwing the tree out of balance. Momma and I had decorated the tree from inside the house; it looked better from there.

There were still too many red lights on the right, I thought. I had told Momma but she didn't listen. When the tinsel garland broke, I thought it was our chance to throw out the motley assortment of ornaments and have an elegant tree: white spruce with blue lights and blue ornaments like the ones in the windows at Bullock's. But Momma tied the silver garland together and the tree looked as it has ever since I can remember.

It doesn't matter, I told myself as I ran up the steps to the porch. This would be our last Christmas without Harold and John.

I dropped the newspaper to the floor. It hit with a splat. I tugged at my sopping shoes and finally got them off. I carefully pulled away the wet stockings from between my toes.

It was strangely quiet inside, not the usual shouting and laughing when there was a meeting. I placed my shoes on the newspaper and entered the house in my stockinged feet. A rush of warm air and the smell of Momma's cooking greeted me.

"Oh ho, here she is!" Uncle Yang sounded like Santa Claus. "Soaking wet. Come over here and stand by the heater." He grabbed my hand and led me to the fake fireplace where orange-blue flames danced along the row of gas jets.

"Hi, Uncle Yang. Where is everybody?" I shook the hem of my skirt. Droplets of water sizzled on the hot stone heater, sending warm air up my thighs. "I must be a mess," I said, looking in the mirror over the mantel. I was startled to see a strange face staring back at me. "Oh," I said, dropping the hem of my skirt. He had been standing there all the time, hidden by the door when I came in.

"This is Daniel Lee, the son of an old friend of mine. He's from Connecticut," Uncle Yang explained.

"How do you do?" Daniel Lee said without a trace of accent. There wasn't a wrinkle in his khaki uniform.

I turned around to face him. "Hi," I said.

Momma came rushing out of the kitchen. "Faye, your hair's a mess. You look terrible!"

"It's pouring outside, Mom," I said.

"Go change into some dry clothes and comb your hair," she said.

"I'm drying off here."

"Have you met Daniel?" She smiled at him.

"Yes. What's for dinner? I'm starved. Alice and I are going to a movie tonight."

A look of distress came over Momma's face.

"Faye." Uncle Yang walked over to put his arm around Daniel's shoulder. He had to stretch, he was a head shorter than his young friend. "Daniel's been in town looking up relatives and old friends of the family. He's leaving tomorrow. He doesn't know any young people in Los Angeles. I thought you could show him around."

"Oh. Well, Alice and I planned to go to a movie," I began to explain.

"I don't want to interfere with your plans," Daniel said quickly.

"Oh! No interference!" Uncle Yang assured him.

"Faye will be glad to show you around," Momma added.

"Your momma said there's some kind of dance tonight. That would be a perfect place for Daniel to meet young Koreans," Uncle Yang said. "I promised his father I would look after him."

"I wasn't planning on going," I said.

"Now you have someone to take you," Uncle Yang smiled at Daniel.

"No really, I don't want to impose on anyone," Daniel insisted.

"You're only young once, my boy. You kids go out and enjoy yourselves. Use my car." Uncle Yang pulled the keys from his pocket and pressed them into Daniel's hand.

Daniel's face turned red. "Would you like to go to dinner?" he asked me. "Your friend is invited too."

I hadn't noticed his soft elongated eyes before. They pleaded innocent to Uncle Yang's machinations.

"I'll phone Alice," I said.

Momma followed me into the hall. She waited while I dialed and waited while I explained everything to Alice. She waited until I hung up and followed me into my bedroom. "Why does Alice have to go? He's a nice boy. Comes from a good family. Such good manners," she said.

"He's square," I said.

"What's that?" she wanted to know.

"That means he's . . . well, he's. . . Oh, never mind." A 'square' would sound good to her: someone who did not jive, who used correct English, and was conscious of his manners. I brushed my hair then rummaged through the closet and pulled out a crumpled shoebox.

I had thrown out the white ankle-strap shoes once; threw them into the trash can after Willie's funeral. But I could not stand the thought of wasting the money and retrieved them before the garbage was collected. Except for a few scuffs, they were like new.

"Why don't you wear your other shoes?" Momma suggested.

"They're soaking wet."

"I'll go see," she said as she started out of the room.

I called her back. "I told you, they're soaking wet. I can't wear them. It doesn't matter anyway. You're sending me out with a guy I don't care anything about. I don't know him, I don't like him, and I don't want to go out with him." I rolled the stockings off my legs and threw them into the wastebasket.

Momma bit her lip. "Uncle Yang says he's a fine young man. Very intelligent. He's going to be a doctor. His father came from a prominent family. Uncle Yang says. . ."

I cut her off. "If Uncle Yang thinks so much of him, maybe he should go out with him." I began to dig in the dresser for a pair of stockings. I found some in the back of a drawer, still wrapped in white tissue.

"Faye, be nice," Momma implored.

"I'm going, aren't I?" I slipped a stocking over my feet. "But the next time, you and Uncle Yang had better ask me before you set anything up." I fastened the stockings to my garter belt.

"Aren't you going to change into a dress?" she asked, watching me step into my shoes.

I smooth out my skirt and yanked the wrinkles out of my jacket. "No. I'm already wearing white sandals in December for him."

She paused, then said, "Never mind. You look nice. White shoes, black shoes . . . it doesn't matter in California."

As Dan and I were leaving the house, I promised Momma we would be back by midnight.

"Oh, never mind," she said. "Any time is all right."

We rode into the blinding rain, seeing only what fell in the path of the headlights. The edge of the beams took in the curb where a river of rain rushed into storm drains.

I directed Daniel to Alice's house. She was waiting for us.

"This is Daniel. He's from Connecticut," I told her as she climbed into the car.

"All my friends call me Dan." He pulled a gold cigarette case from his pocket and snapped it open. "Cigarette?"

"No thanks," Alice said as she nudged me in the ribs. She spoke for both of us.

Dan lit his cigarette then started the engine. The heady smell of tobacco soon filled the Model A. He left the choice of restaurant to us. We knew only those in Chinatown and decided on the Red Pagoda.

"What do you do for amusement in this city?" he asked.

"Well, before the fellows went into the service, we went bowling, to the movies, to the beach on hayrides." I looked to Alice for help. "What else?"

"Dancing and weenie-bakes," she said.

"Concerts? Plays?" he asked.

"Sometimes," she lied. I nudged her for lying.

The rain slackened then stopped altogether. The skies began to open and Dan turned off the windshield wipers. Through the bathed glass, L.A. was dazzling.

"Do you realize how fantastic a December night in Los Angeles is? New Haven is buried in snow and it's so cold your very speech freezes in the air," Dan said.

"Really?" I said without thinking.

He seemed amused by my response. "Yes. You take the words and warm them in your hands then send them on their way," he said.

"Or leave them hanging there?" I said. I allowed him a moment to catch on, then said, "It sounds as cold as Sunchoun."

"As where?"

"Sunchoun, Korea. My family went there when I was a little girl. Froze my toes walking to school one morning." I was surprised I still remembered.

"No permanent injury, I trust."

"No. But oh! It was painful. My teacher carried me to the stove and rubbed my feet until I was able to feel my toes again." The memory of it became more vivid. I was so grateful that I had sworn never to forget my teacher.

"That was wise. So you've been to Korea. You must tell me about

it. I hope to go there someday. Have you been there, Alice?" he
asked.

"Who me?" Alice had been toying with the handle strap and
staring out the window. "It's too primitive. Outhouses and dirt
floors and flies. No, thank you," she said.

"It's not all like that," I protested. "We had servants and slept on
clean *ondol* floors. You get used to the outhouses."

"Even in winter?" Dan asked.

"You might freeze more than your toes, but you rush back to the
house to throw yourself on the heated *ondol* floor. I loved it in
Korea," I said.

"People always say that about places they've been. They forget
the unpleasant part," Alice said. "You'd better start looking for a
parking space," she told Dan. "We have arrived in Chinatown in
fantastic Los Angeles."

She was being sarcastic. She never used the word 'fantastic'. But
Dan was not aware of that.

At the Red Pagoda, Dan held the heavy carved cinnabar doors
open for us. He helped Alice out of her raincoat. Her red polka-
dotted dress was beautiful. She knew instinctively the hairdo and
dress that brought out the best in her and Dan seemed to notice.

"Would you like a drink?" he asked.

"No," Alice said, answering for both of us again.

"Yes," I said. "I'll have a ginger ale."

While Alice and I discussed the menu, the waiter stood over us
tapping his pencil on a paper pad and Dan sat sipping on his scotch
and soda. Every now and then, the waiter reached over to tap his
pencil on the menu. "This good," he would say, making unsolicited
suggestions. Alice and I ignored him and decided on our usual
combinations.

"Be sure the vegetables are crunchy," I told the waiter. "Not too
much sugar on the sweet and sour pork. Bake the fish crisp on the
outside, moist on the inside."

"Yah, yah," the waiter nodded, closing the menu as he impatiently grabbed them from our hands.

As he rushed away, Alice raised her voice after him. "Black
mushrooms and rice, don't forget."

We saw the back of his head bob as he pushed on the door to the
kitchen. Alice and I smiled at each other.

"Chinese waiters are so pushy," I explained to Dan. "They try to tell us what to eat. Are there many Chinese restaurants where you live?"

"No. I'd have to go to Boston or New York. But even those cities have nothing comparable to this." He swept his hands to take in the scrolls of Chinese calligraphy on the walls and the silk lanterns overhead.

"San Francisco has the best Chinese restaurants," I said, taking a sip of ginger ale.

"Have you been there too? You've traveled quite a bit."

I gulped, nearly driving the drink down the wrong pipe. "No. I've read about it. Alice can tell you what a stick-in-the-mud I am."

"She reads too much. Never takes anything as it comes. Always makes matters difficult for herself," Alice said.

I gave her a look. A simple 'yes, she's a stick-in-the-mud' would have been sufficient. I sucked on the cellophane straw until I struck air.

"Tell me about the dance," Dan said. "Who sponsors it and who attends?"

Alice responded. "A Chinese youth organization puts it on every year. Naturally, most of the ones who go are Chinese. Before the war, Cavaliers and Mugunghwas used to pair up to go. They're our Korean clubs. Now, only those who happen to be around show up. It's supposed to be semi-formal but no one cares what you wear anymore."

"One of the benefits of war. A uniform is de rigueur at any event," Dan said as he leaned back to give the waiter room to unload the tray of food.

"Is what?" I asked. I turned the lazy Susan until the baked fish was in front of him.

"De rigueur. Good form," he explained. "A French word. Surely you've read about France," he teased. He dug his chopsticks into the fish and plucked off a piece of delicate white meat. "Umm, delicious," he murmured as he chewed.

"French? Of course," I replied. "It's de rigueur for well-read persons." I juggled a slippery black mushroom with my chopsticks and brought it to my mouth. I thought it was the tastiest mushroom I had ever had.

The Royal Palms Hotel was five minutes away from the restaurant. The flocked purple wallpaper and gilded mouldings were attempts at elegance, but I found them outlandish. Fake palm trees bordered the dance floor. Girls dressed in airy marquisette or shiny satin gowns glided between the columns of simulated bark. Boys with hair oiled into high black pompadours ducked to avoid the drooping artificial fronds. Beaded bags made of counterfeit jewels dangled from the tiny wrists of petite girls who had been pinned with corsages by men wearing rented tuxedos or G.I. uniforms.

"I'm sorry. I have no flowers for you," Dan apologized.

"That's all right," I said. "I'm not dressed for it."

Alice had stopped talking altogether. I felt responsible for her glum expression; she had come on my account.

The band struck up the first measures of 'The Jersey Bounce'.

"Alice is great at jitterbugging," I told Dan. "You should dance with her."

"Are you sure? I hate to leave you alone," he said.

"I don't mind sitting this one out. I'd rather watch," I insisted.

He saw that I meant it and led Alice to the dance floor. He swung her out, twirled her under his hand, pulled her in, then held her close to do their fast steps together. He was loose and danced beautifully.

The band quickened the tempo when they played 'The Jersey Bounce' one more time. Some dancers moved aside to give Dan and Alice room. A crowd began to form, clapping the beat, sharing the heat of the dance with Dan and Alice. Flashes of red polka-dots and khaki gabardine were all I could see through the crowd.

"Who is that character?" a voice demanded. I had been craning to see the dancers and did not see him approach.

"C.K.! When did you get back?"

"A few days ago. Want to dance?"

"Not really."

"Me neither," he said, and plopped himself into the chair next to mine. He had a half empty glass in his hand, but he looked as if he had drunk more than that. "I tried to cut in. Alice was glad to see me but he, whoever he is, says, 'I don't think you're in any condition to dance'." His mimicry oozed with scorn. "Phony bastard. Who the hell is he?"

"He's all right. He's from Connecticut. The son of a friend of Mr. Yang. Alice is helping me show him the town."

He laughed. "You always were a kidder, Faye."

"Sure," I said. "Are you home for good?"

"Phasing out. It won't be long."

"I'll bet your folks are happy you're back. My mom keeps saying, 'Thanks to God, my boys are safe.'"

He smiled at my simulation of Momma's voice. "Are they out?" he asked.

"Just Harold. John's making his way across the Pacific. Beth wants him to go back to school after they get married. Harold's in Seattle with his girl. They're engaged. Did you know there were Koreans in Seattle?"

"Why not? They're all over the damn place." He swilled his drink. "Even in Connecticut."

"What's new with you?" I asked. I felt something was; he seemed different.

He shrugged. "Been to war, came back and. . . ." He took another swallow. "Came back and found my buddy's girl dancing with a smoothie from Connecticut."

"I told you, Dan's with me. Alice came because I asked her to," I insisted.

He leaned toward me and put his arms around my shoulders. "You look terrific, Faye. Godamn shame what happened to Willie. Jesus, I felt like hell when I heard about it. What a great guy. Good old days, right? Fun and games. I know it sounds crazy but Willie was lucky. He missed the fuckin' war and all its foul ups. He got in on the best part of life and didn't wait to get picked off by a bullet . . . or see anyone else get it."

"He didn't really have a choice," I said.

He snickered. "Who does?" He paused to toy with the ice cubes. "We've had some great times."

The music stopped. Dan and Alice were weaving their way toward us.

"How about our dance?" C.K. asked Alice. He put down his glass and stood up.

"Sure, if you think you're up to it," she said.

"Up to it? Why wouldn't I be up to it? You sound like a stuffed-shirt." He took Alice by the hand and led her away.

"Is he always like this?" Dan asked.

"No. He's out of sorts tonight. Trying to drink it off. He's nice, really."

Dan put his hands on the back of the empty chair and leaned toward me. "We're alone now. I don't see how you're going to get out of dancing with me," he said.

"I don't either. Well, let's get it over with," I said without think-ing. "Oh. I didn't mean that the way it sounded. It's just that I'm not much of a dancer."

"I doubt that," he said, taking my hand.

The music was slow. Unlike most of the men I knew, Dan's shoulders came higher than my chin. He drew me close and began to hum softly, as if to make it as easy as possible for me to follow him. The lights had been dimmed for 'Autumn in New York'. Hollywood sparkled through the rain-streaked windows. Silhouet-ted against the city lights, real palm trees swayed in the wind, rain dripping from the tips of their serrated leaves.

My feet were killing me. C.K. had whisked Alice away, leaving me to dance with Dan all night. While the Model A rattled towards home, I leaned over to unbuckle my shoes and slipped my feet half way out, sighing with relief as I freed my toes.

"You may not realize it, but this evening has meant a great deal to me," Dan said. We were alone; Alice had left us to go home with C.K.

"It was only a dance."

"It was more than that to me. I've never been to an event where so many other people looked like me. I guess you find that unbe-lievable. You haven't grown up among others unlike yourself."

"Yes, that's true."

"I don't know if I can explain what it's like," he said. "First of all, you would have to know New Haven. Then you would be familiar with the assumptions of a WASP society."

"Wasp?"

"White Anglo-Saxon Protestant," he explained.

"Oh, like Beverly Hills?" I asked.

"No, not at all. It's conservative with a Puritan tradition. Morality denuded of imagination. Beverly Hills, on the other hand, strikes me as being based on imagination denuded of morality."

"Stop!" I shrieked. He was driving through a boulevard stop.

He drove on through. "I'm sorry, but I didn't want to risk having us go through the windshield. And I doubted we would have been caught."

I was speechless. I had never broken the law before.

"So there we were," he went on, "my family and I in the middle of New Haven. After high school, I received a scholarship to Yale, an endowment of a missionary family for a 'qualified male of Asian ancestry'. By day I was a Yaley, by night the number one son of a Korean patriot." He slowed down, we were approaching a signal. "Do I turn here?"

"No. At the next one. Left," I said.

"Funny how most of us go through life as it presents itself, giving it little thought or scrutiny, just trying to get along. Then something happens that forces us to question the very premise of our existence," he said. He paused for my response.

"Uh huh."

'All my life I have been told of my father's dream to return to his homeland. It was assumed that I would be part of that dream. Hence, my reason for going into medicine. Someday, I'm going to go to Korea to work for my father's people. Ah, there it is. Did you notice? I said, 'my father's people'."

"What's wrong with that?"

"Most of my life has not been spent with my 'father's people' but with the other people of this country. I live among one group of people while my commitments are to another. WASP assumptions require that I be one thing and my ancestry demands another."

"Oh," I said. "Did you know that the water in Europe is undrinkable and the plumbing is bad?"

He seemed taken aback by my question. "Is that so? But how can one fault a civilization that produced a Michelangelo, a St. Thomas Aquinas, a Goethe?" he said.

"That's what I say."

"Alice mentioned that you liked to read."

"I'm not a real bookworm. It's just a way for me to see how other people live. I haven't found a book yet written about the people I know." I said it with a smile on my face; it was supposed to be a joke.

"That could be another form of isolation," Dan said soberly. "Unless one becomes part of that 'other' world."

I laughed. "Me? In Yoknapatawpha County, however it's pronounced, or in upstate New York? What would I do there? Marry into a good family to raise children who in turn would marry into good families?" It was supposed to be another joke.

"But Faye, we do live in the United States. You and I do speak English to one another. I do wear the uniform of this country. We are part of this society. Segments of it may not be completely accessible to everyone, but we who live here have something in common. If not physically then intellectually. In many cases, experientially."

I could not follow him. "I don't know. I could never be one of *them*. I don't know if I would want to be. I really have no need to be." We were approaching the corner. "Turn here," I instructed, "this is my street. There's my house." I pointed to it. The wind had blown the newspaper down the steps. My shoes had toppled over but were still drying on the porch.

Dan parked the car and turned off the ignition. "Before we go in . . . before we face Uncle Yang, I wondered if you would mind if I wrote to you."

"Me? What about?"

"Whatever comes to our minds."

"I'm not much of a letter writer."

"Just talk to me in your letters," he said and got out of the car to open the door for me.

—2—

"Thank goodness he's gone," Alice said. "You deserve a medal for putting up with him." It was morning, but the telephone had jarred me from a deep sleep.

"I thought he was nice," I said, yawning.

"Wha-at? That stuffed-shirt?" She took a moment to recover. "C.K. didn't like him either."

"C.K. was in a bad mood," I said. I sat on the chair and tucked my nightgown under my thighs to keep me warm.

"I can't believe you went for him," she said.

"What are you getting all riled up about? It was only one date."

"Wasted my whole evening," she said.

I leaned back and lifted my feet to the seat of the chair, pulling my nightgown over the bend of my knees to cover my legs. "Oh, Alice, I'm sorry. You were a peach to go with me."

"He was so. . . .so. . . ."

"Smooth?"

"I was going to say 'phony'."

"That's not nice, Alice. He was pretty polite to both of us. He got roped into it too, you know."

"C.K. . . . ." she began.

"C.K. was drunk. Pie-eyed. He was rude."

"You can't blame him. He was ready to kill himself."

"Because of Dan?" I said with skepticism.

"Didn't he tell you? His father kicked him out of the house. Blamed C.K. for commanding a Japanese battalion."

"Wait a minute. You don't mean Japanese Japanese. You must mean American Japanese," I said, rubbing my toes to keep them from going numb. I sneezed.

"Of course, what do you think?" she said impatiently. "He and his men got a special commendation from Eisenhower. Mr. Kim called C.K. a traitor for fighting with the Japanese. Said he was a disgrace to the Koreans. Broke C.K.'s heart."

"Wha-at? What's wrong with Mr. Kim? C.K. only did what he was ordered to do. They were fighting for the U.S."

"I guess his father's afraid of what the Koreans would say."

A feeling of disgust came over me. I began to sort out the sense and nonsense of what Alice was telling me. "Who cares?" I said finally.

"Faye!"

"Well, I'm mad! Mr. Kim is being stupid. He's fighting the wrong war. What does he think an American Japanese soldier goes through fighting for a country that's at war with his family's homeland? I mean, figure it out, Alice. Who are we for? What are we fighting against?" I pressed my fingers against my nose to stifle a sneeze.

"There you go again, Faye. Can't you just feel sorry for C.K. and let it go at that?"

I stood up. "Obviously, I can't." My whole body convulsed as I sneezed. "I'm freezing, Alice. I'll call you later," I said and hung up.

I crawled under the covers to warm up. What a crazy riddle, I thought, to be *yet* not to be. Poor C.K. It really wasn't his fault.

I didn't tell Momma right away; I didn't want her to blow it all out of proportion. I waited a couple of days then made her promise not to bring it up at her meeting before I would tell her.

She heard me out without saying a word. She took time to think after I had finished, then clacked her tongue. "I feel sorry for Mr. Kim. I know how he feels. I feel sorry for C.K. He didn't do anything wrong." She shook her head. "Mr. Kim shouldn't have kicked C.K. out. He's his only son. He needs his family."

I wasn't sure if she meant Mr. Kim needed his family or C.K. did.

She sighed. "It's hard to be Korean living in the United States. Especially for you children. For me, it's not so hard. I know I'm one hundred percent Korean."

Love swelled in my heart for Momma. I was afraid she was going to blame C.K. I walked over and put my arms around her. She patted my hands then picked up her sewing. "This is going to be the last one, the last necktie I sew."

I sat down in the chair next to her. "What will you do?"

"I'm going to rent the boys' room to Uncle Min."

"Uncle Min?"

"He's going to write a book about Korean politics. He wants me to help him."

"What will you use for money?"

"He saved quite a bit from the broadcasts he made for the American government during the war."

"Broadcasts?"

"Propaganda to tell Koreans in Japan to sabotage Japan's armaments. It was a secret. He couldn't tell anyone what he was doing."

I straightened out the stack of neckties that were ready to be wrapped. So, Uncle Min would be living with us. I always thought that if Momma ever got together with a man, it would have been Uncle Yang. But then, Uncle Yang was not a scholar.

I looked at Momma while she sewed. Her silky black hair was streaked with gray. It had happened when I was not paying attention. She had spent years bent over the table, but her back was straight. I could not remember when she first began to wear glasses. Her deep-set eyes were still clear, still capable of turning to fire when she was angry.

"I guess Uncle Min won't be going back to Korea," I said.

She shook her head. "What for? The South Korean government says the KPR is a communist group. We can't get into North Korea either." She waved her hand in the air. "My land in Qwaksan is gone." Qwaksan was gone and there was no money to show for it. The land was Momma's only holding in her homeland and it had been taken away from her; her only holding in the world. Suddenly, I felt as if I had been stamped with stupidity. *That* was what I was supposed to understand. She had hung onto Qwaksan as long as she could. I wanted to cry.

"Gosh, Momma, being one hundred percent Korean isn't easy," I said.

She smiled as she bit off the thread. "You're not a baby anymore," she said, tossing the necktie to me. "That's it. The last one." I set it on top and wrapped up the ties for her.

Rrring!

"I'll get it," I said. I opened the door to a postman. He was not our regular mailman.

"Air-mail Special Delivery letter for Faye Che . . . Choo . . ." he stammered.

"Chun," I said.

"From Connecticut." The gold on his teeth glittered as he smiled. "Must be important," he said with a wink.

I stepped out on the porch to sign for it. He handed me the letter and left. I sat on the steps and studied the envelope. Layers of postal marks had obliterated each other. I had never seen so many postage stamps on one letter. Dan's writing was small and the loops were open. The space between the lines was even. I felt as if we were again meeting for the first time.

I took a deep breath then tore open the envelope.